SEVEN MEN OF VISION
An Appreciation

SEVEN
MEN
OF
VISION

An
Appreciation

by

ELIZABETH JENNINGS

VISION

Vision Press Limited
11–14 Stanhope Mews West
London SW7 5RD

ISBN 0   85478 253 2

© 1976 by Elizabeth Jennings

Printed in Great Britain by
Clarke, Doble & Brendon Ltd., Plymouth
MCMLXXVI

CONTENTS

ACKNOWLEDGEMENTS

The Author gratefully acknowledges use of material by the following authors:

Exile by St-John Perse, translated by Denis Devlin, copyright © 1949 by Bollengen Foundation Inc., New York, N.Y., copyright © 1971 by Princeton University Press, reprinted by permission of Princeton University Press and Mrs Alexis Leger.

Eloges by St-John Perse, translated by Louise Varese, copyright © 1956 by Bollengen Foundation Inc., New York, N.Y., copyright © 1971 by Princeton University Press, reprinted by permission of Princeton University Press and Mrs Alexis Leger.

Anabasis by St-John Perse, translated by T. S. Eliot, copyright © 1938, 1939 by Harcourt, Brace & World, Inc., copyright © 1966 by Esme Valerie Eliot.

Collected Poems by W. B. Yeats published by Macmillan & Co. Ltd., London, and The Macmillan Company of New York, by kind permission of Michael Yeats and Miss Anne Yeats.

Poems by Boris Pasternak, by kind permission of the translator, Eugene M. Kayden, published by the University of Michigan Press, Ann Arbor, 1959.

Dr Zhivago by Boris Pasternak, by kind permission of the translator Manya Harari and William Collins Sons & Co. Ltd.

Fifty Poems by Boris Pasternak, translated by Lydia Pasternak Slater, 1963, reprinted by kind permission of the publishers Allen & Unwin Ltd.

ACKNOWLEDGEMENTS

Collected Poems by Lawrence Durrell from the new and revised edition published by Faber & Faber Ltd, 1968, reprinted by kind permission of the publishers.

Complete Poems by D. H. Lawrence, edited by Vivian de Sola Pinto and Warren Roberts, published by William Heinemann Ltd in 1964.

Flight to Arras by Antoine de St-Exupéry, translated by Lewis Galantiere, 1939, by kind permission of William Heinemann Ltd.

Wind, Sand and Stars by Antoine de St-Exupéry, translated by Lewis Galantiere, 1942, by kind permission of William Heinemann Ltd and Harcourt Brace Jovanovich, Inc.

Chapter V, 'David Jones: A Vision of War', is based on the Virginia Gildersleeve Lecture which Elizabeth Jennings delivered at Barnard College, New York, in the spring of 1974.

FOREWORD

The writers who are being studied in this book may, at first sight, seem a rather arbitrary collection of people. In one sense they are—they bear little relation to one another and they are not even all English. The reason for my choice of them is simply this—they seem to cast a great illumination over this troubled century; they have joy, a joy they have only attained through their own suffering and their own kind of surrenders.

And, naturally, this book is personal in so far as my choice, what I see in these writers, cannot but be personal if one is a human being living at this time. I am well aware of the *lacunae* here—Joyce, Orwell, Aldous Huxley, Virginia Woolf, and Teilhard de Chardin, for instance. I have quite deliberately left out Orwell and Huxley because 1984 and *Brave New World*, as well as *Brave New World Revisited*, are too specific and also too melancholy for the argument of this book. Virginia Woolf is omitted for a different reason. She was a very great and successful experimentalist but only a very few of her books, such as *To The Lighthouse* and *The Waves* possess the joy of a vision, that joy which becomes a part of other people's minds. Joyce is not here because his work, though undoubtedly great, does not transmit a vision or, if it does, it is often a bleak one.

I am not merely concerned with my chosen writers but with what lies behind them. A number of other obvious men, such as Eliot and Edwin Muir, are omitted only because I have written about them already elsewhere.

This is not a book about mystics, though sometimes more than

9

a fitful flash of mysticism does arise. It is not dominated by a theory or, if it is, then the theory is only tentative, something found in my chosen writers but not, I hope, ever imposed on them by me. When I speak of a vision, I mean something which emerges brilliantly in several different ways from these studies; my approach is a hopeful humility, and also gratitude. And that is all I ask from the reader.

Note: Fantasy worlds such as those presented in J. R. R. Tolkien's *Lord of the Rings* and C. S. Lewis's *Out of the Silent Planet* sequence are omitted from this study because of the deliberate air of unreality which is present in these works; science fiction, even the very best, is excluded for the same reason.

I

W. B. YEATS

A Vision of Joy

About one thing, those who used to be called "The New Critics" were entirely right; they persuaded us to read, examine, and, let us hope, enjoy a writer's work before we begin to enquire into his biography. Perhaps only the greatest works stand up to this kind of intense scrutiny but this, surely, is a criterion by which all literature, whether poetry or prose, should finally be judged. Biographies always cast some light and autobiographies a great deal more, but as Eliot said, "The rest is not our business".

In general, then, the finer the writer the less we need to know about his life and the reason for this is that what we know emerges essentially, if we are sensitive enough to see it, from his work. So, for this particular enquiry, Yeats's middle and late poems will be considered without any recourse to his own fascinating, even tantalizing *Autobiographies*. That book is a work of art in itself, but not relevant here. The middle and late poems are much more to my purpose. Even the greatest writers leave a few finger-prints on their work, sometimes when they are not referring to themselves at all. Yeats, especially in his late poems, seldom removed himself entirely from his poetry; indeed, he wrote a few absolutely personal poems.

Yeats's *Byzantium* is both the historical Byzantium and Byzantium brought under the lens of a poet's clear eye and then transformed, by means of imagery, into a world of his own. This poem, and others which are not concerned with Byzantium at all, are, nonetheless, also a part of the poet's total vision. Through

11

the particularities of a poet's world, a vision, a unique one, is transmitted to us; we can not only enter it but live in it.

Why did Yeats select Byzantium as the place, where he could set in order some of his own visions, make poems? The immediate and, therefore, over-simplified answer to this, is that Byzantium both fires the imagination and also makes the human mind ask questions. The mind recalls all that sprang from the era of Constantine, while the eye has seen the reality of, or in reproduction, the mosaics, the lasting colours which spread from Constantinople to Ravenna, Rome and many other places. (But Byzantium was a city and a civilization long before Constantine entered it. So it has a resonance, even a mythical quality which Yeats could exploit for his own purposes.) For Yeats, all this was the raw material for his poems, though at first it was colour and light which were the most important elements of his visionary experience. Like all artists, he wanted to use his visions, incorporate them into his own particular medium and give them a lasting value. But in doing all this, in the actual making of the poems, Yeats never at the time had any conscious audience or public in mind. No important artist ever does but, later, there always comes a time when he does want to show and share his artefact and when he himself has, in however small a degree, lost interest in it and is striving after something else.

There is a grandeur in Yeats's later poems that has nothing to do with pride, self-sufficiency or over-assurance; it is a grandeur that this poet possesses or is possessed by, which then quickly (or so it seems to us who do not know about the heart-ache of transcribing a vision) becomes poems, a peopled world, a place that carries complete conviction. No-one who had only read Yeats's earliest poems could possibly have predicted this amazing later development. So astringent a critic as Eliot called Yeats the greatest poet of his century; he was not a man to use such language lightly. And Auden, in his poem in memory of Yeats, wrote,

> Follow, poet, follow right
> To the bottom of the night,
> With your unconstraining voice,
> Still persuade us to rejoice . . .

That is precisely what Yeats's world does for us; it gives us joy, a very special kind of joy. Again, in the poem entitled *Lapis Lazuli*, Yeats insists that

> . . . Hamlet and Lear are gay;
> Gaiety transfiguring all that dread.

In a late, very short poem, Yeats expresses poignantly the difficulty which he experienced in attaining this vision, a vision of joy and of wholeness. This great poet never forgot that man is flesh as well as spirit, and he knew well the demands the flesh makes. These are the lines which I am thinking of, with their honesty, humility and brevity :

> You think it horrible that lust and rage
> Should dance attention upon my old age;
> They were not such a plague when I was young;
> What else have I to spur me into song?

Out of this "plague", many of Yeats's finest visionary poems sprang but, at an earlier period, we have a foretaste of his joyous, transcendent view of the world.

The early, perhaps the most familiar Yeats to readers of anthologies shows us a Romantic poet with only a small grasp of the troubles that lie beneath the smooth texture of human lives. They are lacking in passion, though never in lyricism. The middle and especially the later work present us with a man who has suffered but seen beyond his suffering and brought back that brilliance he has perceived to us in wonderfully wrought poems, poems "in and out of time", that is to say, poems which understand human nature and also human history.

The odd thing is that Yeats's prose book, *A Vision* carries far less conviction than his poems. This is largely due to the fact that, in his later years, the poet dabbled in most of the forms or quick ways—apart from drug-taking—to so-called visionary experiences that were available; I mean, *planchette*, alchemy, spiritualism, every possible kind of attempt to gain second-sight, or what scientists now call Extra-Sensory Perception. But no true or great poet, let alone a visionary one, needs these short-cuts which are often traps and almost always illusions. So *A Vision* is only marginally interesting not for its contents but for the

13

insight it gives us into the man who wrote it. It invites our questions, it really gives us no acceptable view of the world. It will not, therefore, be examined here. In this sense, but *only* in this sense, Yeats was as Auden wrote in his memorial poem, ". . . silly like us", but Auden wisely added, with great perception, "your gift survived it all". There are no short-cuts to true visionary poems; they arise from other, far more complex matters, most particularly, probably, from the individual character of the poet himself.

In many ways the early poems of Yeats were extremely conventional, although they do show the care for technique, rhythm and form which are essential to any poet who is to develop and become of lasting importance. Yeats's *Autobiographies*, quite apart from the tone and liveliness of the actual prose, tell us much about the poet's life but I do not think one could forecast from them (despite their date) with absolute certainty the middle and late poems from the skilful early ones. One sees an excellent writer, certainly, but not the man who was to write *Sailing to Byzantium*, *Lapis Lazuli* or *The Circus Animals' Desertion*. Like A *Vision*, *Autobiographies* will be set aside here. Yeats had to live through passionate experiences of love, friendship and a deep interest in politics and the troubles of Ireland to achieve his vision of life. So, full maturity came to him fairly late; the complete vision caught him unawares, one might say. His middle period is also of great importance because it adumbrates the great last poems. The most essential of these are to be found in the volumes entitled *The Wild Swans at Coole* (published in 1919), and most of the books which precede *Last Poems* (1936–39). In these books there are poems of great insight, poems which present us with a personal world made general. The artistry increased as Yeats grew older and it kept pace with his vision. He took hold of all the forms and rhythms which the expression, or transmission, of his vision required; his technique is perfect yet natural. There is a wonderful ease about these poems, as well as an adamance. Communication is absolute. But we must never forget that such ease of expression requires a life-time to discover. It is the complete opposite of facility,

The first poem to examine in *The Wild Swans at Coole* is the title poem, and the essential stanza out of the five is the third. It is full of observation, love and insights beyond simply the loveliness of these swans; Yeats writes,

> I have looked upon those brilliant creatures,
> And now my heart is sore.
> All's changed since I, hearing at twilight,
> The first time on this shore,
> The bell-beat of their wings above my head,
> Trod with a lighter tread.

Yeats is filled with a sense of glory about these birds but he knows that both the glory and the birds which caused it are transitory. Yet, although the poem's fifth stanza ends on a note of disillusionment, the fourth ends with three lines which show that the poet believes that, season after season, these birds will be about their business, and so he writes in noble language:

> Their hearts have not grown old;
> Passion or conquest, wander where they will,
> Attend upon them still.

"Passion or conquest" are continuous themes through Yeats's poems from this volume onwards. And so is the personal element. The poet's passion is wonderfully united with the wonder of these wild swans. This kind of vision is genuine; no magic such as *A Vision* displays is necessary. The poet's clear eye and his powerful imagination are all that is needed. There is no faking of any kind.

The only other poem which I want to examine in *The Wild Swans at Coole* is called *Presences*. It is a very mysterious but not obscure poem; it begins,

> This night has been so strange that it seemed
> As if the hair stood up on my head . . .

Yeats is speaking from a dream but a very vivid one which could, if one wanted to undertake the task, be paraphrased. I think, however, that just to read it with wonder and sympathy yields much more of the indubitable vision that is being transcribed here. The poet recalls how the women in his dream

> ... had read
> All I had rhymed about that monstrous thing
> Returned and yet unrequited love.

Yeats recognizes the subtle difference between returned love and unrequited love; the difference is both one of degree and kind. He had known it himself and it springs out of this dream which he turns into a very beautiful poem; it ends with words about three of the women who had appeared in his dream and whom he transforms into a vision. I say it is a vision because the language, though very simple, perhaps for the very reason that it is simple, succeeds in touching something extremely profound. It also, like all visions, whether religious or otherwise, leaves us to imagine. No true vision can be wholly transmitted; because of its very nature it is ineffable, beyond language. Here, then, are the last four lines of *Presences*

> Till I could hear their hearts beating:
> One is a harlot, and one a child
> That never looked upon man with desire,
> And one, it may be, a queen.

In *Michael Robartes and the Dancer* which was published in 1921, three very well-known poems appear, which must be examined though not taken to pieces—that obsessional occupation of so many literary critics for whom poems are collections of words rather than works of art or attempts at works of art. The first of these poems is very important to this study but often almost ignored; it is called *An Image from a Past Life* and is a dialogue between a man and a woman. The poem is really strictly more about past love than past life and the man starts the poem by saying, "Never until this night have I been stirred . . ." The woman's heart is "smitten through", she says, although she feels, through the man's vision, a renewal of life. She is afraid, however, because the dialogue has spoken of "Image of poignant recollection". He tries to reassure her by telling her that his vision must not frighten her, turn her away from him and "all that to this moment charmed" her.

What the woman fears is that a woman in the man's past still has power over him and, as a result, is a threat to her now. What frightens her is "A sweetheart from another life".

But the man tries to reassure her by telling her she is only "imagining" that what he has seen could usurp or in any way spoil his feelings for her; indeed, all that he has felt in the past has given him "images to make him fonder" of her. But the woman will not be pacified and this simply written but intricately thought out poem ends with her words,

> I do not know, that know I am afraid
> Of the hovering thing night brought me.

And there Yeats ends the poem; there is mystery but it is human mystery. There is a problem which cannot be solved and, since he is a great poet, Yeats makes no attempt to give any facile solutions.

Easter 1916 also appears in the *Michael Robartes* volume and is, of course, about the Rising in Ireland in that year. Its most notable feature is that in spite of all the horror (which Yeats does not describe; he only mentions some of the people involved) "a terrible beauty is born". So, this poem gives us a vision of joy, joy wrung out of bitter anguish. The poem, which is written with great artistry and enormous control, is given life by the recital of some of the actual names of real people and, at other times, by leaving them nameless. Yeats is not sentimental but he is passionately concerned about all who have been caught up in "The Rising" and identifies himself both with their suffering and their patriotism:

> I have met them at close of day
> Coming with vivid faces
> From counter or desk among grey
> Eighteenth-century houses.
> I have passed with a nod of the head
> Or polite meaningless words,
> Or have lingered awhile and said
> Polite meaningless words
> . . . . .
> All changed, changed utterly:
> A terrible beauty is born.

From these casual encounters with people who have become caught up in this time of terror, Yeats can, nonetheless, extract a beauty. The people are transfigured by what has happened to them. Later he remembers how an old woman whose "days were spent / In ignorant good-will", once had a sweet voice and was a good rider. Another, a man who

> ... might have won fame in the end,
> So sensitive his nature seemed ...

seems to have perished uselessly. Yet another who was "drunken" and "vainglorious" and who had done "bitter wrong" to some of Yeats's close friends is, most magnanimously, included in this compassionate catalogue and plays his part in Yeats's poem; the reason for this is that he has lost his life "In the casual comedy". Bloodshed, Yeats feels, has changed him, he is "Transformed utterly". And immediately follows the refrain, "A terrible beauty is born".

Nature itself is involved in this appalling catastrophe, or rather in Yeats's vision of it. He continues:

> Hearts with one purpose alone
> Through summer and winter seem
> Enchanted to a stone
> To trouble the living stream.
> The horse that comes from the road,
> The rider, the birds that range
> From cloud to tumbling cloud,
> Minute by minute they change;
> A shadow of cloud on the stream
> Changes minute by minute ...

The repetition here of "minute by minute" is remarkably effective. Yeats also introduces moor-hens and moor-cocks. But, the theme, not a message, of *Easter 1916* is acceptance, not resignation or anger or disillusionment but a complete understanding of men and of how, when they truly are dedicated to a cause, they think just even fighting may ennoble them. The poet is aware of the dangers of cynicism and writes,

> Too long a sacrifice
> Can make a stone of the heart.
> O when may it suffice?
> That is Heaven's part, our part

18

> To murmur name upon name,
> As a mother names her child . . .

The human warmth here is deeply touching and precisely placed. A little later in the poem, Yeats declares hopefully,

> For England may keep faith
> For all that is done and said.

In the last few lines of *Easter 1916*, the poet shows us the courage of the Irishmen and ends with his awe-inspiring refrain:

> I write it out in a verse—
> MacDonagh and MacBride
> And Connolly and Pearse
> Now and in time to be,
> Wherever green is worn,
> Are changed, changed utterly:
> A terrible beauty is born.

These men are transfigured by their faith and courage, but they are immortalized in the lines Yeats has written about them.

This poem tells us a good deal about Yeats the man. He does not eschew bloodshed; on the contrary, he believes it can be, paradoxically perhaps, both terrible and beautiful; but it can only be these things if the attitude of men is one of loyalty, not of hatred or bitterness.

The third poem to be considered from this volume is entirely visionary; it is *The Second Coming*. "Gyre", which appears often in Yeats's middle and later poems, means, of course, turning in a spiral or circle and is a poetic form of "gyration", as well as a very happy abbreviation. *The Second Coming* uses this word in its first line and gives us an extremely vivid picture of aerial activity. The poem then moves at once into its main theme. It seems best to note the first eight lines before we examine them more closely:

> Turning and turning in the widening gyre
> The falcon cannot hear the falconer;
> Things fall apart; the centre cannot hold;
> Mere anarchy is loosed upon the world,
> The blood-dimmed tide is loosed, and everywhere

> The ceremony of innocence is drowned;
> The best lack all conviction, while the worst
> Are full of passionate intensity.

This is a dark vision, on the surface almost a hopeless one. Anarchy and blood seem to have complete power, and not only innocence but the ceremony, the dignity of it "is drowned". Hopeless too seems the statement that "the best" have lost "all conviction" while the "worst" are the ones who are "full of passionate intensity". It is strange that Yeats, a man of tremendously intense passion, should think of those who have this sort of intensity as "the worst". I think we must take it that in this particular vision, passion of any kind is useless. The rest of the poem, fourteen lines, shows a man striving for hope in what appear to be hopeless conditions; Yeats writes,

> Surely some revelation is at hand;
> Surely the Second Coming is at hand.

This Second Coming would be the end of the world and therefore elucidates the uselessness of "passionate intensity" and also explains why the best men cannot believe that this Coming is really at hand. With the words "The Second Coming!" the poet becomes ecstatic and the nature of his vision, by no means a Christian one, but a personal one brought to the pitch of generality, begins to unfold itself. It is a highly visual ecstasy and also in a very few words expresses the poet's own perplexity about its meaning. After mentioning "The Second Coming!", Yeats immediately writes,

> ... Hardly are those words out
> When a vast image out of *Spiritus Mundi*
> Troubles my sight ...

The poet experiences a strange vision of a creature,

> A shape with lion body and the head of a man,
> A gaze blank and pitiless as the sun ...

This is bleak, dark and the poem concludes with a view of Christianity that makes that hopeful religion appear hopeless; Yeats, surprisingly, can see no joy in it and declares,

... now I know
That twenty centuries of stony sleep
Were vexed to nightmare by a rocking cradle [Christ's],
And what rough beast, its hour come round at last,
Slouches towards Bethlehem to be born?

It is true that *The Second Coming* ends on a question but the "rough beast" about whom Yeats speaks cannot be Christ, for he would be the person, God—made—Man according to Roman Catholic and Anglican beliefs, to be born in Bethlehem, and an apparently helpless baby could not be equated with a "rough beast". What we have to bear in mind is that this poem is the *Second* Coming, so it could well be the poet's vision of the end of the world, and a terrifying one it is. But good poetry states, it is not its task to explain. Indeed, Yeats's vision of what Christians call "The Abomination of Desolation" might well be like this. Poetry of Yeats's kind, though so intensely passionate, is never negative. The vision in *The Second Coming* is only bearable because it is both humble and controlled; the humility comes from the depths of Yeats's heart, the control from his great craftsmanship.

Tht fourth poem I want to look at in *Michael Robartes and the Dancer* is a very different one from *The Second Coming*. It is fairly long and is entitled *A Prayer for my Daughter*; the poem is in no way obscure and although it concerns all that Yeats wishes his daughter to find when she grows up, it tells us also the qualities he admires most in all men and women. The scene is set, the language rich but never precious, and the theme carried eagerly forward and, with great rhythmic, emotional and intellectual control sustained to the end of the poem. The poem begins by setting the scene:

Once more the moon is howling, and half hid
Under this cradle-hood and coverlid
My child sleeps on ...

The only "obstacle" to the child's peace is a great wind "Bred on the Atlantic", and then the poet tells us

... for an hour I have walked and prayed
Because of the great gloom that is in my mind.

The poet is melancholy but on his daughter's account, not his own. The roaring sea and tossing wind are at one with his mood, a mood that carries the poet away into a state of vision. After he has spoken of "the murderous innocence of the sea", that natural force which, unwittingly can, with its "frenzied drum", do so much harm, Yeats speaks his prayer, his wish for his daughter in very simple words; first he asks,

> May she be granted beauty and yet not
> Beauty to make a stranger's eye distraught,
> Or hers before a looking-glass . . .

He desires desperately that his daughter should be without vanity, should not overvalue physical beauty or think it an end in itself. He asks that she may have "natural kindness" and something even more rare:

> . . . maybe
> The heart-revealing intimacy
> That chooses right . . .

Yeats then moves, with perfect decorum, to Helen of Troy who has become, mostly through other poets, the perfect beauty, the absolute of a man's desire; but this poet is subtle and sees Helen's disappointment and those of other much-loved women, even Venus herself. He knows that

> It's certain that fine women eat
> A crazy salad with their meat . . .

and so he longs for greater, more profound and lasting gifts for his daughter. Yeats has an unusually intuitive understanding of women; if he had not, there would be no visionary element in this poem at all. He goes on to tell us what he really wants for this child of his:

> In courtesy I'd have her chiefly learned;
> Hearts are not had as a gift but hearts are earned
> By those that are not entirely beautiful . . .

Courtesy is an important part of all love; beside it, physical beauty alone is worthless. A little later, Yeats expounds further:

May she become a flourishing hidden tree
That all her thoughts may like the linnet be . . .
. . . . .
O may she live like some green laurel
Rooted in one dear perpetual place.

"Dear" is a perfectly placed and poised adjective in this context. Yeats has yet another quality to add to his "Prayer", perhaps the subtlest of all:

An intellectual hatred is the worst,
So let her think opinions are accursed.

This is in line with all Christian teaching, for it is the mind, not the emotions which can do most harm; the mind is the real wrecker of all personal relationships, not passion.

So the poet's daughter, still a small child, must lack "all hatred" and find again "radical innocence", learning that this is "Heaven's will". Even if "every windy quarter howl" and human faces "scowl", this child, the poet desires, when grown-up, may be happy. Here we have a vision in which the poet hopefully foresees for his daughter an almost Eden-like joy and grace. Ceremony is constantly on Yeats's tongue so, naturally, he wishes a bridegroom for her and a house "Where all's accustomed, ceremonious", and just before the end of this wonderfully self-effacing poem, he writes,

How but in custom and in ceremony
Are innocence and beauty born?

This poem ends with hope and hope always also means a trustful love, a reciprocity.

The Tower, published in 1928, is Yeats's next book and it opens with one of his best-known, though not necessarily best-understood, poems, Sailing to Byzantium. Byzantium is, for Yeats, a city enchanted by his own imagination, a lasting city; the poem is also about old age and the after-life in which, in his own idiosyncratic way, Yeats believes. The poem opens with an admission that the poet's homeland is no place for the old; it is perfect for young lovers, "salmon-falls" and "mackerel-crowded seas". Briefly it is a place for sensuousness and sensuality and energy, where the intellect is almost completely neglected. So he decides to sail

> ... the seas and come
> To the holy city of Byzantium.

When Yeats dies he wants to become gathered "Into the artifice of eternity". But before death, he recognizes that an "aged man" is "paltry" unless the soul within him can rejoice, "clap its hands", "sing / For every tatter in its mortal dress". Singing cannot, at this time, be learnt; the "magnificence" of all that the flesh had once created can and must be celebrated. Hence, quite logically, Yeats wishes when he dies that his "bodily form" shall not be any "natural thing" but a work of art in itself. He writes of,

> ... such a form as Grecian goldsmiths make
> Of hammered gold or gold enamelling
> To keep a drowsy Emperor awake;
> Or set upon a golden bough to sing
> To lords and ladies of Byzantium
> Of what is past, or passing, or to come.

Byzantium is what to a Christian would be Heaven and Yeats believes in the joy of his form of eternity. It is a unique vision but one which is consistent with all that Yeats feels about great art and great periods of history.

The poem to be considered visionary in every way in *The Tower* is *Leda and the Swan*, a famous anthology piece nowadays and for some time past. The story is taken from a legend, but Yeats also adds to it a magic of his own. He transforms the poem in two ways, first by giving a tremendous sensual strength to the story and, second, by placing it in history. Thus, Leda's thighs are "caressed" by the swan's "dark webs" and "He holds her helpless breast upon his breast". The girl is terrified yet also carried away by passion:

> How can those terrified vague fingers push
> The feathered glory from her loosening thighs?
> And how can body, laid in that white rush,
> But feel the strange heart beating where it lies?

Then this legend changes into a vision which in a few lines shows us all the grandeur, as well as the horror, of the Trojan

War. The sudden change of mood and material here is handled
with consummate mastery. The vision *is* the poem, we feel. The
immense passion of Leda and the swan is what so powerfully
evokes

> The broken wall, the burning roof and tower
> And Agamemnon dead.

But as all visionaries are human, Yeats rightly ends his poem
with a question put with a sense of wonder:

> Did she [Leda] put on his knowledge with his power
> Before the indifferent beak could let her drop?

The bird is "indifferent", has had his will and flown or swum
away, but a whole legend has flowered and, expressed in words,
become lasting.

In *Leda and the Swan* we can see the essential parts of Yeats's
ever-increasing and growing vision. There is no fantasy here,
no make-believe. There is myth, certainly, but myth used for a
purpose; yet "used" is really not the right word. Yeats, like all
true visionary poets, leaves little space between the vision and
the expression of it. By this, I do not mean that he does not work
for words, for images, for the precise expression, but rather that
what he sees and later writes down seem like the same thing.
With Durrell, there is the drawing back and *then* the seeking for
expression, almost always a sensuous one. Perhaps Yeats shares
this quality of unity and immediacy more truly and deftly with
D. H. Lawrence than with any of the writers who are studied
here; but that is the only other thing he does share with Lawrence. So much else differs in these two writers. One is Yeats's
care for ceremony, others are Lawrence's absolute subjection to
subject-matter which is so essential to his way of looking at our
world. Yet I think that the most vital difference is in Yeats's care
for the mind, and Lawrence's very near repudiation of the mind,
the mind as intellect that is to say.

Among *School Children*, also in *The Tower*, has a natural link
with *Leda and the Swan*, partly because it actually mentions that
legend but also because, although it starts with a very ordinary
scene, it opens out into the grand vision which was to fill Yeats's

mind to the end of his life. The scene is a school which the poet
is being shown round as a distinguished visitor; he is "A sixty-
year-old smiling public man". He gazes at the young girls and
many thoughts fill him, thoughts which gradually (the poem
has eight regular, eight-lined stanzas) assume the form of a vision.
He reflects first upon Leda or, perhaps, a woman who had during
youth a body as beautiful as Leda's; as she grows older this
woman beside "a sinking fire" (the poem is everywhere concrete
in its imagery; there are few abstractions and none for their own
sake only), can tell of something "harsh" or "trivial" which,
nonetheless, "changed some childish day to tragedy". The actual
listening to this woman, and Yeats admits that he is now day-
dreaming, makes the poet feel at one with her, "blent" "from
youthful sympathy".

Now, he returns to the real girls before him, sitting at their
class-room desks, and wonders if when, younger still, they felt
Leda's "grief or rage"; he regards them as "daughters of the
swan" and thinks of Leda's loveliness. Here, the vision begins
and Yeats's "heart is driven wild" because now a woman he
has once known, "floats" with all her brilliance before his mind's
eye. He wonders if this woman, now a "present image", was
made in the Renaissance (time has ceased here to have any meaning for Yeats) and fashioned by a "Quattrocento finger". Again,
as in *Sailing to Byzantium*, works of art are always images of
immortality. Of himself, Yeats then declares,

> And I though never of Ledaean kind
> Had pretty plumage once—enough of that . . .

He swiftly and humourously introduces this memory of himself
as a handsome, passionate young man and wants "to smile on all
that smile" and show "There is a comfortable kind of old scarecrow". The homeliness of this is both effective and affecting.

Yeats, still retaining homely dreams, now tells us that the
woman who has so powerfully entered his mind and heart, could
be his mother and he ponders on what she would make of him.
So far, this poem seems more like transformed autobiography
than a vision, but we may be sure that it is not when Yeats
writes of Plato, Aristotle and Pythagoras, Greek philosophers

who had, and have, greater power than kings. He fastens upon
Pythagoras who

> Fingered upon a fiddle-stick or strings
> What a star sang and careless Muses heard:
> Old clothes upon old sticks to scare a bird.

The scarecrow is to reappear in Yeats's *Last Poems*, a frail yet
powerful, solid thing, which the poet links with the soil. Stanza
VII tells us that "Both nuns and mothers worship images . . ."
The word "worship" is not strictly true for the Roman Catholics
whom Yeats is thinking about; they venerate statues but they
only "worship" God. But the poet does not mock women who
put up candles. The fact is that they resemble "Presences", are
a reappearance of a theme, almost an obsession; we have met
before those Presences

> That passion, piety or affection knows,
> And that all heavenly glory symbolise . . .

The poet's full vision is revealed to us with his usual splendour
even though his words are simple, in the final stanza of this
poem. "Labour" is emphasized, for there can be no vision,
Eastern, Western, widely-known or personal, unless it is worked
for; but it cannot be forced, it can only be prepared for. Here
Yeats has a paradox for though "Labour is blossoming or danc-
ing", it is not itself the vision. *That* is given us in the last four
lines of this magnificent, eloquent, perfectly shaped poem. Again,
we note that Yeats asks a question:

> O chestnut-tree, great-rooted blossomer,
> Are you the leaf, the blossom or the bole?
> O body swayed to music, O brightening glance,
> How can we know the dancer from the dance?

Here is the essence of the vision, and it is a mystery and
accepted as such. Art and Nature are used to embody it. The
struggle to impart the vision is over and we are left suffused by
its wonder. Even the paradox is explained, has fallen away; there
is no obscurity at all.

The last poem from *The Tower* to be considered here is a
short lyric entitled *The Fool by the Roadside*. It is important

because it reveals the fundamental humility of a poet who was often regarded as an arrogant man. The visionary element resides in the recognition that folly and things "Transparent" as "the wind" may lead to wisdom; this is not stated but runs throughout the two six-line lyrics of the poem. Here are some of the lines relevant to my theme:

> When thoughts that a fool
> Has wound upon a spool
> Are but loose thread, are but loose thread;
>
> When cradle and spool are past
> And I were shade at last
> Coagulate of stuff
> Transparent like the wind,
> I think that I may find
> A faithful love, a faithful love.

As well as a strong belief in the after-life, another very important thing is again shown here; it is hope. For Yeats, life is nothing without passionate and tender love, and so, he is certain, eternity will give him such a love, entirely "faithful".

In his next book, *The Winding Stair and other Poems* which was published in 1933, Yeats has one of his best poems of this period; it is called A *Dialogue of Self and Soul*. Many things enter this poem but the essential theme is immortality; "self" and "soul" remind us of the original meaning of Existentialism (formulated long after Yeats wrote this poem, of course) which was that man is born with his existence and makes his essence; in this way—and Yeats would subscribe to this—free-will is of extreme importance. A *Dialogue of Self and Soul* alludes to astrology, history, religion, and philosophy, but the words and the rhythms, the deft use of half-rhymes are, as always now with this poet, clear. The surface of the poem is lucid, but to apprehend Yeats's vision completely we need to plumb the depths, reach the profundities. A clue resides in the *Self* speaking in the second part of this poem (the whole of it is written in nine stanzas). Some parts of the poem may sound arrogant, but not when we have read these later lines:

> What matter if I live it all once more?
> Endure that toil of growing up;
> The ignominy of boyhood; the distress
> Of boyhood changing into man ...

Here we are reminded vividly of those wise words of Keats, in a letter about adolescence, which he calls "the space of life between". All possible pride is removed from this poem when we read later, the *Self* still speaking, that Yeats is

> ... content to live it all again
> And yet again, if it be life to pitch
> Into the frog-spawn of a blind man's ditch ...
>
> I am content to follow to its source
> Every event in action or in thought ...

These lines come very near the end of the poem, but, because they are crucial to our sharing the poet's magnificent vision, I have considered them before commenting on *My Self* and *My Soul* (it is always important to remember which is speaking) in the first part. The second part of this dialogue is spoken entirely by *My Self* and is therefore obviously more personal—though the lofty vision lifts the personal element onto a more general plane, as all great poetry must be lifted, and there is no doubt about the greatness of this poem.

In this *Dialogue, My Soul* speaks first and talks of "the winding ancient stair", and conjures *Self* to

> Fix every wandering thought upon
> That quarter where all thought is done.

This stanza ends with the question, "Who can distinguish darkness from the soul?" As in *Sailing to Byzantium*, Yeats's *Self* replies that works of art can but, here, also so can weapons, "Sato's blade", for example, a blade that is cherished for its beauty and antiquity, not for the part it may have played in bloodshed. The poet then turns to the simple yet also intricate art of embroidery; his *Soul* now asks questions:

> Why should the imagination of a man
> Long past his prime remember things that are
> Emblematical of love and war?

29

His *Self* replies, referring to an important Eastern dignitary and warrior; the gist of this reply is that the pure antiquity of this sword give it a sacredness:

> ... about it lie
> Flowers from I know not what embroidery ...

Yeats "sets" these things

> For emblems of the day against the tower
> Emblematical of the night,
> And claim as by a soldier's right
> A charter to commit the crime once more.

Yeats was never a pacifist, always the reverse so long as the cause of fighting seemed to him just. His feelings about war in general reveal themselves in his highly idiosyncratic *Oxford Book of Modern Verse* where he omits Wilfred Owen who said of his own poems, "The Poetry is in the Pity", simply because the poet-anthologist considered that "passive suffering is not a subject for poetry"; he was not condemning the soldier, Owen, who fought in the trenches in France and died, so ironically, a week before Armistice Day, but his attitude towards war. Both men were great poets but great poets in entirely different ways —hence Yeats's otherwise inexplicable omission of Owen from the Oxford anthology.

But to return to *A Dialogue of Self and Soul*—the poet's *Soul* answers his *Self* in this way: (a "quarter" is undoubtedly a reference to astrology and all magic, in which Yeats in his later years, took such a great interest):

> Such fullness in that quarter overflows
> And falls into the basin of the mind
> That man is stricken deaf and dumb and blind,
> For intellect no longer knows
> *Is* from the *Ought*, or *Knower* from the *Known* ...

Then, at once, follow lines which are entirely at variance with Christian teaching:

> That is to say, ascends to Heaven;
> Only the dead can be forgiven;
> But when I think of that my tongue's a stone.

Yeats is wrong and, being a highly educated man, knows that he is wrong or, rather, at variance with Christian dogma when he declares that "Only the dead can be forgiven". But it is no part of this book's purpose to delve deeply into the differences between Christian and other visionaries' modes of thought and belief; they simply need to be noted. The essential, most important part of this poem is the splendid affirmation of its last line, "Everything we look upon is blest."

The next two poems which I want to consider in *The Winding Stair* are very short. The first throws much light both on Yeats's beliefs and his vision. The first is called *Symbols* and in three rhymed couplets manages to convey all that his work is increasingly moving towards. It is a remarkable poem because it is brief without being either elliptical or obscure. We see how all these later poems are linked together by the mention of an "old watch-tower" in the first line; again, Yeats's passion for art and history appears in the phrase "All-destroying sword-blade" at the beginning of the second couplet. In the second line of that couplet, Yeats's prevailing Fool appears, here called "wandering". The final line binds everything together: "Beauty and fool together laid."

A fool, as in Shakespeare's *King Lear*, has a strange wisdom which so-called wise men lack; "beauty" is both that of a greatly loved human being and also of lasting art. This small, in length, poem is a kind of key to Yeats's whole view of the world.

The other, even shorter poem from *The Winding Stair*, called *Spilt Milk*, is important because it tells us, very simply, just what Yeats believed about thought and action. The poem is only one rhymed quatrain and needs to be quoted completely:

> We that have done and thought,
> That have thought and done,
> Must ramble, and thin out
> Like milk spilt on a stone.

The operative word here is "ramble". Yeats knows about wandering and seeking what he desires. Again, the simile about "milk spilt" is homely but also exact and carries great weight. Yeats is a master at handling the homely as well as the ceremonious.

Over and over again, he links what appear to be disparate elements with perfect decorum in his poems.

The last poem I want to look at closely in *The Winding Stair* is *Byzantium*. It may be related to *Sailing to Byzantium* but has a greater power and vision than the earlier poem. Here, Yeats is concerned with, almost taken over by, the last three lines of the first of five stanzas:

> All that man is,
> All mere complexities,
> The fury and the mire of human veins.

Beside his vision, any complexities at all seem trivial. In the poem's second stanza, the poet sees "shades" and "images" and, once more, "the winding path" (not a staircase now). But he ends this stanza with a triumphant assertion:

> I hail the superhuman;
> I call it death-in-life and life-in-death.

Yeats explains this anomaly by returning, in a different way, to his prevailing theme of wishing to become, when dead, part of a lasting, indeed immortal work of art. Here, however, he uses the word "miracle". This third stanza begins:

> Miracle, bird or golden handiwork,
> More miracle than bird or handiwork,
> Planted on the star-lit golden bough . . .
> . . . . .
> In glory of changless metal . . .

The penultimate stanza speaks of the Emperor of Byzantium and the power, as Yeats pictures Byzantium, of the place itself. What seem of most relevance are the lines which soon follow:

> And all complexities of fury leave,
> Dying into a dance,
> An agony of trance,
> An agony of flame that cannot singe a sleeve.

The last stanza of *Byzantium* shows us Yeats entirely carried away by his vision. It is hard to believe that the wording of his experience and the experience itself are not one. Of course, they cannot be because there is complete, technical control over language here, as always with Yeats. But he is ecstatic and says "Spirit after spirit!". These spirits are "Astraddle on the dolphin's mire and blood". It is "The golden smithies" (the artists, the craftsmen) who "break the [sea's] flood" and also "Break [explain or drive away] bitter furies of complexity". Simplicity returns and the poem ends on an affirmative note. Assured of the power of the Emperor's smithies, the poet cries out with joy,

> Those images that yet
> Fresh images beget,
> That dolphin-torn, that gong-tormented sea.

So the gong—a man-made thing—has, in Yeats's vision, power over the natural force of the sea itself.

I want to turn now to a consideration of a number of poems in Yeats's *Last Poems* because these poems are not only, from the literary point of view, his greatest achievement, but because they throw light, reveal more clearly his vision of this life and the next. The poems in this volume were written between 1936 and 1939. *The Gyres*, the first poem in the book, is about the end of the world, a subject treated by Yeats before but now differently. "Tragic joy" is what makes the falling-apart of all things endurable. "Rocky Face" stands for all who are prepared to see that "the centre will not hold". The gyres are turning everything topsy-turvy:

> For beauty dies of beauty, worth of worth,
> And ancient lineaments are blotted out.
> Irrational streams of blood are staining earth . . .

Reason has lost its power; so too have philosophers—Empedocles represents them. Yeats ends the first of these three stanzas,

> Hector is dead and there's a light in Troy;
> We that look on but laugh in tragic joy.

Even the sack of Troy means nothing. But rejoicing is essential to Yeats's vision and he does not mourn for "a more gracious time" or for "painted forms or boxes of make-up". What, then, remains? We are told in the last stanza, that a resurrection is to occur; the people and animals whom "Rocky Face holds dear" will return; now, Rocky Face becomes God but not precisely the Christian conception of him; he will give everlasting life:

> Lovers of horses and of women, shall,
> From marble of a broken sepulchre,
> Or dark betwixt the polecat and the owl,
> Or any rich, dark nothing disinter
> The workman, noble and saint, and all things run
> On that unfashionable gyre again.

There is some obscurity again. It is the "lovers of horses and of women" who will be given the power to bring back to physical, as well as spiritual, life "The workman, noble and saint . . ." Oddly, even the saint, after death, has disappeared, in Yeats's view, into darkness. Men who love women and horses have a greater power to give life than they have. This poem puts forth a view that is so private as not to be tenable. But, as a personal view, it must be taken seriously; within the context of all Yeats's late poems it coheres. It endures as a splendid work of the imagination, not as theology or philosophy. *Lapis Lazuli*, which follows *The Gyres* is a much better, clearer poem because it does not make such enormous claims on the reader as *The Gyres*. I would say it is one of the very finest poems Yeats ever wrote. It is important because it is the most adamant, the most exultant affirmation he put into verse of his belief that life is fundamentally joyful. The poem owes its title to the fact that these superb lines spring from Yeats's scrutiny of some Chinese figures made of lapis lazuli. It is very surprising what ideas or poems can spring from a small work of art or a little living creature. Eliot said something interesting about this once when talking about the poems of Marianne Moore; he declared that it did not matter what started a poem off; what was important was the finished product. That was what must be evaluated and cared for; so the end was, ultimately, of much greater importance than the beginning, the initial impulse.

Yeats starts this poem by chiding "hysterical women" for being "sick of" art and of poets who "are always gay" and for considering that they should be worried, and doing something about war (there is an apparent contradiction here with Yeats's view of Wilfred Owen). The poet eschews this attitude and illustrates his own feelings about it (and we must never forget that he was not a man who was a pacifist, far from it) by referring to two of Shakespeare's greatest tragic heroes, Hamlet and Lear. So everything is thus seen *sub specie aeternitatis*; these characters from plays are immortal in the minds of men, but they are something else as well, and that something is the heart of Yeats's vision of life. He writes,

> ... Hamlet and Lear are gay;
> Gaiety transfiguring all that dread.
> All men have aimed at, found and lost;
> Black out; Heaven blazing into the head:
> Tragedy wrought to its uttermost.

However much "Hamlet rambles" and "Lear rages", they cannot *alter* anything; they may move us to experience things we have never dreamt of, but Yeats's vision takes us even further; his absolute faith that "Hamlet and Lear are gay" is not facile. The third part of this poem, which is not written in regular stanzas, tells us why.

The crucial lines in this part of the poem are

> All things fall and are built again,
> And those that build them again are gay.

From what we have already seen about Yeats's view of immortality, we know that by building up again, he does not mean just the material erecting of houses or cities or of works of art. Great art, *under* these forms, has a lasting quality of its own. So, before he talks about building up, Yeats gives examples of the kind of people who do this. Some people, if they read such a poem as *Lapis Lazuli* superficially or casually, might suppose that Yeats's attitude is a callous one. That would be very ill-judged and wrong indeed:

> Old civilisations put to the sword.
> Then they and their wisdom went to rack:
> No handiwork of Callimachus,
> Who handled marble as if it were bronze,
> Made draperies that seemed to rise
> When sea-wind swept the corner, stands ...

After the assertion that all these people are gay, Yeats moves
to the Chinese work of art which evoked this poem:

> Two Chinamen, behind them a third,
> Are carved in lapis lazuli,
> Over them flies a long-legged bird,
> A symbol of longevity . . .

Yeats, in spite of all his ideas about and beliefs in immortality,
wanted to stay on this earth as long as possible. Hence the
"symbol of longevity". But now he writes of this work of art
as if the people carved are alive; here the poem becomes visionary,
rises from the ground and uplifts us too:

> . . . doubtless plum or cherry-branch
> Sweetens the little half-way house
> Those Chinamen climb towards, and I
> Delight to imagine them seated there;
> . . . . . .
> On all the tragic scene they stare.

And the poem ends with complete conviction:

> Their eyes mid many wrinkles, their eyes,
> Their ancient, glittering eyes, are gay.

This is no idle wish on Yeats's part for immortality but an
affirmation of joy, a vision that transcends all that so cumbers
and misleads us. The poem is undoubtedly great, it carries us
away into speculations of our own as well as remaining in the
mind with all its careful detail and statements.

An Acre of Grass is a very personal poem entirely concerned
with the power a man must exercise, however difficult, to the
very end of his life. As an artist, Yeats feels this especially in-
cumbant upon him; he must not give in when "strength of body
goes". He states plainly that "My temptation is quiet". He
means, here, passivity. In the second stanza of this poem, written
in four stanzas of six lines each, he recognizes that he needs far
more than simply what comes at the end of most men's days, and
he cries out against it, defies it:

> Here at life's end
> Neither loose imagination,

> Nor the mill of the mind
> Consuming its rag and bone,
> Can make the truth known.

Yeats desires power and vision and so prays thus:

> Grant me an old man's frenzy,
> Myself must I remake
> Till I am Timon and Lear
> Or that William Blake
> Who beat upon the wall
> Till Truth obeyed his call.

The poet realizes he must summon up his strength himself, not expect it to come upon him without effort. The vision of the "Truth" he seeks may now be commanded, not just waited for. The last line of the final stanza is reminiscent of Eliot's "Why should the aged eagle spread its wings?"

What Yeats want is the kind of richness of mind that "Michael Angelo [sic] knew"; such a visionary mind could

> ... pierce the clouds,
> Or inspired by frenzy
> Shake the dead in their shrouds

—or, otherwise, be forgotten by mankind. Yeats wants to live on and he wants his work to be remembered; he was fortunate, for both these things happened. He died when he was writing at the height of his powers. What he called "frenzy" was really a visionary power, something that took him over. But there is nothing wild in his last poems, as we shall see in the few others to be examined; his poetic technique becomes, if possible, more deft than ever, his ear more acute. All these last poems are a unique apotheosis in English poetry. Yeats makes his personal experiences general by communicating them in such exultant rhythms and simple but exquisite words. He writes more and more about the art of poetry itself, as can be seen in *Those Images*, a poem of four four-lined verses which again mentions the eagle. The poet is speaking, throughout the poem, of how he receives the symbols for his poems; he feels that he has some control over them, but not much. This is in accordance with all that good or great poets have written about the making of poems. Though Yeats feels able to give orders to his poems, he does so largely in an impersonal way:

> I never bade you go
> To Moscow or to Rome.
> Renounce that drudgery,
> Call the Muses home.

He wishes his poetic faculty or Muse (a word dulled and debased by careless usage) to

> Seek those images
> That constitute the wild,
> The lion and the virgin,
> The harlot and the child.

This is an odd assembly, but all four have one thing in common, namely, power. The lion has his animal strength, the child, through its innocence, the ability to command, the virgin the impregnability that comes from chosen purity of mind and body. But what power has the harlot, one might ask? That over the desires of men would, I believe, be the answer. In the final stanza of this poem, Yeats states decisively just what he does want his images to do:

> Find in middle air
> An eagle on the wing,
> Recognise the five
> That make the Muses sing.

"The five" are, of course, the lion, the eagle, and the three people who have been discussed.

Long-Legged Fly is the next of Yeats's last poems which I want to consider. It has a magical, a truly mysterious refrain; each stanza contains it.

> *Like a long-legged fly upon the stream*
> *His* [in the second of the three stanzas, *"Her"*] *mind*
> *moves upon silence.*

This is a perfect summing-up of contemplation. The other eight lines of each stanza are more concerned with action. The result is that we are given a unique blending of the preparation for a vision and the vision itself; and always the language is absolutely concrete, never abstract. The first stanza is concerned specifically with civilization, that it should not fall into decadence. Julius Caesar is mentioned but, just before he is, two gentle lines occur, lines which are meant to be an indication of how civilization can be maintained:

> Quiet the dog, tether the pony
> To a distant post . . .

The second stanza continues this theme. Yeats is strangely aware of just when peace and stillness are essential, so he writes,

> That the topless towers be burnt
> And men recall that face,
> Move most gently if move you must
> In this lonely place.

The poet is referring to the Trojan War and Marlowe's lines about Helen,

> Is this the face that launched a thousand ships
> And burnt the topless towers of Ilium?

It seems, at first, strange that war should be mentioned but this is not only part of Yeats's vision, but also a part of history as well. Out of the worst wars in the past, the greatest art has usually followed. I think we should recall here the lines from *Lapis Lazuli*,

> All things fall and are built again,
> And those that build them again are gay.

This is the vision of joy which leaps from all the best last poems. As for history, we only have to recall the great works of art which appeared after times of great strife—the Renaissance, for example. Before the refrain, this second stanza has a beautiful touch of human simplicity. Yeats speaks of someone "part woman, three parts a child" who, thinking in her innocence that no-one is watching her, practises "a tinker shuffle / Picked up on a street". Such innocence is also part of civilization and part of Yeats's vision. He never falters when he is combining the grand with the extremely simple—in his own words, "the ceremony of innocence".

The last stanza of *Long-Legged Fly* shows us Yeats wishing girls "at puberty" to keep "The first Adam in their thought", and he does this by conjuring the reader to "Shut the door of the Pope's chapel". This is not, of course, a contradiction of the desire to retain innocence; Yeats is writing again of Michelangelo (or, as he calls him, Michael Angelo) here painting the marvellous Adam on the ceiling of the Sistine Chapel:

> There on that scaffolding reclines
> Michael Angelo.
> With no more sound than the mice make
> His hand moves to and fro.

The most vivid description of Michelangelo lying, and sweating, on his back painting is given in that great artist's own sonnets.

I think it is true to say that Yeats wishes adolescent girls to rejoice in what Christians call "the happy fault" of The Fall of Man; if there had been no symbolic eating of the forbidden apple, there would never have been a need for art. Yet there is something else in these lines where Yeats so brilliantly makes the past seem like the present; he wants young girls to be told early of the beauty of human love and passion, so what better picture of man could there be than Michelangelo's Adam? Yeats states decisively that this is not for children; one line of this tightly-packed yet lucid stanza says, "Keep those children out". The refrain of this last stanza refers to Michelangelo as he is working.

This is a very subtle poem, but Yeats expresses the ideas drawn from his vision of the world with such simplicity and so lyrically that he shares it with us completely. Everything has been assimilated and now, in the poem, is expressed.

There are only two more poems by Yeats which I want to write about. The first is called *Why should not Old Men be Mad?* It is a grand gesture on the part of old age, a celebration of its powers. A few familiar images appear, but the form is unlike those of many of the last poems; the poem is written in ten rhymed, four-beat couplets.

Yeats begins this poem by showing how promising boys have become "a drunken journalist". Again, a girl who once knew the whole of Dante's works married "a dunce". Then there was a Helen, obviously a young woman of great beauty, who dreamt of doing social welfare work and finally mounted "a wagonette to scream". Yeats is at great pains to show us that promise or beauty in youth may very often come to nothing. He then makes an abstract statement:

> Some think it a matter of course that chance
> Should starve good men and bad advance . . .

He does not remain abstract for long, however, but continues his theme thus.

> That if their neighbours figured plain,
> As though upon a lighted screen,
> No single story would they find
> Of an unbroken happy mind,
> A finish worthy of the start.

Yeats considers these ideas very prevalent, heart-rending, and true. "Young men", he says, "know nothing of this sort" but "Observant old men know it well". Old men have acquired wisdom and they are well aware of the injustices of life. These injustices are something Yeats cannot endure and so he ends his poem thus,

> And when they [old men] know what old books tell,
> And that no better can be had,
> Know why an old man should be mad.

So old men, in Yeats's view, understand how the disillusionments of life can drive old men mad. He never supposes that he himself is mad; he is, rather, very angry at what appears to be an element of determinism in life. This infuriates him because he believes firmly in free-will.

This poem, though at certain points argumentative, is like the aftermath of a vision, the coming down to earth. For this reason it is important to include it in this book.

The last poem to be examined is entirely different, Yeats at his finest in every way. It is called *The Circus Animals' Desertion* and, on one level, is about the making of a poem. Before we enter this poem, I think it should be said that Yeats stated of himself and his fellow-poets, "We were the last Romantics". It is an odd claim since few of Yeats's own poems, except perhaps the very early ones, owe anything to the early nineteenth-century English Romantic poets. But they did share one thing—a desire to join a cause, in the case of Wordsworth and some of his contemporaries, it was the French Revolution, in the case of Yeats and his, the Irish "Troubles" (*Easter 1916* was a visionary example of this). In every other way, Yeats is a classical poet; he can see a vision, hold it, withdraw from it and then share it with his readers. His love of history and myth is also classical in its scope and power. On the other hand, he does share with earlier Romantic poets, a method of personal writing, whether he is wearing a mask or not. *The Circus Animals' Desertion* brings all his greatest qualities together.

The poem is written in five, regular, rhymed stanzas. It begins with the poet re-exploring how he discovered his images and themes in the past. In old age, he is feeling that he cannot find images any more—any new ones, that is to say. So, this poem is a splendid juxtaposition of art and, much more important, a vision accepted wholly by the complete man. Yeats says that "maybe" he is "a broken man" but this very poem proves triumphantly that he most certainly is not. Then this marvellous moment comes in the first stanza :

> I must be satisfied with my heart, although
> Winter and summer till old age began
> My circus animals were all on show . . .

This is not disillusionment or resignation; it is a dynamic acceptance, as will be made clearer as we look at this poem more closely. It is not obscure (Yeats seldom is), but because this is undoubtedly a great visionary poem, we want to take care that we miss nothing. One reading almost stuns us, but further readings are necessary to discover everything—in short, all the riches that are here.

In the second stanza of *The Circus Animals' Desertion*, Yeats seems to have reached near-despair, which he communicates to us in this way:

> What can I but enumerate old themes?
> First that sea-rider Oisin led by the nose
> Through three enchanted islands, allegorical dreams,
> Vain gaiety, vain battle, vain repose,
> Themes of the embittered heart, or so it seems . . .

The poet feels deserted, but he is resolute, defiant, adamant. Love and passion have not deserted him, nor has fanaticism, but now these viewpoints appear to be mere dreams,

> And this brought forth a dream and soon enough
> This dream itself had all my thought and love.

The Fool, the Blind Man, Cuchalain, all symbols from the poet's past poems, are now "Heart-mysteries" and Yeats admits that "It was the dream itself enchanted me". He has reached great self-knowledge and profound wisdom; his vision has come together again, but now more enduringly. Yeats tells us, in a few words, what have been the misleading things in his past life:

> It was the dream itself enchanted me:
> Character isolated by a deed
> To engross the present and dominate memory.

And, casting off all that he feels has led him and his work astray, he writes,

> Players and painted stage took all my love,
> And not those things that they were emblems of.

But this is not the end; no end is ever tragic or disillusioned with Yeats. Just as "Hamlet and Lear are gay" for him, so is the world, yet it is not simply gay; there is much more to his vision than that, and this we see in this poem's last stanza.

Yeats, in this stanza, tells us that, although his images "Grew in pure mind", they began from something quite different. Here, he is in line with Christian theology. He recognizes from what slight homely things poems can start, and so he writes, as a reaffirmation, of

> A mound of refuse or the sweepings of a street,
> Old kettles, old bottles, and a broken can,
> Old iron, old bones, old rags, that raving slut
> Who keeps the till . . .

All great poets know this, but few express it within a poem and make a great poem about the truth of the art of poetry. Yeats speaks in the first person all through this poem but he makes the personal, general; his images are his own unique possessions which he communicates to us and shares with us through his poetry. Thus, *The Circus Animals' Desertion* is a visionary poem about how poets, especially old, wise, mature ones work. These last words have a beautiful, direct simplicity :

> . . . Now that my ladder's gone,
> I must lie down where all the ladders start,
> In the foul rag-and-bone shop of the heart.

What, we may ask, precisely is this "ladder". It is, surely, a symbol for the fantasy flights of verse which Yeats knew as a young man. The "rag-and-bone shop of the heart" is "foul" because man is flesh and spirit, his motives are mixed, he is moved by lust and staggered by love. To end a poem with a line such as the last one of *The Circus Animals' Desertion* and still leave the reader with a very powerful sense of dignity and grandeur is an amazing achievement. Yeats has lifted the curtain from the stage of his particular poetic world and revealed the truth of his vision, and what we feel, on seeing it, is a tragic pity, not for Yeats but for the general condition of man.

II

D. H. LAWRENCE

A Vision of the Natural World

This is a study of D. H. Lawrence as a visionary, not of the man who, with his novels and a number of paintings, gave people a liberating attitude towards sexual experience and love, but rather of the poet who wrote ecstatic poems. In his poems Lawrence lost himself, steeped himself in all animals, trees and flowers. Out of this imaginative immersion he wrote in a sensuous, but scarcely ever merely sensual way of what he had found and, like all visionary writers, he passed his experiences on almost as completely as they came to him. All visions, whether religious or secular, must necessarily lose a little of their initial brilliance when they are put into words or paintings, but a great genius (and there is no doubt that Lawrence was this) both loses and gains when he begins to communicate. He loses in so far as some experiences cannot of their nature be transcribed completely into words, but he gains in that language was Lawrence's medium, so that words came naturally and inevitably to him, untarnished, accurate and rich without ever being cloying.

Snake is probably his best-known poem and, if not his finest, reveals to us how he could actually enter into the sensations of the animal kingdom, whatever form they took, and also into the very growth of plants. Lawrence did very much more than identify himself with the natural world or just describe it; he entered it with the liveliest senses and the deepest compassion at one and the same time. We can see this in the following lines from *Snake*:

45

In the deep, strange-scented shade of the great dark carob-
tree
I came down the steps with my pitcher
And must wait, must stand and wait, for there he was at
the trough before me.

The poet enters into the movements of the snake by subduing
his own much more intricate human feelings and thoughts. So
Lawrence continues thus:

He reached down from a fissure in the earth-wall in the
gloom
And trailed his yellow-brown slackness soft-bellied down,
over the edge of the stone trough
And rested his throat upon the stone bottom,
And where the water had dripped from the tap, in a small
clearness,
He sipped with his straight mouth,
Softly drank through his straight gums, into his slack long
body,
Silently.

This is more than observation. There has been, very obviously,
close observation certainly, but the poet has moved far beyond
that. Seeing was for him a means, not an end. His beautifully
modulated lines, his deliberate repetitions and alliteration help
him to enter into the snake's sensations. Lawrence's human self
is set aside and all he cares about is the activity of the snake. But,
of course, only a human being of transcendent vision and a
complete control over language could write down all this and
share his view of the natural world with us. And, while identifying himself with this snake, Lawrence at the same time maintains
a human respect for him, a love of the creature simply for what
he is. This is very like Hopkins's understanding of, for example,
the "inscape", the individuality of a particular bird and, indeed,
also of all nature. So, a little further in this poem, Lawrence continues,

The voice of my education said to me
He must be killed,
For in Sicily the black, black snakes are innocent, the gold
are venomous.

And voices in me said, If you were a man
You would take a stick and break him now, and finish him off.

But this is something the poet cannot bear the idea of; such
a killing seems to him almost as bad as killing or even threaten-
ing his own compassion and love of creatures and trees and
flowers. We must note the great artistry in Lawrence's particular
kind of *vers libre*, its complete lack of arbitrariness, its use of
repetition. He, feeling as if he were the reptile itself, questions
himself and also states specifically the care he has for this snake
which he has just come upon for the first time:

But must I confess how I liked him,
How glad I was he had come like a guest in quiet, to drink
                                        at my water-trough
And depart peaceful, pacified, and thankless,
Into the burning bowels of this earth?

Lawrence desires no gratitude from the snake. On the contrary,
so much is he steeped in it and its life, that to be able to receive
the snake's gratitude for water would almost, to Lawrence, be
like thanking himself for something. Yet there is a complete
lack of sentimentality about this poem because while Lawrence
can contemplate the snake, he can also go on questioning himself,
probing his motives:

Was it cowardice, that I dared not kill him?
Was it perversity, that I longed to talk to him?
Was it humility, to feel so honoured?
I felt so honoured.

The key-word here is "honoured". Lawrence recognizes that
though it can harm, even kill, the snake is no part of the evil,
fallen world of men; he feels himself into the very skin of the
snake but is haunted by human, accusing voices:

And yet those voices:
If you were not afraid, you would kill him!

But Lawrence admits that he *is* afraid yet, and this is very important to his whole approach to the natural world, he is far more
honoured and happy just to behold the snake:

47

And truly I was afraid, I was most afraid,
But even so, honoured still more
That he should seek my hospitality
From out the dark door of the secret earth.

This "dark door" is a clue to the way in which Lawrence longs
to and succeeds in entering the animal world. It is a dark and
often dangerous place for man to enter, but he enters it, becomes
one with the snake. There is nothing in him of the person who
tries to tame what is wild nor, on the other hand, of the man
who enjoys killing, destroying nature. Tiger-shooting or fox-
hunting would have been anathema to Lawrence.

More and more he enters into the secret life of the snake, this
creature who is quite unaware that he has much more than a
very compassionate man near him who is risking, for a little
time, his life. So, when the snake had drunk "enough", he

... looked around like a god, unseeing, into the air,
And slowly turned his head,
And slowly, very slowly, as if thrice adream,
Proceeded to draw his slow length curving round
And climb again the broken bank of my wall-face.

Then, with a reluctance that frightens him, Lawrence realizes
that he must do something about the snake because it is deadly.
And so,

... I put down my pitcher,
1 picked up a clumsy log
And threw it at the water-trough with a clatter.

I think it did not hit him,
But suddenly that part of him that was left behind con-
                    vulsed in undignified haste,
Writhed like lightning, and was gone
Into the black hole ...

Here we reach the heart of Lawrence's feelings, the passion
he felt and the vision of the natural world as he saw it. He has
not killed the snake, he has only banished him, cast him away,
taken away his freedom but he writes,

... immediately I regretted it.
I thought how paltry, how vulgar, what a mean act!
I despised myself and the voices of my accursed human
                                                  education.

And I thought of the albatross,
And I wished he would come back, my snake.

The albatross which Lawrence mentions is, of course, a reference
to the albatross which the Ancient Mariner shot in Coleridge's
ballad. But Lawrence calls this reptile whom he has only en-
countered once, and by chance, "my snake"; the identification
is complete. He curses what he has learnt, he wishes to be a
creature who could live in contented ignorance were it not for
the existence of man. So the vision reaches a great height in this
poem's last lines:

For he seemed to me again like a king,
Like a king in exile, uncrowned in the underworld,
Now due to be crowned again.

And so, I missed my chance with one of the lords
Of life.
And I have something to expiate;
A pettiness.

Such is the strength of Lawrence's care for creation that merely
throwing "a clumsy log" at the snake seems to him to be a cruel
act; even though he calls this "A pettiness", and thus flings aside
all possibility of sentimentality, he feels there is something he
ought to expiate. For him, the snake is "one of the lords/Of life"
and he has meddled with it, interfered with its ordinary, daily
activity.

This is a very powerful poem indeed. The passion and vision
are tremendously strong, but so also is the control of language
and rhythm. Words are leashed by the careful, inevitable line-
lengths; there is great artistry here and not a flaw in style or
in the way in which the poet's thoughts and feelings are expressed. If this poem represents "the spontaneous overflow of
powerful feeling", then the overflow is checked, stemmed, and
so the poem becomes all the more potent because of the simple

words which are used and which are partly responsible for giving
the impression of restraint. The surface of the poem is unruffled
but beneath the actual words and repetition, very great passion
is communicated to us; it is not an exaggeration to say that in
this one poem we are given a completely new vision of the world.

Lawrence wrote a long poem called *Man and Bat* which bears
some resemblance to *Snake* although, in this poem, when the
poet, on entering his room at noon in Florence finds a bat there,
his immediate response is disgust and fright:

> The venetian shutters I push wide
> To the free, calm upper air;
> Loop back the curtains . . .
>
> *Now out, out from my room!*

But the bat will not go and Lawrence has a very vividly expressed
struggle with the creature. Then, after the battle, he realizes
something and this makes him identify himself with the bat,
enter into its sensations:

> He *could* not go out,
> I also realized . . .
> It was the light of day which he could not enter,
> Any more than I could enter the white-hot door of a blast
> furnace.
> He could not plunge into the daylight that streamed at the
> window.
> It was asking too much of his nature.

Here Lawrence shows that unique understanding and compassion
for life which make him able, as no other English poet can do
so completely, to succeed in thinking as a man yet, *at the same
time*, enter completely into the life of other living creatures or
trees or plants. So he can say,

> Worse even than the hideous terror of me with my hand-
> kerchief
> Saying: *Out, go out!* . . .
> Was the horror of white daylight in the window!
>
> So I switched on the electric light, thinking: *Now
> The outside will seem brown* . . .

The battle between a man and a beast is over; sympathy has changed the poet's attitude. Lawrence's care is now almost entirely for the bat, yet he has not, at this point, altogether forgotten his disgust. And so he continues,

> But no.
> The outside did not seem brown.
> And he did not mind the yellow electric light.
>
> Silent!
> He was having a silent rest.
> But *never!*
> *Not in my room.*

It is not simply that the poet is disgusted by the bat; he cannot endure its helpless flounderings and plungings, its blindness; and, though he may say "Go out!" and "Out, you beast", and though he says these things and describes with great colour and excitement his dilemma and his feeling that the bat is "like something unclean", he cares. He is far more concerned with the bat, identified with it (the powerful, straightforward language proves this) than with his own emotion. So he writes,

> What then?
> Hit him and kill him and throw him away?
>
> Nay,
> I didn't create him.
> Let the God that created him be responsible for his death . . .
> Only, in the bright day, I will not have this clot in my
> room.

This last admission in no way diminishes Lawrence's concern; rather, it enhances the conflict. Much as he hates the presence of the bat in his sunlit room, he is full of a terrible sadness when the bat, by so floundering and knocking himself about the room, finally dies. Great tenderness resides in these lines:

> He fell again with a little thud
> Near the curtain on the floor.
> And there lay.

And the next lines are full of passion. For a creature whom almost everyone is frightened of, Lawrence can feel like this:

Ah death, death
You are no solution !
Bats must be bats.

Only life has a way out.
And the human soul is fated to wide-eyed responsibility
In life.

All anger, all fear and disgust have gone; Lawrence's simple admission that "Bats must be bats" and his reference to human beings' "wide-eyed responsibility" take the form of willing himself, sometimes easily and with joy, sometimes with anger and suffering, into the very fibres of all that is Nature, all life, in short. And this goes to the very depths of Lawrence's being; it has nothing at all in common with the ordinary man and woman's care about cruelty to animals. It is something profoundly religious in Lawrence, the essence of his vision.

We must understand too, that Lawrence's extraordinary ability to identify himself with non-human, living created things had nothing to do with the famous "pathetic fallacy", that is to say, the ability to become other creatures fitfully (and fitfully is the operative word here) or, which happens far more often, merely think you can become a part of animate or even inanimate objects. Lawrence's vision was both higher and deeper than this, often so deep that, as with all visionaries, it sometimes took him into very dark places. But this was his whole way of life also. No single word can sum it up. Pantheism does not fit this poet at all, and certainly not the kind of pantheism which we find in the earlier Wordsworth. Lawrence had a vision shared by no-one else and he was and is, for that reason, inimitable. He founded no tradition, but he certainly changed men's minds and hearts.

This seems a fitting time to abandon for a moment members of what is called, roughly, the Animal Kingdom and look at what Lawrence does with trees. His poem called *Cypresses* is a perfect example of this wide, deep imagination of his, of the genius that amounts to a fresh vision. Here, once more is a complete identification with these particular trees as well as a love of them which is handed on to us by the wonderfully used

language, rhythm and repetitions of the lines of the whole poem.
It begins,

> Tuscan cypresses,
> What is it?

> Folded in like a dark thought,
> For which the language is lost,

[but this poet *has* found the language].

> Tuscan cypresses,
> Is there a great secret?
> Are our words no good?
> . . . . .
> Ah, how I admire your fidelity,
> Dark cypresses!

Just before these two lines, Lawrence compares the cypresses
with the then "Darkly monumental" and indecipherable language of the Etruscans. And then he goes on to speak of "The
long-nosed, sensitive-footed, subtly-smiling Etruscans". This
poem was written in Fiesole which is just ouside and above
Florence and is famous for its view of that treasure-crammed city
as well as for its Roman amphitheatre and its trees and the
almost fabulous scents mingled of so many natural things. Lawrence, though he has entered entirely into the life, the very sap,
of the cypresses, can still call them "vicious"; perhaps because
he lets them overwhelm him, though never to the detriment of
the control in which he writes about them, he is able to use this,
in other contexts, strongly offputting adjective. But Lawrence
loves all things for their danger and this is the whole point of
Cypresses; the constant allusions to the Etruscans are really the
poet's movements into the life of the trees:

> The smile, the subtle Etruscan smile still lurking
> Within the tombs,
> Etruscan cypresses.

Yet the poet also wishes to bring back the cypresses to a state,
a world of pure innocence, a time before The Fall of Man, and
he scorns that idea when he writes,

What would I not give
To bring back the rare and orchid-like
Evil-yclept Etruscan?
For as to the evil
We have only Roman word for it,
Which I, being a little weary of Roman virtue,
Don't hang much weight on.

Lawrence eschews most established religions, whether very old
or very new and although, in his novels and letters, he attempts
to provide a religion of his own, he never does this in his poems
or travel books. This matter is well put in some words of a poem
by Auden, "The full view indeed may enter". Also, good poetry is
always intensely recalcitrant to the didactic, the preaching voice.

It is true that the dark mysteries of Mexicans, the Aztecs,
fascinated Lawrence, but this fascination, shown so vividly in
his novel *The Plumed Serpent*, held him because of its mysteries
rather than for its beliefs. These mysteries appear far more
vividly and directly in his poems where they assume the form of
genuine visions, something much loftier than great insight. In
the last line of *Cypresses*, however, the Mexican Montezuma,
rejected by America, is mentioned. He takes his place among all
that Lawrence hates so much in "what man has made of man";
these are the lines that complete this very beautiful poem, where
depth of feeling is so perfectly linked with simplicity:

Evil, what is evil?
There is only one evil, to deny life
As Rome denied Etruria
And mechanical America Montezuma still.

History is evoked here but comes with perfect decorum because
so much of *Cypresses* is concerned with Lawrence's "Etruscan
cypresses".

Before returning to Lawrence's animal poems, I think we
should examine his poem entitled *Bare Fig-Trees* because in it
there is a brief reference to a great religion, Judaism, and to
mythology; the poem, of course, is primarily concerned with the
fig-trees. It was written in Taormina. Lawrence travelled much
and this shows in his poetry, largely because of its subject-matter.
Bare Fig-Trees begins with a passionately felt celebration and

54

understanding of them, which is something far more profound than mere description.

> Fig-trees, weird fig-trees
> Made of thick smooth silver,
> Made of sweet, untarnished silver in the sea-southern air—
> I say untarnished, but I mean opaque—
> Thick, smooth-fleshed silver, dull only as human limbs are
> dull
> With the life-lustre,
> Nude with the dim light of full, healthy life
> That is always half-dark ...

Quickly, Lawrence, after this half-dark (the darkness which so often intrigues him, whether complete or partial), enters into the life of these bare fig-trees by using comparisons, similes:

> And suave like passion-flower petals,
> Like passion-flowers,
> With the half-secret gleam of a passion-flower hanging
> from the rock ...

Secrets are an important part of Lawrence's world, but he does not want to solve them completely; rather, he wants to be immersed in them, and this is yet another way in which he enters fully into Nature. He observes minutely, yes, but swiftly he also sees that life must be preserved and loved. This is the heart of his genius and vision and he finds the precise words and rhythms and repetitions by means of which he can share with his readers his own vision of the world. He wants us to become part of it too. His desire is to give as abundantly as he can. So now these fig-trees are compared with sea creatures:

> Rather like an octopus, but strange and sweet-myriad-
> limbed octopus;
> Like a nude, like a rock-living, sweet-fleshed sea-anemone,
> Flourishing from the rock in a mysterious arrogance.

Lawrence's visual imagery is always startling and he shows in this poem his rare ability to combine a wide and profound view of the visible world together with a sense of the mysterious, perhaps, almost, of the numinous. What is so interesting is that this poet gives freely his living beasts, trees and so on "arrogance", while he himself maintains assurance, an audacity that enables him to move us, communicate with us so deeply and compassionately. It also enables him to move from the specific, the brilliantly presented particular, to very orginally presented generalities. Thus, immediately after "a mysterious arrogance", we have these lines:

> Let me sit down beneath the many-branching candelabrum
> That lives upon this rock
> And laugh at Time, and laugh at dull Eternity,
> And make a joke of stale Infinity,
> Within the flesh-scent of this wicked tree,
> That has kept so many secrets up its sleeve,
> And has been laughing through so many ages
> At man and his uncomfortablenesses . . .

The poet speaks of great generalities but only to repudiate them; in fact, these lines alone might be taken as a summing-up of Lawrence's whole view of the world, the tangible, durable, strange-smelling world that has a kind of lastingness which has nothing at all to do with the abstract. The poet introduces his slight reference to Judaism almost immediately after the last quotation:

> Let me sit down beneath this many-branching candelabrum,
> The Jewish seven-branched, tallow-stinking candlestick
>   kicked over the cliff
> And all its tallow righteousness got rid of,
> And let me notice it behave itself.

Now Lawrence is feeling disgusted with Jewish smugness, the Pharisaical attitude, yet he does not drag this in simply to express personal venom but only because the shape of the bare fig-tree brings to his mind the Jewish candle-stick. This is proved in the splendid lines which follow, where the poet is indeed entering the very sap of the tree:

> And watch it putting forth each time to heaven,
> Each time straight to heaven,
> With marvellous naked assurance each single twig.
> Each one setting off straight to the sky
> As if it were the leader, the main-stem, the forerunner,

Intent to hold the candle of the sun upon its socket-tip,
It alone.

Every young twig
No sooner issued sideways from the thigh of his predecessor
Than off he starts without a qualm
To hold the one and only lighted candle of the sun in his
socket-tip.
He casually gives birth to another young bud from his
thigh . . .

The way in which Lawrence speaks of the tree as a person, a man, indicates his complete identification with it. It is essential that he sees first very carefully the shape of the tree, but from close observation he moves to imagery and from this his vision springs.

A further examination of Lawrence's tree and flower poems seems necessary because it gives us a deeper understanding of his animal poems. In the plant kingdom he is always at ease, but in the animal kingdom he can, largely because of our own human nearness to animal instincts, enter even more profoundly. Lawrence is humble, he sees himself as simply a part of a world of wonder. Where his human need to accuse and upbraid himself arises, as in *Snake*, he is willing to let it, wishing both to be at one with the reptile and also recognize his responsibilities as a man. In his best poems, these two things fuse; there is no dichotomy, only a revelation to the poet which is put into perfect words for us.

In *Bare Fig-Trees*, mythology is introduced when the poet compares the trees to "the snakes on Medusa's head"; after this, the poem cries out, "Oh naked fig-tree!" The poet is here wholly ecstatic. *Bare Almond-Trees* is a complete celebration of and identification with these other trees. It's only specific references to places are to Sicily and Etna, which are to be expected since this poem was written in Taormina. The beginning of the poem carries us, as it has carried the poet, into the rich sensuous life of these trees, even though they are now seen without their blossoms. Their very existence, whatever the season, is sufficient for Lawrence's vision of them:

Wet almond-trees, in the rain,
Like iron sticking grimly out of earth;
Black almond trunks, in the rain,
Like iron implements twisted, hideous, out of the earth . . .

Repetition is a constant device with Lawrence but never a
mere mannerism. And, as in other poems, the fact that a tree
as a member of the natural world may appear to be ugly never
deters the poet, never puts him off. On the contrary, it is, for
him, an invitation to look at the growing thing even more
closely. So, he continues *Bare Almond-Trees* like this:

Out of the deep, soft fledge of Sicilian winter-green,
Earth-grass uneatable,
Almond trunks curving blackly, iron-dark, climbing the
slopes.

Lawrence is again at home with the dark world, the world of
secrets and mysteries. But he loves the light too, and the world
of minerals and soon compares these almond-trees with steel.

You have welded your thin stems finer,
Like steel, like sensitive steel in the air,
Grey, lavender, sensitive steel, curving thinly and brittly
up in a parabola.
What are you doing in the December rain?

The questioning, the sense of wonder never leave Lawrence; the
whole world is to him always newborn, fresh for him to enter.
And delight is also a part of this amazing vision so accurately
expressed.

He is even able to feel a certain unity with the terrifying
forces of Nature for, in *Bare Almond-Trees*, he goes on to write
with great vigour and spontaneity:

Do you feel the air for electric influences
Like some strange magnetic apparatus?
Do you take in messages, in some strange code,
From heaven's wolfish, wandering electricity, that prowls
so constantly round Etna?
. . . . .
Do you telephone the roar of the waters over the earth?
And from all this, do you make calculations?

Lawrence has a startling vision here of the world both before man existed and of the discoveries he later made, and so he identifies himself with what these almond-trees are enduring; it is significant that they are fragile, utterly open to all storms yet also like lava which may at any time start pouring out of the crater of Mount Etna. So his poem concludes with a strange mixture of dread (for the trees) and also of exultation:

> Sicily, December's Sicily in a mass of rain
> With iron branching blackly, rusted like old, twisted,
> > implements
> And brandishing and stooping over earth's wintry fledge,
> > climbing the slopes
> Of uneatable soft green!

Even the last line of this poem has the strong tenderness which Lawrence feels for all living, vital things (whether swayed by storms or, in the case of reptiles and animals, moved by their own volition). He faces his own fear and casts it out by becoming one with all that is growing or tossed about around him. This is yet another part of his vision of the world, or even the whole universe.

It is time now to turn back to the Animal Kingdom and look at *Mountain Lion*, a poem written in Lobo, Mexico. After the second line, "Dark grow the spruce-trees, blue is the balsam, water sounds still unfrozen, and the trail is still evident", come three lines which open out Lawrence's whole approach to the world, his all-embracing acceptance, wonder and compassion:

> Men!
> Two men!
> Men! The only animal in the world to fear!

It is man, with all his own personal venom and fear as well as his destructive weapons, who is more terrifying than any lion. Simply, and with his customary and constant, though never tedious, use of repetition, Lawrence sets his scene:

> Two Mexicans, strangers, emerging out of the dark and
> > snow and inwardness of the Lobo valley.
> What are they doing here on this vanishing trail?

"Dark" and "inwardness" are important words here. We know Lawrence's fascination with dark things and places, but now we learn of the introspection he dislikes so much, his vision is seen outside himself, in the whole world; it is there he wishes to lose himself. Very soon we come to the lion and the man who caught it:

> It is a mountain lion,
> A long, long slim cat, yellow like a lioness.
> Dead.
> He trapped her this morning, he says, smiling foolishly.

Lawrence understands this man's emotions; he himself has felt something very like them about the snake and the bat, but he is now concerned with the beauty of the creature herself; man, for the moment, is forgotten:

> Lift up her face,
> Her round, bright face, bright as frost.
> Her round, fine-fashioned head, with two dead ears;
> And stripes in the brilliant frost of her face, sharp, fine
>   dark rays,
> Dark, keen, fine rays in the brilliant frost of her face.
> Beautiful dead eyes.

The poet goes in search of the lion and finds "her lair", "in the blood-orange brilliant rocks that stick up, a little cave". At once he mourns for her but, as usual, quite without sentimentality. He imagines the abundant life that was once in this now dead lion:

> So, she will never leap up that way again, with the yellow
>   flash of a mountain lion's long shoot!
> And her bright striped frost-face will never watch any more,
>   out of the shadow of the cave in the blood-orange rock,
> Above the trees of the Lobo dark valley-mouth!

After entering the lair, Lawrence looks out upon a desert and the snow on distant mountains. He ends the poem in a way which might seem inhuman if one did not know how much and steadfastly he cared about all men and women. But the crucial part of his vision is declared explicitly in these final lines about the lion:

And I think in this empty world there was room for me
                     and a mountain lion.
And I think in the world beyond, how easily we might
                  spare a million or two of humans
And never miss them.
Yet what a gap in the world, the missing white frost-face
                of that slim yellow mountain lion !

Here the identification of man with beast is total. Indeed, momentarily at least, Lawrence shows more admiration for the animal than for men.

An examination of the four poems called *The Evangelistic Beasts* gives us a great understanding of Lawrence's attitude towards Christianity. *St Matthew* is the first of these. After beginning

> They are not all beasts.
> One is a man, for example, and one is a bird.

Lawrence says "I, Matthew, am a man". He goes on at once to Christ himself, speaking as if he himself were St Matthew:

> That is Jesus.
> But then Jesus was not quite a man.
> He was the Son of Man
> *Filius Meus*, O remorseless logic . . .

There is, initially, more argument in this sequence of poems than in any of Lawrence's others, and he is not at his best with religious or philosophical disputation. He has quoted Christ's words, " 'And I, if I be lifted up, will draw all men unto me'," and then, as Matthew says,

> I, Matthew, being a man
> Cannot be lifted up, the Paraclete
> To draw all men unto me,
> Seeing I am on a par with all men.

Lawrence cannot believe that Christ is both God and man. Nor can he accept at all (none of us can *understand* such a mystery) the doctrine of the Blessed Trinity. But suddenly he changes the whole tone of the early lines and starts to show us what he, as Lawrence, yet also still as St Matthew, means by

61

being uplifted; this is a very strange vision, quite unlike any other writer's. So, he says,

> I, on the other hand,
> Am drawn to the Uplifted, as all men are drawn,
> To the Son of Man
> *Filius Meus.*
>
> *Wilt Thou lift me up, Son of Man?*
> How my heart beats !
> I am man.
>
> I am man, and therefore my heart beats, and throws the dark
> >   blood from side to side
> All the time I am lifted up.
> Yes, even during my uplifting.
>
> And if it ceased?
> If it ceased, I should be no longer man
> As I am, if my heart in uplifting ceased to beat, to toss the dark
> >   blood from side to side, causing my myriad secret streams . . .

Now we are back with the Lawrence who can steep himself in all natural things, enter places. This is the man who loves the world of the senses. As he says,

> I might be a soul in bliss, an angel, approximating to the
> >   Uplifted;
> But that is another matter;
> I am Matthew, the man,
> And I am not that other angelic matter.

Lawrence, as Matthew, has no wish for the kind of spiritual life which the Gospels tell us of :

> So I will be lifted up, Saviour,
> But put me down again in time, Master,
> Before my heart stops beating, and I become what I am not.

There is no blasphemy here; Lawrence is simply entering fully into his conception of St Matthew, just as he does with animals, trees, and flowers, all the tangible world, in fact. We must not think Lawrence is afraid of death; he only wants to endure and enjoy all that this planet is composed of. And this poem proceeds,

Put me down again on the earth, Jesus, on the brown soil
Where flowers sprout in the acrid humus, and fade into
                                        humus again.
Where beasts drop their unlicked young, and pasture, and
                              drop their droppings among the turf.
Where the adder darts horizontal.
Down on the damp, unceasing ground, where my feet belong
And even my heart, Lord, forever, after all uplifting:
The crumbling, damp, fresh land, life horizontal and
                                        ceaseless.

Nowhere in this poem is there a trace of mocking at Christianity;
Lawrence isn't even trying to set up his own adamant assurance,
his personal, powerful, unique vision against those of the
Christian mystics. He is only stating, showing to us his vision
—namely that the world we can know by our senses is sufficient
for him, is, in his own word, "ceaseless" for him. His vision is
of a different order from those of the Christians for whom he
shows great respect, even reverence; but his own view of the
world of man is different both in kind and in degree; the *kind*
is clearly the most important from the point of view of this
study. Lawrence has become so unified with the natural world
that, being a genius, he can only transmit that vision, the dark
and the light, which he finds there. But, in the following lines
of this poem we can see that his strong intelligence, his wish
to understand and share, makes him able to see the Christian's
point of view, even, at times, to partake in it; but, when he *does*
partake in it he changes it, perhaps unconsciously, into a part
of his own vision. Above all, he hates destruction, whether of
men or beasts or flowers or of trees. What he seeks, suggests, and
so often finds is a unity which he can express in his poems.

Matthew will "take the wings of the morning, to Thee,
Crucified, Glorified" but he insists on being "put down, Lord, in
the afternoon" and with a homely touch Lawrence adds,

> And at evening I must leave off my wings of the spirit
> As I leave off my braces ...

It is the earth which Lawrence, identified with Matthew, can
know with all his senses that the poet most cares about. This

may not be good theology, but it is not intended to be theology. Lawrence glories in, is willing to become one with, all natural things, beautiful and tame or frightening and cruel or ugly. And this is a noble vision. So, Matthew wishes to return to earth in the afternoon in order that he may join in all the created, sensuous life that is going on in the evening

> ... while flowers club their petals at evening
> And rabbits make pills among the short grass
> And long snakes quickly glide into the dark hole in the wall
> hearing man approach ...

Lawrence, speaking as the Evangelist, is a man who will approach all this and so much more. I do not think it is blasphemous to say that as Christ was "all things to all men" so, in all his poems about natural life, Lawrence shows a fierce desire to become what they are; and this is a courageous and humble desire. It also shows great reverence for life, a wish that nothing man has made will spoil it. The vision is passionate and it coheres; in short, it is seamless.

This poem, in which Lawrence so successfully becomes St Matthew, continues, with lines about a fish:

> And I must resume my nakedness like a fish, sinking down the
> dark reversion of night
> Like a fish seeking the bottom, Jesus ...

Lawrence who was far better informed than many people think then uses the Greek word for fish, the symbol of Christianity which can be seen so often in the Catacombs in Rome.

Identified with St Matthew, Lawrence must inevitably identify himself with Christ's message to his Apostles, but he does so in his own way; he does not tamper idly with what Roman Catholic Christians regard as accepted truths, he only changes them for his own purposes, but quite openly; there is never any deceit. Because of this, the St Matthew poem can continue thus:

> Over the edge of the soundless cataract
> Into the fathomless, bottomless pit
>
> . . . . .
> Utterly beyond Thee, Dove of the Spirit;
> Beyond everything, except itself.

Nay, Son of Man, I have been lifted up.
To Thee I rose like a rocket ending in mid-heaven.
But even Thou, Son of Man, canst not quaff out the dregs of
                                        terrestrial manhood!
They fall back from Thee.

There is something deeper than defiance here. The poet, putting
himself in what he feels to be St Matthew's position, cannot
help showing his own vision—not his own personality but his
profound, wide view of the world, where all that he cares for
is alive. Materialism never comes into the matter. Now, very
logically, after Matthew has seen the "Bat-winged heart of
man",

Afterwards, afterwards
Morning comes, and I shake the dews of night from the wings
                                        of my spirit
And mount like a lark, Beloved.

It is wonderful the way in which Lawrence can become St
Matthew and yet retain his usual extraordinary ability to enter
this world he loves so much. He can see and feel the beliefs of
St Matthew, so that, in these four *Evangelistic Beasts* poems, he
is doing, with great ease, a kind of double-identification, and
doing it with simple, life-brimmed language. After he has made
Matthew say

But remember, Saviour,
That my heart which like a lark . . . hovers morning-bright to Thee,
Throws still the dark blood back and forth
In the avenues where the bat hangs sleeping, upside-down
And to me undeniable, Jesus.

We know now what Lawrence felt and thought about a bat, his
private war with him, but here he never forgets the "Saviour",
Jesus, and he goes on to the Holy Ghost thus:

Listen, Paraclete.
I can no more deny the bat-wings of my fathom-flickering spirit
                                        of darkness
Than the wings of the Morning and Thee, Thou Glorified.

Lawrence speaks, paradoxically, on intimate yet also defer-
ential terms to the Holy Trinity. He concludes *St Matthew* as
he, speaking as Matthew, is "the Man" while also declaring
that "Thou art Jesus, Son of Man / Drawing all men unto
Thee . . ." The last lines of this poem speak of "the wings of
the morning", and "the zenith's reversal . . . Which is my way,
being man" [the lack of a capital letter for "man" here is
important]. But I think we must admit that it is Lawrence's
interpretation of Matthew rather than Matthew himself who
declares, "God may stay in mid-heaven, the Son of Man has
climbed to the Whitsun zenith". Yet Lawrence understands
precisely what Whitsun signifies and he ends his poem as a
prayer ends with the humble "So be it".

With St Mark's symbol, a lion, Lawrence's approach is slightly
different from the one he has towards St Matthew's emblem.
The poem begins with short lines but later opens out into
another identification, very like his poem about the mountain
lioness; the difference here, however, is that the Christian
religion, or Lawrence's version of it, enters in. Here are the
opening lines:

> There was a lion in Judah
> Which whelped, and was Mark.
>
> But winged.
> A lion with wings.
> At least at Venice
> Even as late as Daniele Manin.
>
> Why should he have wings?
> Is he to be a bird also?
> Or a spirit?
> Or a winged thought?
> Or a soaring consciousness?
>
> Evidently he is all that,
> The lion of the spirit.

Lawrence gives us this vision, then quickly moves to another
one—a real *tour de force*:

Ah, Lamb of God,
Would a wingless lion lie down before Thee, as this winged
                                                    lion lies?
    The lion of the spirit.

This writer never for a moment doubts the spirit of man, but he
also sees a spirit, something incorporeal as well as sensual, in
plants and animals. So, at this point, St Mark's lion becomes
like any other lion in a most powerful recreation:

Once he lay in the mouth of a cave
And sunned his whiskers,
And lashed his tail slowly, slowly
Thinking of voluptuousness
Even of blood.

Simple words like "sunned his whiskers" blend perfectly with
the strong "voluptuousness" and suggestion of blood.

Now Lawrence moves further into the lion's being, as far as
a man can go. He is one with the beast as he "fell to frowning,
as he lay with his head on his paws". But quickly a contrast
between the meek lamb and the lion is introduced in this truly
religious poem. The lion sees "in a shaft of light a lamb on a
pinnacle" and

Going out to investigate
He found the lamb beyond him, on the inaccessible pinnacle
                                                    of light.
So he put his paw to his nose, and pondered.

This lion is now completely Lawrence himself and the lamb is
The Lamb of God, part of another vision, understood but not of
the same kind as the poet's. The Lamb is Christ and he speaks as
Christ spoke:

"Guard my sheep," came the silvery voice from the pinnacle,
"And I will give thee the wings of the morning."
So the lion of the senses thought it was worth it.

We are clearly meant to see this vision as both unattainable
and a kind of trap. So, after an apt reference to Carpaccio, a
Venetian painter, Lawrence suddenly begins to show Christ's
ways and teachings as a threat. But, it is very important to

remember that this springs from the lion in Carpaccio's picture, though there is, a little later, an unmistakable note not of cynicism but of mockery. We soon see that orthodox Christianity is not for Lawrence, and we begin to see why his own vision and beliefs are different. The humour in some of the following lines takes away the sting of rancour or bitterness. This poem is far too potent for bitterness, as, indeed, any really fine, passionately felt poem is—even when we do not agree with all the poet is saying.

Lawrence, surely mistakenly, in this poem where he almost becomes the lion of St Mark, uses the animal as a strong defence and argument against the gentle but firm teaching of Christ. Of the lion, he continues,

> There is a new sweetness in his voluptuously licking his paw
> Now that it is a weapon of heaven.

There is a new ecstasy here recognized by Lawrence and so blended into his vision. But later he certainly makes fun of Christian teaching, though it is a child's fun not a violent grown-up's crude, ignorant attack. The poet speaks of "the faithful sheep-dog of the Shepherd" [a desire for freedom is clearly indicated here], "thinking of his voluptuous pleasure of chasing the sheep to the fold / And increasing the flock, and perhaps giving a real nip here and there, a real pinch, but always well meant." Here, there is certainly irony but, oddly, it is rather on the side of the Christian than of the pagan. Nonetheless, a genuine note of slight mockery enters into some lines which come a little later:

> Then the proud lion stalks abroad alone,
> And roars to announce himself to the wolves
> And also to encourage the red-cross Lamb
> And also to ensure a goodly increase in the world.

Lawrence's rather ambiguous attitude towards Christianity itself is seen most strongly in the four *Evangelistic Beasts* poems. On the one hand he recognizes both the beauty and terror of the created world, while, on the other, he puts himself inside the Evangelists' emblems which, for him, become as alive as

the creatures he has written of before. What seems certain is
that there are two things which Lawrence objects to in Christianity; one is its laws and discipline, the other, which is part of
the first, what seems to him its interference with man's freedom. But, by the very act of expressing his own visions, Lawrence is, inadvertently, subscribing to the great Christian dogma
of free-will; he may say what he likes. More important than
that, he feels he can express his own vision of the world and is
in no danger of having it invalidated. No real Christian could
ever say that his view is any kind of hoax. It is, put very simply,
a different vision with Lawrence, and it never makes any claims
to be a mystical one. So, the poem about St Mark ends as gently
as the one about St Matthew does:

> Look at him, with his paw on the world
> At Venice and elsewhere
> Going blind at last.

That final line is very fine and full of meanings within meanings.

With the St Luke poem, Lawrence has a tremendous opportunity to exert all the strength he has in entering into an
animal's life, for the bull is St Luke's emblem; but, despite this,
the Christian element is not forgotten. The poet moves strongly
straight into his poem:

> A wall, a bastion,
> A living forehead with its slow whorl of hair

[how detailed and exact this language is]

> And a bull's large, sombre, glancing eye
> And glistening, adhesive muzzle . . .

Even if you have never seen a bull rampaging in a field or a
bull-ring, the full force of this animal comes to us almost as
potently as it does to Lawrence. A few lines further on, Lawrence
writes,

> Horns,
> The golden horns of power,
> Power to kill, power to create
> Such as Moses had, and God,
> Head-power.

The poet evokes the Old Law in *the Old Testament* but he forgets that the Christian God, the God-made-Man who changed that Law and died for mankind, never killed; he only allowed man the free-will to choose whether to destroy or to make.

This is a fiercely felt and fiercely expressed poem. The reader feels that Lawrence is far more interested in the bull than in St Luke. Some lines, such as the following, are almost thunderous in their impact:

Thud! Thud! Thud!
And the roar of the black bull's blood in the mighty passages of
his chest.

. . . . .
The urge, the massive, burning ache
Of the bull's breast.
The open furnace-doors of his nostrils.

Quickly, however, Lawrence thinks that the bull has been weakened, has become a "Massive old altar of his own burnt offering". After some consideration—and this is a probably unwitting tribute to Christianity—this visionary poet declares,

Since the Lamb bewitched him with that red-struck flag
His fortress is dismantled
His fires of wrath are banked down
His horns turn away from the enemy.

By attempting to tame the bull, man, it seems to Lawrence, has tampered with his great natural strength; one is bound to feel that if man had not done this with wild creatures, he would never have been able to civilize himself; but then, civilization is to Lawrence more an evil than a good thing. He does not argue about this, and he does not rave either. He only puts forward his own point of view. In this, perhaps only in this, Lawrence's visions resemble those of Blake; both are un-Christian, highly personal, but always compassionate.

Lawrence states that the bull "serves the Son of Man" and he feels by doing this the beast has become weaker, less than himself:

And hear him bellow, after many years, the bull that serves
>> the Son of Man.
Moaning, booing, roaring hollow
Constrained to pour forth all his fire down the narrow sluice
>> of procreation
Through such narrow loins, too narrow.

The poet forgets that if man had not tamed or caged wild animals, he could not have survived at all. On this level, Lawrence's vision lacks a sense of reality, yet it is, nonetheless, a perfectly sane vision. Man, with Lawrence, is always on the same level as an animal, occasionally a lower one, never a higher one. This point of view makes him write

Is he not over-charged by the dammed-up pressure of his own
>> massive black blood
Luke, the Bull, the father of substance, the Providence Bull,
>> after two thousand years?
Is he not over-full of offering, a vast, vast offer of himself
Which must be poured through so small a vent?

Too small a vent.

There is a certain amount of indignation here, but there is also some, though not perhaps enough, understanding. Lawrence is really nearly always writing of a world before The Fall, a world in which no-one could be harmed; he also forgets that St Luke was a physician and the Patron Saint of Doctors. But this passionately vehement writer wants the bull to

... charge like a mighty catapult on the red-cross flag
[of the Lamb of God], let him roar out challenge on the world
And throwing himself upon it, throw off the madness of his blood.
Let it be war.

In Eden, there was no war and, in most contexts, Lawrence loathes war, but he thinks animals like bulls have a natural birthright for fighting, that it is part of their nature. So the man who feels guilty about killing a poisonous snake, has no compunction about a wild animal being given every opportunity to kill men. It is a strange, rather inconsistent vision, but it is still a vision. So St Luke ends very quietly

71

And so it is war.
The bull of the proletariat has got his head down.

The mention of "the proletariat" in this important part of the
poem weakens the whole poem slightly. We are brought down
to earth abruptly, and for a rather foolish political intention.
But there is no doubt at all of the great power in the rest of
this remarkable poem.

The poem about St John is a fairly brief poem; in it, Lawrence
has a sublime conception of the eagle, this Evangelist's emblem,
but, as with St Mark's lion, he wants it brought out of the skies
or from "The Word of God" and changed into an eagle who
can die. The end of the poem is satirical but it begins with great
vigour and vividness:

John, oh John,
Thou honourable bird,
Sun-peering eagle.

Taking a bird's-eye view
Even of Calvary and Resurrection
Not to speak of Babylon's whoredom.*

High over the mild effulgence of the dove
Hung all the time, did we but know it, the all-knowing shadow
Of John's great gold-barred eagle.

John knew the whole proposition.
Even the very beginning.

Lawrence then quotes the beginning of St John's Gospel " 'In
the beginning was the Word / And the Word was God / And
the Word was with God' ". Once more, he does a double identification, both with John and with the eagle. But Lawrence does
not like what he feels Christianity has done to the world;
especially he thinks that it has increased man's sense of sin and
guilt. So of Christ, he says, without what, at first sight, seems
like condescension,

* The last phrase being a very unpleasant reference to what the Roman
Catholic Church has often been called.

> As for innocent Jesus
> He was one of Nature's phenomena, no doubt.

Then, immediately, Lawrence becomes ecstatic about St John, "the beloved disciple".

> Oh that mind-soaring eagle of an Evangelist
> Staring creation out of countenance
> And telling it off
> As an eagle staring down on the Sun !

When we examine the next few lines of this perhaps best of the *Evangelistic Beasts* poems, we can see much more clearly what Lawrence's attitude towards God and Christianity is. Certainly, he is not setting his vision in opposition to it:

> The Logos, the Logos !
> 'In the beginning was the Word.'
>
> Is there not a great Mind pre-ordaining?
> Does not a supreme Intellect ideally procreate the Universe?
> Is not each soul a vivid thought in the great consciousness stream
> of God?

So Lawrence admires, even celebrates, this vision yet, as always, he does not want the tangible things of the Universe to be forgotten; this, then, is a Christian, as well as a very personal poem. Where Lawrence struggles most is in his feeling that the intellect was and is made to dominate sensuous things. He does not argue this in these poems—good poems, with the exception of some childish satire, perhaps; rather, they state, they express the fruits of *all* the poet's struggles, whether intellectual or sensual.

Lawrence commends the "high-soaring Mind" but he dislikes the tamed "Jesus' pale and lambent dove" because he feels that it is "cooing in the lower boughs / On sufferance". He returns to marvel at "the Word" which was "the first offspring of the almighty Johannine mind, / Chick of the intellectual eagle". Yet, Lawrence wants to "put salt on the tail of the Johannine bird ... John's eagle" and to

Shoo it down out of the empyrean
Of the all-seeing, all-fore-ordaining ideal.
. . . . .
For the almighty eagle of the fore-ordaining Mind
Is looking rather shabby and island-bound these days . . .

The poet wants a new bird, he sees a new vision, so that out of the "poor old golden eagle of the word-fledged spirit . . . a new conception of the beginning and end / Can rise from the ashes". And with an almost terrible cry, Lawrence writes,

Ah Phoenix, Phoenix,
John's Eagle!
You are only known to us now as the badge of an insurance
Company.

All through this poem Lawrence has been at one with both St John and his eagle but this brilliant poem ends on a note of deep regret and sadness:

The nest is in flames,
Feathers are singeing,
Ash flutters flocculent, like down on a blue, wan fledgeling.

This final natural description is as beautiful as some of Hopkins's very different poems about birds. Unlike Yeats in *The Second Coming*, Lawrence seems here to have no hope that a new vision "is at hand". But *St John* is a visionary poem, despite its dark ending.

Although it does not come within the group of poems about animals of every conceivable sort, or those about flowers and trees, it seems essential to look at Lawrence's longish poem, *The Ship of Death*; it is very important to this study because, being entirely concerned with death, it is a vital part of Lawrence's vision of life and death. Death for Lawrence means oblivion, but that does not stop him urging us and himself to prepare for it, and the image he uses for this preparation is a voyage. So this poem opens

Now it is autumn and the falling fruit
and the long journey towards oblivion.

The apples falling like great drops of dew . . .

The seasons have their risings and fallings, deaths and resurrections endlessly repeating themselves. A man like Lawrence lives with, as well as in all the seasons. He uses a word from *Hamlet* and also, later, a phrase, when he remarks, ". . . O tell me, is it quietus?" and, repudiating suicide writes very softly, almost in the manner of a prayer,

> O let us talk of quiet that we know,
> that we can know, the deep and lovely quiet
> of a strong heart at peace!

> How can we this, our own quietus, make?

> Build then the ship of death, for you must take
> the longest journey, to oblivion.

We must prepare ourselves peacefully for death, be ready for the long voyage towards it. In an odd way, this sounds almost Christian except that Lawrence has no faith in personal or, indeed, any kind of immortality, except the return to dust, dust from which plants and trees grow; and those plants and trees provide food for men and animals. So this is a kind of immortality, the immortality Lawrence passionately cares about. But in the next few lines, there is hope, because the poet talks of "the old self and the new". The new self will be the self after death transcended, and it will be transcended in this way:

> We are dying, we are dying, so all we can do
> is now to be willing to die . . .

Then Lawrence tells us how to prepare "the ship of death", and the details of this are reminiscent of Egyptian burials where every tiniest *material* necessity was placed near the mummy in his coffin. I think, however, that Lawrence is not referring to this because he does not believe in the after-life in which the ancient Egyptians had such faith. No, the ship must be prepared, "fitting and ready for the departing soul":

> There is no port, there is nowhere to go
> only the deepening blackness darkening still

blacker upon the soundless, ungurgling flood
darkness at one with darkness . . .
. . . . .
She [the ship] is gone! gone! and yet
Somewhere she is there.
Nowhere!

After the bleak line, "It is the end, it is oblivion", Lawrence
sees a momentary gleam of hope, but it is uncertain, must not
be taken absolutely seriously; yet the very fact that it is there,
that he is aware of it, lightens the darkness of this strange
vision, makes it bearable. And, as always, there is not a suggestion of the facile about it:

And yet out of eternity [he admits eternity], a thread
separates itself on the blackness,
a horizontal thread
that fumes a little with pallor upon the dark.

Lawrence sustains this hope to the very end of *The Ship of
Death* and, thus, leaves us satisfied:

The flood subsides, and the body, like a worn sea-shell
emerges strange and lovely . . .
and the frail soul steps out into her house again
filling the heart with peace.

Swings the heart renewed with peace
even of oblivion.

The last line, "For the voyage of oblivion awaits you", reminds
us that the poet is not sure of an after-life such as the great religions present for our faith, but eschewing dogma, he leaves
the matter a complete mystery.

I want now to make two explorations of Lawrence's flower
poems, *Bavarian Gentians* and *Sicilian Cyclamens*. They come
well after an examination of *The Ship of Death* because they
show so well Lawrence's life-enhancing power and his joy in all
living natural things. Pluto and Persephone are mentioned in
Bavarian Gentians but the most important part of the poem is
Lawrence's absolute union with these flowers:

Not every man has gentians in his house
in Soft September, at slow, sad Michaelmas.

Bavarian gentians, big and dark, only dark
darkening the day-time, torch-like with the smoking blueness of
Pluto's gloom,
ribbed and torch-like, with their blaze of darkness spread blue
down flattening into points, flattened under the sweep of white day
. . . . .
lead me then, lead me the way.

Lawrence is fascinated by the particular darkness of these
gentians, he longs to become them. So he continues,

Reach me a gentian, give me a torch !
let me guide myself with the blue, forked torch of this flower
down the darker and darker stairs, where blue is darkened
on blueness . . .

And the poem ends with one line which enshrines the vision.
The bride and groom referred to are, of course, Pluto and
Persephone:

among the splendour of torches of darkness, shedding darkness on
the lost bride and her groom.

As we know, according to the myth, Persephone spent Autumn
and Winter with Pluto. The light and the dark in this poem are,
however, felt in and through Lawrence himself; he is in total
unity with the gentians.

In *Sicilian Cyclamens* the mood is even more ecstatic; the
description flowers into the desire to know the flowers with the
closest possible intimacy a man may have with Nature:

Beautiful
Frost-filigreed
Spumed with mud
Snail-nacreous
Low down.

The shaking aspect of the sea
And man's defenceless bare face . . .

. . . . .
Dawn-rose
Sub-delighted, stone-engendered
Cyclamens, young cyclamens
Arching
Waking, pricking their ears
Like delicate very-young greyhound bitches . . .

This comparison of the plant with the animal kingdom shows just how profoundly Lawrence loves them both, becomes one with them, however short their life. He continues with poetry which is like an invocation:

Ah Mediterranean morning, when our world began!
Far-off Mediterranean mornings . . .
. . . . .
Rose cyclamen, ecstatic fore-runner!
. . . . .
Whispering witchcraft
Like women at a well, the dawn-fountain.

We are being taken back to the world of innocence, the Garden of Eden. But we are also quickly introduced to history since Lawrence proceeds:

Greece, and the world's morning
Where all the Parthenon marble still fostered the roots of
the cyclamen.

The whole of Greece and the Parthenon in particular are only important in their relationship with the cyclamens. For Lawrence, Nature always matters more than art although, paradoxically, he himself uses consummate art to convey his own vision.

Like all Lawrence's beast and plant poems, *Bavarian Gentians* and *Sicilian Cyclamens* throw as much light on the poet as they do on his subject-matter. By this, I most certainly do not mean that he uses members of the plant and animal kingdom to give a message or put over a theory. On the contrary, what he tells us about himself inadvertently is that he can be lost in Nature, find a vision there and always communicate it with the most mesmerizing use of language and in an inimitable rhythm.

78

The last poem by Lawrence to be looked at closely is *The Song of a Man Who Has Come Through*. It does not bear any special formal resemblance to what we usually call songs, but the poem's rhythm, the sheer power of Lawrence's customary pulsating lines where there is again, much deliberate repetition and alliteration carry us through this comparatively short piece; it is a song of joy, a triumphant thanksgiving for the whole of existence. It starts,

> Not I, not I, but the wind that blows through me !
> A fine wind is blowing the new direction of Time.
> If only I let it bear me, carry me, if only it carry me !

Lawrence longs for a total identification with the wind. He knows and says that to permit this to happen, he must be "sensitive", "subtle", and "delicate", he must not be merely passive. The poem soars as it continues :

> If only, most lovely of all, I yield myself [yielding is
>   an active thing] and am borrowed
> By the fine, fine wind that takes its course through the
>   chaos of the world
> Like a fine, an exquisite chisel . . .

It is interesting that Lawrence, who usually hated implements that could do man, animals, trees or plants damage, mentions a chisel here. But, in this context, he uses the chisel as a simile (and also the "tip of a wedge") to tell us how he wishes he could be

> Driven by invisible blows,
> The rock will split, we shall come at the wonder, we shall
>   find the Hesperides.

A vision of absolute happiness is given here and, although, towards the poem's end, he asks "What is the knocking at the door in the night?" he never loses his great hope, his love of life. I think we must remember here that Lawrence was, for most of his life, a sick man. He suffered, as all great poets suffer and, like them too, without self-pity. His sufferings included physical illness but also a complete failure of understanding of his writing and painting by the English general public. One man, Aldous

Huxley—an entirely different kind of artist, a truly cerebral writer—understood Lawrence's vision, ideas and work almost perfectly.

It seems fitting to end this study with the last two lines of *The Song of a Man Who Has Come Through*. They are wholly affirmative and an answer not only to the "knocking at the door", but also to all who question the validity of Lawrence's insight into the wonder of the natural world. There is no fear at all:

> No, no, it is the three strange angels.
> Admit them, admit them.

III

LAWRENCE DURRELL

The Vision of an Observer

Lawrence Durrell is the visionary as observer, though this sounds rather like a paradox. In his poems, however apparently steeped in his subject-matter he appears to be, he is always outside. If that were not so, he would not be able to write about so many places, climates, and people. The end of the poem such as the following shows us the man, excited by all he sees, thrilled in all his senses, yet still, somehow, apart from it all. Here are the lines:

> ... The dispiriting Autumn moon
> In her slow expurgation of the sky
> Needs company, is brooding on the dead,
> And so am I now, so am I.

These lines sum up perfectly Durrell's whole attitude to the world. He is always the watcher, maybe the sunburnt, smelling-of-oranges-and-garlic one, but always the man who stands aside, the one who cannot settle, who has always been a wanderer, whether in Cyprus, Greece, or Nîmes or elsewhere. He is the restless writer *par excellence* but he always stays long enough in one place to accept all that it brings to his senses and his mind; with Durrell, the intellect is never far away, but it is the imagination which illuminates his vision and makes his poems so memorable to us. So, Lawrence Durrell looks at the real world but makes it new, makes it a vision by the careful and exciting words and rhythms in which he writes about it. The same is true of his travel books, but the poems are what are really important; many of them undoubtedly will last.

Where Durrell becomes truly a visionary is in the way, as the title of one of his prose books shows, he can catch the "Spirit of the Place", however beautiful, and transform its evanescent beauty with his mind as well as with his passions. But, unlike D. H. Lawrence, he never loses himself in a place of a creature or plant. His findings are illuminations, but the man who writes is elusive, always on the move.

Durrell is a man moving through history, but because he is a poet, the past is always the present for him; as an archaeologist digs, so do his observant eyes uncover the past, simply by seeing. This is the heart of his very individual kind of vision. He leaves things alone but he stores up in his memory what he has seen, and more than what he has seen—briefly, what he has known with all his acutely aware senses.

The sense of wonder never leaves Durrell. One might suppose that a man who has travelled so much, mainly in Mediterranean places, would become so accustomed to them that he would take all their splendours and particular marvels for granted. This is never so; he is always a Northerner wandering in hot countries, constantly amazed by what he observes, constantly basking in it, yet never entirely becoming immersed in it. Mostly there is joy in his poems and travels, a feeling of the luxuriance of Nature, but there is also often sometimes nostalgia, a little sadness, an awareness of being no part of all this but of belonging elsewhere. This is what gives Durrell's work its individuality, as much as his scrupulous, dazzling vocabulary and imagery do.

Here is a man who is almost in love with the sun and who has been able to travel and live for certain periods in some of the hottest parts of Europe. But he has never lost his English identity. English people go to the South because they yearn for a warmer climate. But Durrell is not just a tourist; nothing that he sees or feels is casual and his writing has an absolutely original tang of its own. I do not think it would be possible to mistake any of his poems, or any phrase in a particular poem, for that of any other writer. Like all men who have a vision, he is precise in depicting it, his descriptions are never vague.

Lawrence Durrell is also a highly civilized, an educated man, but he never makes the mistake of loading his writing with too much learning. What he is after is clarity and his finest poems bear witness to this. He sees a city, smells a flower, and from such things has his own vision which he builds into a world with words. One of his books of poetry is called A *Private Country* but the title is really a contradiction. Nothing Durrell writes down is meant to be hoarded for himself. It is the true poet's natural modesty which makes him give a volume of poems a title like that.

In one sense, Durrell's world is a timeless one. He has lived in countries like Greece where, in spite of political upheaval, life goes on in much the same way, the seasons have a purity and an accuracy almost unknown in the North; this is especially true of the Greek islands which some of his poems are about. But despite this quality of timelessness, the writer is constantly aware of history, the past, the present, sometimes even the future and, being an observer, he is more keenly aware of this than the inhabitants of the countries he knows so well but in such a different way.

Durrell never ceases to be keenly attuned to history. In a poem called *Sarajevo*, he sums up in two lines precisely how the 1914–18 World War began; brevity is always a gift with him—the couplet is:

> A village like an instinct left to rust,
> Composed around the echo of a pistol-shot.

The carefully selected and precise adjective, the story of a whole civilization are re-created in a few lines here.

When I say that Durrell is essentially an observer, I do not mean that he is in any possible way a passive writer. On the contrary, his world is dynamic, pulsating with life. But he does differ from D. H. Lawrence in his poems in that he never allows himself to be completely steeped in his vision; he does not want to lose himself. Lawrence does.

Unlike Lawrence too, Lawrence Durrell is a highly educated,

even a learned man. Yet his learning never obtrudes or comes between the immediate findings of his senses and his thought; his observation is primarily that of the eyes and other senses, but frequently remarks are made which could only come from a man who has thought deeply. The poem called *On First Looking Into Loeb's Horace* is a good example of this particular quality.

Here, the poet re-creates Horace and his surroundings, a Horace who is "This lover of vines and slave to quietness". Durrell sees the mind and the senses of the great Latin poet working at one and the same time:

> Surely the hard blue winterset
> Must have conveyed a message to him—
> The premonitions that the garden heard
> Shrunk in its shirt of hair beneath the stars . . .

In no part of this poem, which is a longer one than most of Durrell's, does the writer identify himself with Horace. He does something else; he *understands* him, and not only because he knows his work but also because he has visited the places where the poet lived. So this poem is a perfect mingling of sensuousness and reflection. As always with Durrell's poems, the language and imagery are felt to be exactly right yet also completely new. He continues,

> Here, where your clear hand marked up
> "The hated cypress" I added "Because it grew
> On tombs, revealed his fear of autumn and the urns" . . .

A little further on, we have the following lines, where Durrell shows not just a state of mind but a whole life in a few lines.

> A burning heart quite constant in its station.
> . . . . .
> He will not know how we discerned him, disregarding
> The pose of sufficiency, the landed man,
> Found a suffering limb on the great Latin tree
> Whose roots live in the barbararian grammar we
> Use, yet based in him, his mason's tongue . . .
> . . . . .
> Disguising a sense of failure in a hatred for the young . . .

On First Looking Into Loeb's Horace continues with Durrell's idea of Horace's vision, the vision of a man

> Who built in the Sabine hills this forgery
> Of completeness, an orchard with a view of Rome;
> Who studiously developed his sense of death . . .

Here the poet is philosophizing, examining the intellect of another poet far from him in time but close to him in spirit. It is not cynicism which makes Durrell begin the last stanza of this poem with the following lines; it is compassion and sympathy:

> So perfect a disguise for one who had
> Exhausted death in art—yet who could guess
> You would discern the liar by a line,
> The suffering hidden under gentleness . . .

Durrell sees something of himself here but he does not introduce himself, there is no subjectivity, no attempt to identify himself with Horace. Durrell's complete comprehension, amounting to vision, of Horace the man, occurs in the last three lines of the poem which are simply some words which Horace wrote about himself which indicate great self-knowledge:

> . . . "Fat, human and unloved,
> And held from loving by a sort of wall,
> Laid down his books and lovers one by one,
> Indifference and success had crowned them all."

It is, possibly, the cool, appraising intellect which prevents Durrell, even in his most sensuous poems, from ever entering completely into them. Yet there is never a battle between the mind and the senses but rather a marriage of them. The mind selects the precise verb or adjective and then lets the imagination have its way with them; the writer, however, is always standing at a little distance, like a man touched by the sun, with his nostrils full of the many smells of the South, but one who knows that this is not his home, that he has a home elsewhere or perhaps not one at all.

Maybe Durrell's vision is at its most powerful in his songs. For example, a fairly early poem, called *Echo*, ends with these lines:

Nothing is lost, sweet self,
Nothing is ever lost.
The unspoken word
Is not exhausted but can be heard.
Music that stains
The silence remains
O echo is everywhere, the unbeckonable bird !

This poem is absolutely simple yet it contains one or two words
that are not simple, such as "exhausted" and "unbeckonable".
This is a central part of Durrell's attitude towards language
—his ability to use complex and original words and surround
them with very simple ones. This is his style and it is also the
man. In no very good poet can the two be separated.

The more we examine Durrell's poems, the more inextricably
do his senses and his intellect seem to us to be in harmony, but
it is the play of the intellect that is largely responsible for the
fact that he does not wish to lose himself completely in all those
things which appeal so powerfully to his senses; he is a man with
a strong mind, one lively with ideas. Obviously, some poems
show this more clearly than others. This is the place to examine
some of them.

Deus Loci, a poem in ten ten-line stanzas, makes a good
beginning for this examination; it shows a remarkable sense of
history. The opening lines are

All our religions founder, you
remain, small sunburnt *deus loci*
safe in your natal shrine,
landscape of the precocious southern heart,
continuously revived in passion's common
tragic and yet incorrigible spring . . .

Durrell recognizes that religions are not based simply on men's
mind's but also on their feelings, but it takes great perception to
see this and to say it in such memorable language.

Sheer poetic expertise and an accurate, original use of knowledge are shown in this fine poem. The third stanza begins,

On how many of your clement springs
the fishermen set forth, the foresters
resign their empty glasses . . .

and the fourth one starts with these lines:

> All the religions of the dust can tell—
> this body of damp clay that cumbered so
> Adam, and those before ...

Durrell will not accept Adam as a beginning of the world. Evolution is for him something evocative; and so the sixth stanza of the poem starts with these lines:

> The saddle-nose, the hairy thighs
> composed these vines, these humble vines ...

We may be tempted to say "Yes, but this is only a poet's imagination at work". It is far more than that. A poet's imagination is here seen to be at work on the past and picking out the precise words and rhythms in which to re-create it. Like Auden, Durrell has the great gift of providing the surprising yet exact verb or adjective or, indeed, any part of speech. The English language runs through his mind from which treasures may be hooked or halted and then used; there is no element of chance about this but the constant, attentive senses and the alert mind, which together present us with a definite vision, a vision in time, not a brief snatching-up into eternity. So Stanza 6 of *Deus Loci* has these lines:

> ... on some cracked pedestal
> by the sighing sea sets eternally up,
> item by item, his small mid-day meal,
> garlic and bread, the wine-can and the cup.

The poet here moves us to precisions in a few perfectly selected words.

At the beginning of Stanza 7 of *Deus Loci*, Durrell becomes very eloquent; the first line runs, "Image of our own dust in wine!" But the eighth stanza of the poem is more meditative in mood and the poet returns to his stance of observer, of the observer of men and of events:

> Your panic fellowship is everywhere,
> not only in love's first great illness known,
> but in the exile of objects lost
> to context, broken hearts, spilt milk ...

Here the poet is referring not only to religion but to men's super-
stitions, of which the Deus Loci is itself a part. He knows too
that superstition is quite irrational and so Stanza 9 begins,

> *Deus Loci* your provinces extend
> throughout the domains of logic . . .

It needs a very rational man to see and say this, but Durrell
fittingly ends this poem on an evocative, extremely lyrical note:

> . . . O spirit of place,
> Presence long since divined, delayed, and waited for,
> And here met face to face.

The use of alliteration is necessary, and flawlessly used here. At
times, Durrell almost drowns himself in those things which his
senses find—but never completely or for long. He feels strongly,
as every poet must, but he refuses to be carried away; his absolute
mastery of words and rhythms reveal this. The poet is the observer but a warm, sympathetic, often passionate one.

Durrell is a poet of nostalgia too; a man who has travelled
so much and who is so sensitive to change and atmosphere is
almost bound to be. *Episode* (Durrell worked for the British
Council in Cyprus for a period) shows this quality very well
indeed:

> I should set about memorising this room
> It will be a long time empty and airless;
> . . . . .
> Rice-powder on a sleeve and two dead pillows
> The telephone shook and shook but could not wake.

There is nostalgia of a different kind in *A Prospect of Children*
and, again, not a trace of sentimentality but very strong feeling.
This poem ends,

> What can they tell the watcher at the window,
> Writing letters, smoking up there alone,
> Trapped in the same limitation of his growth
> And yet not envying their childhood
> Since he endured his own?

Here the poet actually calls himself a "watcher". Writing a poem
about Alexandria, Durrell again assumes the observer's role

overtly; he speaks of a "littoral and tides" which were both "objects for my study and my love".

The crucial words here are "study" and "love". Durrell may be an observer but he cares for what he sees, cherishes it in a mind that is always ready for riches. In one sense, all poets have to stand away, a little distance off. The good ones do not scribble down words which immediately come from any kind of experience that has moved them. If they do scribble down ideas or half-lines or images when they are still near to the experience which sparked these off, then they generally emend, alter, sometimes go through many drafts of the poem later. Inspiration—that much-abused word—has to be accompanied always by order and craftsmanship.

But Durrell is an observer also in another way; he refuses to allow the findings of his senses to submerge him or satiate him; the calm mind is always on the alert; thoughts, as well as sensations, throng him, but he always maintains the position of the master and controller. He knews exactly what untamed words, flung down at random, produce. The answer is simple—something quite worthless.

Durrell's sense of history is very strong indeed; he can evoke the past without ever becoming arid. Here is an example of this gift taken from a very short poem called *Manoli of Cos*:

> This is not the rose of all the world,
> Nor the rose of Nostradamus or of Malory:
> Nor is it Eliot's clear northern rose of the mind . . .

That use of the word "northern" reminds us that Durrell is an Englishman. I believe the very fact that he *is* English, taken together, of course, with the existence of his five uniquely sharp senses, makes the South appeal to him so much. Englishmen have always pined for the sun and for the smells and sights of Southern Europe. We only have to recall most of our Romantic poets to realize this. But Durrell's feelings and ideas are always in harmony; that is why his sense of the past and of place are set before us so vividly. This poet certainly loves a "beaker full of the warm South" but he never desires a "dull opiate". He is constantly alert, a watcher who feels, the poet on the threshold.

With love poems, Durrell is especially moving. His approach to love is realistic but it is part of his vision of the world and, indeed, helps to make that world more complete. When I say this I do not mean that this poet tries to make an ecstatic experience of love into one resembling the mystical knowledge of union with God. What I mean is that, for him, love reaches beyond the senses only and is held in the mind before it is set down in the most rigorously selected words and images. So, a personal love affair becomes a kind of sharing. As Auden has said, on the lyric level of poetry, all love is general; this is certainly true of Durrell's love poems. But history enters even poems about love as we can see in these lines from *Heloise and Abelard*:

> Yet in deprivation found
> By a guess
> Love unseal its loveliness.

In poems about love which spring from Durrell's own experience, he always manages to distance the passion while in no way diminishing it. So, *Water Music* starts,

> Wrap your sulky beauty up,
> From sea-fever, from winterfall
> Out of the swing of the
> Swing of the sea.

[The repetition here is deliberate and very effective.] And the second of this poem's three stanzas ends,

> Waves roll, waves toll but feel
> None of our roving fever.

Sometimes, in a poem of place, Durrell uses birth or sexual imagery and so deftly introduces the theme of love. This happens in *Summer in Corfu* in which the second of three stanzas contains these lines:

> ... The black fig
> Desire is torn again from the belly of reason.
> Our summer is gravid at last, is big.

Loneliness is never far away from Durrell's verse and even in the midst of recalling love he remembers that all loves are ephemeral; so, the last stanza of *Summer in Corfu* begins,

> All you, who know desire in these seas,
> Have souls or equipment for loneliness, loneliness,
> Lean now like fruitage.

Although the poet is speaking as an onlooker here, we may be sure that he is remembering and registering his own experiences. Probably, the strongest element in Durrell's love poetry is nostalgia.

Niki has a deep note of sadness. A very short love poem, it begins, "Love on a leave-of-absence came": but it ends,

> (Bitter and pathless were the ways
> Of sleep to which such beauty led.)

Perhaps *Chanel* is the most perfect of all this writer's love poems. A famous scent is what has moved the poet to write the poem, but with beautifully sensuous writing he manages to convey the fullness of an experience of love in nineteen lines only. *Chanel* starts, "Scent like a river-pilot led me there", and, a little later, goes on with four almost chanting lines,

> "Skin be supple, hair be smooth,
> Lips and character attend
> In mnemonic solitude.
> Kisses leave no fingerprints."

Not simply a passing mood but a whole approach to love is given to us in that last wonderful line. The last line of all has a similar quality; the poet leads up to it thus:

> Still the long chapter led me on.
> Still the clock beside the bed
> Heart-beat after heart-beat shed.

By this time, the poet is recollecting his experience and pondering upon it, but his memory quickens within us as it does so clearly in him.

Within the vision of the world which Lawrence Durrell passes on to us there is, as we have already seen a little, a strong sense of history, not simply the dry findings of the scholar but an informed sense of the lives of famous men and the *feeling* of well-known places and buildings, observed by a very keen intellect and actually felt by strong senses. It has already been noted that Durrell owes a little to Auden in his ability to find the precise word, especially the precise adjective and noun, yet here it is also a gift of his own and used for quite different purposes from those of Auden. We know already Durrell's re-creation of Horace. Here are some more of the historical characters which make up his world and inform his vision. He sees people always with understanding and sympathy, sometimes with something even deeper; I mean compassion. This is part of what he writes about Byron in a fairly long poem:

> Before me now lies Byron and behind,
> Belonging to the Gods,
> Another Byron of the feeling
> Shown in this barbered hairless man,
> Splashed by the candle-stems
> In his expensive cloak and wig
> And boots upon the dirty ceiling.

That distinction of "another Byron of the feeling" gives us a very important clue to Durrell's approach to everything. Even though there is never any dichotomy in his poems between the mind and the senses, he is well aware that they are two distinct things. By beautifully chosen words and a flawless ear, he brings the two together. He continues further on about Byron, with great perception,

> ... Picture to yourself
> A lord who encircled his life
> With women's arms; or another
> Who rode through the wide world howling
> And searching for his mother.

These are, of course, two views of the same person. And Durrell gives us also a third:

> Picture to yourself a third: a cynic.
> This weeping published rock—
> The biscuits and the glass of soda-water ...

Byron is shown, in precise words, in the round. Part of this subtle poem is written as though Byron were himself speaking. The last five lines of the poem reveal simply a total understanding of that much misunderstood and complicated man and poet:

> O watch for this remote
> But very self of Byron and of me,
> Blown empty on the white cliffs of the mind,
> A dispossessed His Lordship writing you
> A message in a bottle dropped at sea.

Durrell has also written a poem about the sculptor Maillol in which he displays a most acute insight into the difficulties of a sculptor. The poem is about the clay Pomona which Maillol made. The last stanza begins,

> If art is self-reflection, who he was
> She woke within the side of . . .

The never-to-be concluded theories of the actual making of a work of art are here given another dimension; and when, very near the poem's end, Durrell writes of "the joy in touching / The moistened flanks of her idea", he once again welds mind and sensuousness (almost, here, sensuality) by stating the matter in a few vivid words. For, to write a poem is not very different from shaping a clay figure, certainly not Durrell's kind of poetry. But it is vital to note that there is no "I" mentioned in this poem; the poet is using his own experience as an artist to bring to life the craftsmanship of an artist in a completely different medium. He is trying to understand someone else and succeeding in doing so; but to do this he has to stand aside and reflect.

In a volume of poems entitled *A Private Country*, Durrell has two poems which enlarge the scope of his world—one, a letter, in the form of a poem, called *Letter to Seferis the Greek* (Seferis is the recently dead and great modern Greek poet), the other, *Daphnis and Chloe*, about a myth. Durrell is equally at ease with myth and history, which is yet another sign of a poet with a unique vision. *Letter to Seferis the Greek* contains these lines (the poem is a long one for Durrell):

> No milestones marked the invaders,
> But ragged harps like mountains here:
> A text for Proserpine in tears . . .

Myth is thus referred to here, and most fittingly. But Durrell goes on to record his feelings for this great poet who was also his great friend:

> Something sang in the firmament.
> The past, my friend compelled you,
> The charge of habit and love.
> The olive in the blood awoke,
> The stones of Athens in their pride
> Will remember, regret and often bless.

A later stanza ends with the line, "All these things are simply Greece".

Durrell sets Seferis in his home, his landscape. The picture is complete:

> ... the rotting walls
> Of the European myth are here
> For us, the industrious singers,
> In the service of this blue, this enormous blue.

Here, the poet's own knowledge of Greece is handed to the Greek poet for whom the poem is written. Durrell forgets nothing, neither "this huge magazine of flowers", "the women / Winding up their hair into sea-shells", the "Exhausted rivers ending in the sand", nor the details of Seferis's personal life:

> Your letter of the 4th was no surprise.
> So Tonio had gone? He will have need of us.
> The sails are going out over the old world.

That last line sums up not just an epoch but a whole way of feeling and understanding. But there is a moment of disillusionment in the last lines of this poem (they seem like a premonition now when we know what has happened in Greece many years after this poem was written):

> The calculations of the astronomers, the legends
> The past believed in could not happen here.
> Nothing remains but Joy, the infant Joy
> (So quiet the mountain in its shield of snow,
> So unconcerned the faces of the birds),
> ... somewhere awake,
> Born of this darkness, our imperfect sight,
> The stirring seed of Nostradamus' rose.

94

This is a very warm letter but the poet's feelings are controlled, distanced; a vivid memory helps him to achieve this sort of outlook; if the reader is to share such personal recollections, a certain detachment is essential and Durrell knows this. With the purely mythical figures of Daphnis and Chloe, his approach is more impersonal and yet brings these characters to life partly by overtly comparing Daphnis to Christ in an absolutely unblasphemous way:

> This boy is the good shepherd.
> He paces the impartial horizons,
> Forty days in the land of tombs,
> Waterless wilderness, seeking waterholes ...

But Chloe is a dangerously beautiful, sensual girl who has

> Under the tongue the bee-sting,
> Under the breast the adder at the lung,
> Like feathered child at wing.

There follows a simple line which is also rich with meaning. It is, "Life's honey is distilled simplicity". In one line, Durrell sums up the beauty and the wonder which all myths have. He makes legends live for us because they are as much a part of his world as history is. So,

> This was Chloe, the milk and honey,
> Carved in the clear geography of Time ...

Chloe exists in time because she is part of our memories and imaginations, the tales we read when we were children. Both she and Daphnis have a history within us and it is Durrell who makes us even more vividly aware of them. *Because* he is not utterly caught up with them, not too involved but a joyful celebrator of them, he can do this for us.

When Durrell deals with places in his poems, he maintains detachment, as well as a joy in history. Sensuousness here, once again, never forsakes him. He writes of the Parthenon in a poem with that title

> Put it more simply: say the city
> Swam up here swan-like to the shallows ...

Imagination spreads over that ancient building and brings it to life. Later in this poem, Durrell, still the spell-bound observer, has this line, "Man entered it and woman was the roof". But, almost immediately, the poet's sense of history enters in. This is not excessively learned history, although we know that this poet is a scholar, but essentially a poet's view. A very vital part of Durrell's vision is the short route between what his senses experience and what his mind reflects upon; he can always draw upon a wide range of reading and study and transmute it for his own purposes. In this, he is a kind of alchemist as well as a visionary. The following lines from *The Parthenon* illustrate precisely what I mean:

> A vexing history, Geros, that becomes
> More and more simple as it ends, not less;
> And nothing has redeemed it : art
> Moved back from pleasure-giver to a humour
>
> As with us . . . I see you smile . . .
> . . . . .
> And quickened by self-knowledge
> Men of linen sat on marble chairs
> In self-indulgence murmuring "I am, I am".

Durrell is very quick to observe how men want to identify themselves with, become a part of an ancient building. The seer in him knows that such desires are one way in which human beings try to immortalize themselves.

In the following poem about the island of Delos, the past and the present are brought together very subtly; Durrell does this by writing of the dead and then quickly moving on to the habits, pathetic yet delightful, of women. Here are the lines I mean:

> The statues of the dead here
> Embark on sunlight, sealed
> Each in her model with the sightless eyes :
> The modest stones of Greeks,
> Who gravely interrupted death by pleasure.

Pleasure is given a timeless quality, and the poet ends his poem with an all-encompassing wisdom:

> And in harbours softly fallen
> The liver-coloured sails—
> Sharp-featured brigantines with eyes—
> Ride in reception so like women :
> The pathetic faculty of girls
> To register and utter a desire
> In the arms of men upon the new-mown waters,
> Follow the wind, with their long shining keels
> Aimed across Delos at a star.

"New-mown waters" is a perfect phrase, original yet absolutely acceptable. Durrell has an almost endless power to surprise us both with the originality and accuracy of his language. But this poem, which is called *Delos*, draws together the ancient world and the never-changing passions of men and women. A Greek island is the starting-point for a wholly satisfying and short visionary poem; not a word is out of place and our imaginations are enthralled by and hold on to these lines, these images, this view that is far more than merely a description of a very beautiful place.

During the 1939 War, Durrell spent much time in the Middle East and elsewhere, either in Southern Europe or in Africa. With a number of other friends, including poets such as Bernard Spencer and Keith Douglas, some of his poems appeared in a small anthology fittingly entitled *Personal Landscape*. Durrell's sharp, alert vision remained as vivid as ever and he wrote a number of poems of place during his times abroad in war-time. One of this poet's poems in this book (which also contains some prose) is called *Mythology* and it is a crucial poem in that it gives us a statement in verse of Durrell's attitude towards history and myths. The poem begins,

> All my favourite characters have been
> Out of all pattern and proportion :
> Some living in villas by railways,
> Some like Katsimbalis heard but seldom seen . . .
> . . . . .
> Tibble, Gondril, Purvis, the Duke of Puke,
> Shatterblossom and Dude Bowdler
> Who swelled up in Jaffa and became a tree . . .

Clearly some of these are invented characters recalled from Durrell's childhood. Men often comfort themselves with such recollections in times of war. But I believe that, in our child-hoods, most of us go through many of the real stages and epochs of history. We not only invent characters, we also invent religions and/or play games of the one we may happen to belong to. I shall quote now the last eight lines of *Mythology* because it shows both Durrell's mingling of history with myth and also how alive both of them are to him in adult years. "The poetry was in the pity" is, of course, an adaptation of Wilfred Owen's prose statement about his own great poems which were written during the 1914 War. He wrote "The Poetry *is* [my italics] in the Pity". So Durrell proceeds and concludes this poem thus:

Ramon de Something who gave lectures
From an elephant founded a society
To protect the inanimate against cruelty.
He gave asylum to aged chairs in his home,
Lampposts and crockery, everything that
Seemed to him suffering he took in
Without mockery.

The poetry was in the pity. No judgment
Disturbs people like these in their frames
O men of the Marmion class, sons of the free.

The only reference to war is oblique and it is simply a line a great war poet wrote. We are reminded, when reading the reference to "suffering" here of that wonderful other line of Durrell's—"The suffering hidden under gentleness"—which appears in *On First Looking Into Loeb's Horace*. That poem also appears in this anthology.

For Durrell, then, as for David Jones, history and myth are always here and now. More sensuous than Jones, Durrell has a mind just as keen and just as easily caught up in a vision, though his visions are different ones from Jones's and expressed in a totally different manner. But however visionary he is, Durrell is always also a realist; but we should remember that great Christian mystics have also always been very realistic.

In his approach to places and buildings, Durrell yields to them only momentarily, just long enough to catch their history, their smell, their colour—in short, all that appeals to the senses. But he does not draw back abruptly or retreat in a hurry; with a simplicity which is almost formidable in so sophisticated and self-aware a man, he steps aside so that he may gather together, not exploit, his findings and make them into poems. For him, distance is essential. Most sensuous poets do not need and usually do not want this; but this is precisely what makes Lawrence Durrell such an exceptional and rare writer.

A very close scrutiny of Durrell's long sequence entitled *Cities, Plains and People*, reveals an immense knowledge of many places and people too, as the title of this poem indicates. In the first section we have this wonderfully concise view of Tibet:

> Caravans paused here to drink Tibet.

[those last three words alone are a perfect piece of description which goes beyond description]

> On draughty corridors to Lhasa
> Was my first school
> In faces lifted from saddles to the snows . . .

Durrell never writes of cities or countries which he has not actually seen. It is possible to write a very good poem about a place which one has only seen a photograph or film of, or has heard people speak about or oneself simply read about; Durrell is not that kind of poet. The very first line of this distanced autobiographical poem is "Once in idleness was my beginning", but he is soon speaking of seeing

> . . . the Himalayas like lambs there
> Stir their huge joints and lay
> Against his [the poet's] innocent thigh a stony thigh.

Part I of *Cities, Plains and People* ends with the line, "Until your pain becomes a literature". This is what all good poetry does; it is an alchemy; it transmutes the most intense anguish into gold, that lasting metal, of literature. In Part II, Durrell gathers together a number of famous poets, philosophers and theologians. Thus, we have the following passages where the poet is both withdrawing himself and reviving history, even while he is writing of his own schooldays:

> . . . a window
> Into the great sick-room, Europe,
> With its dull set-books,
> The Cartesian imperatives, Dante and Homer . . .
> . . . . .
> Here he [the use of the third person here is
>   typical of Durrell] saw Bede who softly
> Blew out desire and went to bed . . .
> . . . . .
> Here St Augustine took the holy cue
> Of bells in an English valley; and mad Jerome
> Made of his longing half a home from home.

The poet's nostalgia is deftly passed into the sadnesses and joys of other men. Durrell continues with words about Dante's Beatrice and then very soon, moves to the English Romantic poets:

> (The potential passion hidden, Wordsworth
> In the desiccated bodies of postmistresses

[a witty reference to the small gratuity which Wordsworth received from the Stamp Act]

> The scarlet splash of campion, Keats.
> Ignorant suffering that closes like a lock).

That "scarlet splash of campion" is a marvellously succinct image for Keats's death from consumption. Durrell writes often of suffering but very seldom directly of his own. This, the longest poem which this poet has ever written, goes on in the fifth part of the sequence, to considerations of many other writers, French and English:

> Here however man might botch his way
> To God via Valéry, Gide or Rabelais.
> All rules obtain upon the pilot's plan
> So long as man, not manners, makyth man.
> Some like the great Victorians of the past
> Through old Moll Flanders sailed before the mast,

> While savage Chatterleys of the new romance
> Get carried off in Sex, the ambulance.
> All rules obtain upon the pilot's chart
> If governed by the scripture of the heart.

Two things are very noticeable here—firstly, wit, and, what we have become used to, the observer's stance, his ability to step aside and look at his own past tastes and yet never lose passion. Durrell has that very rare gift—the power to be acutely aware as an observer and extremely passionate at the same time.

The seventh part of *Cities, Plains and People* is much concerned with Budapest (here called Buda), but it ends with this,

> As, like a spring coiled up,
> In the bones of Adam, lay Eve.

In a simple piece of imagery we are given a new vision of *The Book of Genesis*. Now, Durrell moves on to a consideration of Time. With Time, he mingles place; there is nothing abstract here. Time is "lovely and mysterious", has "promises and blessings" and

> So gladly does he bear
> Towards the sad perfect wife,
> The rocky island and the cypress-trees.

Next, Durrell returns to his own individual autobiographical manner where the "him" is really an "I" or "me". He is re-creating his own vision of Greece for us, Greece

> Bearing in rivers upside down
> The myrtle and the olive, in ruins
> The faces of the innocents in wells.

Salt, garlic, "Greek bread", "flawed grapes painted green" entranced him, held him, then released him to tell us, "Here worlds were confirmed in him". Durrell then recalls the Poles ("Red Polish mouth"), and now he is more and more giving us an account of his views of love and linking them with Time and history. So he returns to the first person singular although he is looking back on a past self. After the beautiful line, "Love, the undeclarèd thought," he writes,

> Within a time of reading
> Here is all my growth
> Through the bodies of other selves . . .

He is learning experience at one remove and by reading about others and contemplating their ways of life in a scholarly way; in fact, he is learning how to be objective without being either cold or remote. He concludes his thoughts about learning thus:

> So knowledge has an end,
> And virtue at the last an end,
> In the dark field of sensibility . . .

But Durrell's "dark field of sensibility" is very different from the dark places in which D. H. Lawrence loved to lose himself.

Now, before returning to profound and precisely expressed comments on literature and history, Durrell writes,

> Love bears you. Time stirs you.
>
> . . . . .
>
> Art has limits and life limits
> Within the nerves that support them.

Past and present—in short, history—are then brought together by means of memories of reading great writers from the East and the West. Durrell says,

> Now darkness comes to Europe
> Dedicated by a soft unearthly jazz.
> The greater hearts contract their joys
> By silence to the very gem . . .
>
> . . . . .
>
> Barbarians with secretaries move,
> Whom old Cavafy pictured,
> Whom no war can remove.

Terse and direct as always, Durrell, in *Cities, Plains and People* probably reveals his unique vision, a wholeness, that is never shown quite so satisfyingly in any of his other poems. So he speaks of how he, "a personal world" goes to seek "the yellow emperor", the emperor who

> . . . searching in himself struck oil,
> Published the first great Tao . . .

Durrell may call himself "a personal world" but he is never a personal poet in the way that, for example, Stephen Spender was, only a few years before him. He looks into himself then, almost at once, when he has caught what he wants, turns outward again; he is always more interested in other people and places than in himself; but, of course, as the old Greek words put it, he must "know himself" before he can give us this so vivid vision of our world and our times.

Durrell moves on to literature, both writers and the characters they have created. So we have "Hamlet in the maze", "the *doppelgänger* / Goethe saw one morning", "The magnificent responses of Rimbaud", Faust and then a return to "This personal landscape" [we must recall that this was the title of the wartime anthology to which Durrell contributed] "built / Within the Chinese circle's calm embrace". There is nothing private in all this; we are given the memories of a poet who is a scholar and who can always stand back, keeping a firm perspective yet also a warmth and sensuousness.

Now comes the "Dark Spirit, sum of all / That has remained unloved, / Gone crying through the world". Here we are shown not self-pity but compassion for the whole world which is found "In ferns and birds and ordinary people", and in "this our temporal sun", and in

> The part of living that is loving,
> Your dancing, a beautiful behaviour.

Darkness excites Durrell, though he infinitely prefers light. But of the dark he writes,

> Darkness, who contain
> The source of all this corporal music,
> On the great table of the Breath
> Our opposites in pity bear,
> Our measure of perfection or of pain . . .

If this is not visionary writing, I do not think I know what is. We are quickly now brought back to the recurrent "old yellow Emperor" who has this amazing resemblance to two great men; this is another aspect of Durrell's fullness of vision:

His soul became a vapour
And his limbs became a stake
But his ancient heart still visits us
In Lawrence or in Blake.

Durrell is not referring to the transmigration of souls but to a
spirit, a radiance that he, himself a visionary, observes in other
seers.

We then see light, the visible light again :

All cities plains and people
Reach upwards to the affirming sun . . .

The poet now uses most aptly and dexterously two words from
Freud. The linking of past and present, of thought and feeling in
this sequence, is amazingly successful and subtle yet never
obscure. So Durrell writes,

Ego, my dear, and id [sic]
Lie so profoundly hid
In space-time void, though feeling,
While contemporary, slow,
We conventional lovers cheek to cheek
Inhaling and exhaling go.

This poet can distance himself so satisfactorily that he can be
witty about, even laugh at, himself. Immediately after this
stanza, we go back in time and history to Nostradamus and
Durrell writes:

The rose that Nostradamus
In his divining saw
Break open as the world . . .

And St Augustine of Hippo follows next:

The city that Augustine
Founded in moral law,
By our anguish were compelled
To urge, to beckon and implore.

Durrell wears his learning lightly. The city which the writer is
referring to is of course the ideal *City of God*, the title of a book
written by Augustine.

Now this poem takes a curious but entirely acceptable turn. Durrell begins to have misgivings that he, in his own writing, may somehow corrupt language, the language which he uses with such care and love. Only a poet with a vision (and a vision postulates humility) could write

> ... should I reach,
> By touch or speech corrupt,
> The inner suffering word,
> By weakness or idea,
> Though you might suffer
> Feel and know,
> Pretend you do not hear.

There is also a gentle sweetness about that last line which enhances the strength of the rhythm, language, allusions and imagery of this whole poem.

When we reach the 1945 World War, Durrell speaks of "Bombers bursting like pods"; he has seen, can remember, give to us the changed cities of Europe:

> See looking down motionless
> How clear Athens or Bremen seem
> A mass of rotten vegetables
> Firm on the diagram of earth can lie ...

The poet retains his distance though not his startling vision. Soon, he is writing, with a trace of disillusionment:

> We have tried hoping for a future in the past.
> Nothing came out of that past
> But the reflected distortion and some
> Enduring, and understanding, and some brave.

Here is, indeed, understanding, perception, and a dazzling view. Durrell ends this long poem with a favourite character of his, Prospero, the Prospero who appears occasionally in shorter poems. He is, as it were, a stand-in for Durrell, for Durrell the magic-maker. The last stanza of *Cities, Plains and People* runs thus:

> For Prospero remains the evergreen
> Cell by the margin of the sea and land,

Who many cities, plains, and people saw
Yet by his open door
In sunlight fell asleep
One summer with the Apple in his hand.

The poet finishes his poem by drawing together his own experiences, the sense of timelessness, and a reminder of the Fall of Man; "the Apple" which Prospero holds is surely an unstated assumption that, just as Prospero broke his magic wand and set free his slaves, we must accept both the beauty and limitations of our human condition, since we too have free-will. All this is said quietly but with wonderful lucidity. The vision within this poem ends, as anything vital to do with mankind must end, with a question, but here the question is partially concealed. *Cities, Plains, and People* is surely Durrell's most important, most far-seeing and most controlled poem. Its worth has never been properly understood or sufficiently acknowledged.

In a, for Durrell, moderately long poem called A *Soliloquy of Hamlet*, he sums up many of the qualities we have already noted. Literature and history are brought together and the poet is completely aware of this; throughout, the poem is written in fourteen short sets of couplets. The second part begins,

One innocent observer in a foreign cell
Died when my father lay beside his ghost.

Dumb poison in the hairy ear of kings
Can map the nerves and halt the tick of hearts.

Durrell, distancing himself, is clearly felt in the beginning of the third part:

Guilt can lie heavier than house of tortoise.
Winter and love, O desperate medicines . . .

Many disparate things are brought together in this poem, but the poet's power and vision link them. We never feel any confusion of facts or of feelings. A strong intellect and great passion are always leashed but also always linked. Part IV considers the world's geography: "Here in the hollow curvature of the world", and love enters where

> ... pain forever green winds her pale horn.

> Make in the beautiful harbours of the heart,
> For scholars sitting at their fire-lit puzzles,

> The three-fold climate and the anchorage.

These reflections and the many others in this poem come from Durrell's *doppelgänger*, who is here Hamlet; thus the distance Durrell always needs is maintained.

In Part VI, the poet writes that "Winter and love are Euclid's properties" and, further in this section, adds, for our illumination,

> The heart can bless, or the sad skin of saints
> Be beaten into drum-heads for the truth.

There is a kind of late Classical melancholy in this poem; the poet's vision is sad. He observes and reflects with a slight sense of disillusionment. The figures who enter this long poem are skilfully equated one with another; thus,

"Hamlet is nailed between the thieves of love." Hamlet, seen as Christ, is not a blasphemous idea; rather, it is a typical example of Durrell's constant and rare gift to fuse literature and history together in order to tell us some particular truth. Again, and this is also now in Part VII, the poet cries out for a moment with an absolutely personal authority:

> I hang my heart, being choked, upon a noun.
> I hang her name upon this frantic pothook.

Here, Durrell is talking of the long, hard task of writing poetry and upon the necessity of love to him, wherever it comes from at different times. To put so much into two lines is a feat, but one that does not shout about its skill. Every feeling and thought have been assimilated.

In Part VIII, Durrell probably becomes less the astute observer than anywhere else in all his many poems, though we must remember that he is speaking as Hamlet. But the beautiful imagery gives the little distance which he wants to preserve:

> I close an hinge on the memorial days.
> I perch my pity [*not* self-pity] on an alp of silence.

In Part IX Durrell writes:

> Pain hangs more bloody than the mystic's taws.
> Down corridors of pain I follow patience . . .

This poem, so full of vivid ideas, so crammed with ordered reflections, is as near as Durrell ever gets to autobiography, but it *is* near although many other people are crowded into it. His unique vision of sensuousness and reflection (reflection amounting to wisdom) are to be found here most commandingly, not only because the poem is longer than most of his others but because it brings more important matters together with a remarkable skill. In Part X, he can say so much in just this one couplet:

> Here birth and death are knitted by a vowel.
> A mariner must sail his crew of furies . . .

and a little later in the same Part, Durrell declares,

> I, now, go, where the soliloquy of the sad bee
> O numbs the nettles and the hieroglyphic stone.

Words and phrases like "knitted" and "the soliloquy of the sad bee" in these two couplets save the poem (for Durrell does this kind of linking admirably) from mere arid, philosophical reflection. But there is no doubt that, alongside his unusually powerful senses, Durrell has a penetrating, almost metaphysical cast of mind. It is the latter which always enables him to observe and not be overwhelmed by what his senses find.

In the last Part of this poem, XIV, Durrell actually tells us that he is handing over his experience to others, though he is here speaking to one particular person. His generalizing gift enables all his readers to feel that *they* are that person:

> To you by whom the sweet spherical music
> Makes in heaven a tree-stringed oracle,
>
> I bend a sonnet like a begging-bowl,
> And hang my tabor from the greenest willow-wand.
> . . . . .
> My ash I dress to dance upon the void,
> My mercy in a wallet like a berry bright . . .

The reader's imagination immediately leaps to thoughts of Prospero again and is amazed to find that this poet sees his own death as something like Prospero breaking his wand, giving Ariel his freedom, and himself renouncing his magical powers and becoming an ordinary man. The classical repose remains but the Romantic pleasure in sensuous experience is not abandoned. This seems a fitting point at which to end a study of Durrell the observer-seer poet. I think our final, deepest feeling is gratitude; we have admired all the expertise, all the places and people so vividly and timelessly put before us and, through them, we have learnt to love the man through his vision.

IV

ST-JOHN PERSE

The Worldly Seer

The first thing to be done before we examine the vision of this Frenchman who, like Claudel, was not only a writer but also a man of affairs, connected with diplomacy, a wise man where politics was concerned—the first thing to do is to define the particular form of poetry he chose to use, the prose poem. The prose poem originated in France and only in recent years has it become acclimatized to the poetry of this country. The prose poem is quite unlike any conventional verse which makes use of rhymes or stanzas; we can understand it most clearly if we examine how it differs from *vers libre*. Unlike *vers libre*, it does not rely on end-stops or an apparently loose but, in fact, an essential though varied rhythm. The prose poem differs from prose because it often abandons main verbs, is elliptical, resorts frequently to imagery (particularly to visual imagery), and relies heavily on alliteration, assonance and repetition. Repetition is usually of single words or phrases, not of whole lines. There is nothing in the prose poem which bears any relation to the refrain of conventional, age-old lyrical poetry.

T. S. Eliot who translated *Anabasis* does not think that this poem really needs an Introduction at all. Nonetheless, he does provide us with a very useful short one. The *Anabasis* or, in French, *Anabase*, has no "particular reference" to Xénophon's famous "journey of the Ten Thousand". Eliot says that it is simply a poem about "a series of images of migration, of conquests of vast spaces in Asiatic wastes, of destruction and foundation of cities and civilizations of any races or epochs of the ancient East".

This gives the poet a very wide scope and much freedom of allusion. With St-John Perse depth of thought run side by side with height of vision. Always there is movement. The prose poem is a perfect medium for this kind of writing; it makes allowances for swift, even abrupt, juxtapositions of observation and description. It does, quite literally, bear the reader along. Maps are useless to him, so are even the ordinary modes of travel. The way in which images are used are of extreme importance. So, too, is the celebratory, joyful note throughout these poems.

Eliot insists that the *Anabasis* is poetry because it has a "logic of imagery . . . *declamation*" and a "system of stresses and pauses, which is particularly exhibited by the punctuation and spacing". The two latter methods, he says, belong to poetry, not prose. And we must remember that not only did Perse have a close knowledge of the Far East, but also of the English language.

The poem divides itself into ten parts, beginning with a conqueror arriving on the land of the city he is to found, continuing through seven stages of the establishment of it, including the consultation of augurs, and concluding with the Warrior-Prince's reception with great honours; but he is soon eager to be on the move again.

One might be tempted to compare parts of the *Anabasis* with Yeats's Byzantium. The only similarity is that both cities (though a real Byzantium did exist) are places of the imagination. Otherwise, they are utterly unlike each other. Both are rich in imagery, but the richness is of a different kind; it would not be rash to say that Yeats's solid texture is that of an Irishman, whereas Perse's is always that of a Frenchman who knows not only place, but the long tradition of French poetry which lies behind him, much of which he revivifies by his own poems. So, we must start with *Anabasis*.

The poem begins with a brief song, a song written and translated by Eliot, in prose. There is description, such as,

Under the bronze leaves a colt was foaled . . .
O from the provinces blow many winds . . .

and evocations like, "Hail, daughter! robed in the loveliest
robe of the year". The song ends with this line and now the
full poem starts. The conqueror is speaking sparely, elliptically
but with a great flow and colour:

> Beautiful are bright weapons in the morning and behind us the
> sea is fair . . . The Sun is not named but his power is amongst us.
> and [sic] the sea at morning like a presumption of the mind.

Here is our first entry into the poem. Perse includes us with
himself and his many followers; he never treats us as mere
observers. The vision which we enter, though so swiftly presented, is not abrupt, and it is not abrupt because of the choice
of language, the terseness that does not, such is the poet's craft,
appear like terseness. But Perse wants us to marvel at what he
has seen; indeed, he insists that we do so:

> Glory at the threshold of the tents, and my strength among
> you, and the idea pure as salt holds its assize in the day light.
> Power, you sang on our roads of splendour . . . With salt shall
> I revive the dead mouths of desire!

We note the all-important quality in a poet throughout
Perse's work—namely, the ease with which he links the ap-
propriate concrete language with the appropriate abstraction.
Thus Part I of *Anabasis* ends,

> Mathematics hung on the floes of salt! there at the sensitive
> point of my brow where the poem is formed, I inscribe this chant
> of all a people, the most rapt god-drunken,
> drawing to our dockyards eternal keels!

Here the first note of mystical experience is sounded, is touched
on.

In Part II of the ten sections, Perse begins, with use of repetition, by making the conqueror consider his country, and also
his Queen:

> In busy lands are the greatest silences in busy lands with the
> locusts at noon [the South all over the world is conjured up in
> these few words] . . .

> We step over the gown of the Queen, all of lace with two brown stripes ...
>
> We step over the gown of the Queen's daughter, all of lace with two bright stripes (and how well the lizard's tongue can catch ants at the armpit).

Then the poet asks questions. After the detailed descriptions, the concrete facts of what he, as the King, has experienced with all his senses, his vision, in short, become an evocation which is also a question:

> How, under the wild rose is there no more grace to the world? ...
>
> And the linen exposed to dry scatters! like a priest torn in pieces ...

This vision is unique in that it sweeps us along with it. The poetry has immediacy and the poet wants to share all he is feeling and seeing with us. He calls for our participation.

Part III fittingly begins with men going out in search of barley. There is a hierarchy in this world or city; there are Ambassadors. In between these short vivid pictures, Perse constantly inserts evocations of the sun and of other aspects of nature. The mingling of the grand manner, with rhetoric, with slangy expressions or simple language is as effective as it is with David Jones.

Thus "The Assayer of Weights and Measures" has "bits of straw in his beard", and the poet addresses the sun in this way: "Come, we are amazed at you, Sun! You have told us such lies", and

> ... the streams are in their beds like the cries of women and this world has more beauty
>
> than a ram's skin painted red!

Eliot has pointed out the importance of pauses in these prose poems; Perse achieves this by suddenly moving to a new line as in the last quotation. It is a poetic notation, just as music has its notation, though with music the matter is essential and much more complex. What is especially noticeable about *Anabasis* is the speed with which so much is said and done while there is no obscurity; there is a crystalline quality about the entire poem.

Rhetoric and advice move easily alongside incisive views and pictures of people and landscapes.

Part III continues by giving us an excellent example of this technique:

> Better said: we notify you, Rhetorician! of our profits beyond reckoning. The seas erring in their straits have not known a narrower judge! . . . Roses, purple delight; the earth stretched forth to my desire—and who shall set bounds thereunto, this evening? . . . violence in the heart of the sage, and who shall set bounds thereunto, this evening? . . .

Eliot's is a perfect translation and in the above passages we can see the way vision, exhortation, aphorism, repetition, and questioning do more than link one with another; rather, they flow together. And always there is the strong visual imagination at work, the concrete is never eluded. This can be seen particularly well at the very end of Part III:

> . . . And my soul, my soul keeps loud vigil at the portals of death
> But say to the Prince to be still: on the point of a lance, amongst us,
> this horse's skull!

Part IV is almost entirely given over to an ecstatic celebration of the beauty of the world in general and of the City the poet has seen in particular. Here are some fragments from it:

> Such is the way of the world and I have nothing but good to say of it—Foundation of the City. Stone and bronze. Thorn fires at dawn
> bared these great
> green stones . . .
> and the mariner at sea whom our smoke reached saw that the earth to the summit had changed its form . . . Arrivals of grain! . . . And the ships taller than Ilion under the white peacock of the sky . . . O mules, our shadows under the copper sword! four restive heads knotted to the fist make a living cluster of the blue.

The visual imagery here is dazzling. What is particularly remarkable about this section of the poem is the nearly Eden-like, Utopian vision of the world which it transmits to us. The minute details enhance the sharing of the vision; it was the poet's, now it is ours too. In less skilful hands the many details of this section would seem cluttered, disorderly, and merely random. Here they are not because of the perfect placing and the purity of the language. Thus we have:

> . . . founders of asylums meet beneath a tree and find their ideas for the choice of situations . . . And then came the bankers blowing into their keys. And already in the streets a man sang alone, one of those who paint on their brow the cipher of their god . . .

In this City, everything is provided for. It carries complete conviction yet the reader never forgets that he is partaking of a vision; he feels almost as if he is reading and wondering at an extended *Kubla Khan*. There the poet's experience was interrupted, but he wrote enough to give us an experience that is far from purely a poetic or literary one. In a fuller way, this is exactly what Perse does in *Anabasis* and his other prose poems.

This City of the mind and imagination which, because of the poet's vigour and ease with words, becomes like a real city to us and excitement mounts. There are "the pools of clear shadow" and also "Solitude! the blue egg laid by a great sea-bird, and the bays at morning all littered with gold lemons!" but the bird flies away; there are, too, "huge pieces of dead palm trees and at the end of this section "the body of a woman was burnt in the sands". Thus we are shown that what started as a vision of a world of joy has its dark side. This gives a greater realism, a lasting conviction to the poet's flights of ecstasy. Just as the fitful visions of a personal God of the Christian mystic are preceded by and followed by moments, often months, of darkness, so this secular vision shows us misery and unhappiness. Perse's world is not immune to death itself.

Part V tells us of that basic instinct of man—the desire to conquer other worlds. But the cries of ecstasy of the previous section keep appearing. Solitude is again invoked and Perse reveals something wonderful in such a passage as "squadrons of stars pass the edge of the world, enlisting from the kitchens a homely star". That homely (*domestique*) star lends a simplicity to the wholeness of the vision, just as the "stale smell of morning" does. But it must never be forgotten that the poet, with his evocation and exultation, is well aware of "the pure pestilences of night". Such things do not invalidate this complete creation of a City, seen in a vision and turned into rich, but never too rich, poetry for us.

So, preparations for a move which does actually happen proceed:

> Ah when the star was benighted in the servant-girls' quarters,
> did we know that already so
> many new spears pursued in the desert the silicates of Summer?

Soon the bustle of departure begins as "Those who lay naked in the immense season arise in crowd on the earth . . ." What they cry out, the poet tells us is "that this world is mad!" There is madness indeed in a world where it is suggested that a child "who has not yet, in dreams," stolen a colt's eye may one day do so.

The wonder, the dynamic quality, the set scenes, the desire for solitude, the horror, in this poem remind us of David Jones's vision of a war that happened. But Perse is not limited by stark realities. He sees, or actually is "the Stranger clothed in his new thoughts", who "acquires still more partisans in the ways of silence". Here is no seer only but a person who possesses an "eye full of a sort of saliva" and who feels "there is no more substance of man in him".

Throughout *Anabasis* there is variety but never confusion, there are horrible things from which the poet never turns away, but the keynote throughout is joy. If there were not the dark passages, the joy would be less bright. Part V closes like a slow movement in a symphony with these quiet but potent words: "And the earth in its winged seeds, like a poet in his thoughts, travels . . ."

Something needs to be said about the quick, but never abrupt, changes of mood in the whole poem. They are there for a purpose, planned. There is never any arbitrariness about them; their main purpose, like the concrete details, is to establish a convincing City and its inhabitants' activities in our minds. But they are also something which the poet has himself already experienced, before he started to transcribe his vision. His details, his mood-changes have the same function as the "hints and guesses" in the *Four Quartets*. In every other way these two poems are utterly different. What is shared is a part of what all major poets share—namely, a flawless technique.

Part VI tells sparely yet with a sense of luxurious labour on the part of its inhabitants of the establishing of the City, making it firm and lasting. Perse here brings his City more firmly and, if possible, more vividly before us. Men's "military governments", "alliances by marriage in the midst of dissolute peoples", are of extreme importance for this city and its surroundings but Perse has experienced Eliot's "the point of intersection of the timeless with time", and so we are given sensuous phrases, lines and passages which have a sensuousness that is reminiscent of Durrell's poems. And, as always with St-John Perse, natural beauty, the whole Universe are never forgotten. Sometimes sensuousness is at the service of the citizens' activities, sometimes it comes to us in language that glorifies the world, widens the poet's vision. Here are two examples of the first:

And deflecting a crossing of lights to the corner of terraces, great chargers of gold held up by the handmaidens, smote the weariness of the sands, at the confines of the world . . .

Then came a year of wind in the west, and on our roofs weighted with black stones, all the business of bright cloths abandoned to the delight of wide spaces.

The poet's mood is one of extreme excitement; and so the prose poem is the perfect vehicle for the conveying of his vision. The omission of main verbs allows him to put before us many things very quickly. But it must not be thought that Perse is only concerned with the sensuous world; he is also a thinker. The vision of this City is worked out for us; everything that is essential is provided for; "provinces" may be "prices in the solemn odour of roses", but they *are* priced. This is a living world where rule, law, even haggling must proceed. But language which conveys subtle intuition also enters the poem:

They who at birth have not sniffed such embers [the scent of the roses], what have they to do with us? Can they have commerce with the living? "It is your business, not mine, to rule over absence . . ." For us who were there . . . our joy amongst you was a very great joy . . .

Every literary device is employed to make this vision more accessible to us—alliteration, assonance, repetition—but there is also a great eloquence, as in these words: "Go and say truly: our habits of violence, our horses abstemious and swift upon the seeds of sedition and our helmets sniffed by the fury of the day."

This vision is all-inclusive; it is not the mystic's close, personal union with God. It is an attempt—and a successful one—to present both a creation and a sense of creating to us. The poet has found his perfect form for communicating this and we must bear in mind that all articulate visionaries, whatever the nature of their vision, desire to share it; this, Perse, most triumphantly does. Perhaps what is most wonderful in his writing is the immense knowledge it reveals—a knowledge handed over by a way of ecstatic communication. But it is always knowledge transformed, transmuted, into poetry; for example, in this section of *Anabasis*, we are told of "exhausted countries where the ways of life are to be remade, so many families to be composed like cages of whistling birds . . ."

Then a Master, who could be a prophet, a potentate or a King from the West, announces, "I have faith in my destiny . . ." This Master goes on to speak of "the deeds of peace" and of countries which are "infested with comfort" like "an odour of forum [sic] and of nubile women". Desire, sensuality are all referred to just before the wonderful words: ". . . great traffic of influence in the teeth of rivers . . . messages exchanged on leaves of gold", and then a calmness descends at precisely the right moment (this poet never allows our senses to be glutted):

(the leisurely unfolding of stuffs . . . the sword-rusting sea, and, one evening, descent into the coast provinces, towards our lands of great ease and towards our

"scented girls, who shall soothe us with a breath, silken webs . . .")

This may be a very human kind of peace but it is immediately followed by a return to the earlier talk of "a strange destiny" and of a kind of strength "on this side of the world, the most vast, where power each evening is exiled, all a widowhood of laurels!" Power, glory and peace come together. Magnificence is, at least momentarily, held at bay, and Part VI of *Anabasis* ends gently with these words: "And the still winds harboured in the depths of the desert-like gulfs."

Perse has a unique power for moving from description to exhortation, and an almost magical gift of conjuring up wonders and then subduing them, for his and our benefit, into peace. In this he resembles Prospero in *The Tempest*, but here it is Perse who is the magician, not a Shakespearean character; what they share, however—the gift to spell-bind—is the same, and exercised in a rather similar manner.

As its first line indicates, Part VII is concerned with decisions to undertake more journeys: "We shall not dwell forever in these yellow lands, our pleasance." Perse's vision is never still, never passive; he wants now to show us the restlessness of man, including himself. Exquisite descriptions and lightly touched-in sights are presented: "Colour of immortal things, the whole grassy earth taking light from the straw of last winter—and from the green sponge of a lone tree the sky draws its violet juices." We are to understand that it is Summer, and Summer is always the time when man most wishes to be on the move. The poet says of himself here, "From the crack of my eye to the level of the hills I join myself . . . and my heart gives heed to a family of locusts". Incidentally, throughout this translation, Eliot has most skilfully managed to translate the French alliterations into English ones.

This whole section is filled with calm, the calm of wonder and the calm of a serene, meditative state of mind; colours are subdued but always present. Words such as "gentle", and "quiet", and even "dead" appear. But there is much life in Nature. "The earth here and there ripens the violets of storm; and these sandsmokes that rise over dead river courses, like the skirts of centuries on their route . . ." Then the poet asks this question, "Such gentleness in the heart of man, can it fail to find its measure?" He "speaks" to his "soul", but is also acutely attentive to his earthly vision. He notes that "several great land birds, voyaging westwards, make good likeness of our sea birds"; the pale eastern sky seems to him "like a holy place sealed by the blind man's linen".

The rare skill with which Perse varies the mood of this poem is matched only by the lucidity and completeness of a personal vision which he makes general, available to all of us. And there is never any sense of strain, always decorum, even when discordant events are being depicted. But Part VII is full of peace until the end where the poet is overcome with ecstasy, not the ecstasy of the presence of God, but the ecstasy which comes from the sight of natural beauty, enhanced by the imagination. So he cries out, "Raise stones to my fame, raise stones to silence; and to guard these places, cavalcades of green bronze on the great causeways!"

Perse is celebrating not only his own joy but also the mystery and beauty of silence. He ends Part VII quietly, just as he has ended previous endings. In a few words in brackets he creates reverberations, echoes, and also a deep desire in the reader to continue reading the poem, to enter further into this world, this vision. Here is the line: "(The shadow of a great bird falls on my face.)"

Part VIII is also short and it is a kind of secular Dark Night of the Spirit—of the body also. The language, to match this stage of the poem is sometimes bleak and the syntax elliptical. Thus at the opening, we read "Nomad laws. And ourselves. (Man colour)". Yet though there is a fitting diminution in the earlier rich tone of language, there is no despair. The "solemn rains" are "of a marvellous substance, woven of powders and insects".

It seems important here to examine the reason for Perse's use of parentheses. What is their effect and purpose? At the end of a Part of the whole poem they are always a summing-up of the mood of that poem; at other times, however, they can be exhortations accompanied by a most fastidious care for words and imagery. One of the latter appears in the early section of Part

VIII. It is a definition and also a moment of rejoicing: "(To the scale of our hearts was such vacance [sic] completed!"

The poet is holding language on a leash here to prepare us for what is to come. He admits—and this is very important— "Not that this stage was in vain". He then proceeds to speak of "the darkness of the spirit—infinity of things at leisure on the frontiers of the spirit . . . And again: these shadows—the prevarications of the sky against the earth . . ." The vision is not private; these are many men. Nor is the method allegorical. All is part of a full vision, fully absorbed. Before we come to the most important statement in this part of the poem, we have questions and advice asked: ". . . shall we raise our whip over the gelded words of happiness?—Man, weigh your weight measured in wheat. A country, here, not mine. What has the world given me but this swaying of grass? . . ." As always, Nature is never forgotten. The people *are* the City, but they are also part of a larger world, the world of land and beasts and birds, of skies and empty spaces. Immediately after the mention of "this swaying of grass", we come to the crux of Part VIII.

We, the poet, and his imagined citizens have arrived at "the place called the Place of the Dry Tree". There is also "starved lightning" (a wonderful phase). There follows very fitful peace; we are told that there is a place of the "greater leisures" and "land of grass without memory, the year without ties or anniversaries, seasoned with dawns, and heavenly fires". A mysterious parenthesis immediately follows: "(Sacrified, in the morning, the heart of a black sheep.)" This is surely intended to remain a kind of magic, a dark magic. A decision comes swiftly now: "Roads of the world we follow you . . ." And then this most suffering section ends not with the holy man's handing on of peace but with this strong, pregnant line: "A great principle of violence dictated our fashions." This is man's world more than any world of hope which a holy man may convey to us after contemplation and mystical experience of God.

Part IX of *Anabasis* tells us of the arrival on the borders of a great territory. The journey has been wearisome but the poet is happy about it. It is an arrival at a Western land and no-

SEVEN MEN OF VISION

one will be parched with thirst or stricken overmuch by the sun. However, at the actual borders, the Stranger, the Leader (into whose mouth most of this section is put) does prophesy: " '. . . I fortell you the time of great heat, and the widows crying over the dissipation of the dead.' " But, very soon, he is announcing, " '. . . I foretell you the time of a great blessing and the felicity of leaves in our dreams.' " Here there is hope and a different kind of sensuousness in the choice of language. Most of what follows is entirely secular. The one who prophesies is not concerned with divinities, but with pleasure and happiness. Love-making is spoken of in parenthesis and, a few lines later, we are told that in the night "when the dogs bark", "the time of great heat . . . takes its pleasure from the womb of women".

The mysterious figure of the Stranger stays in his tent and is brought gifts. Women are brought for his pleasure too. But the poet-prophet who now speaks again tells us of "the time of great blessing, and the felicity of springs in our dreams". He declares also that he is the "companion of the grave-corner," yet there is hope to fortell also, for this voice says, "I foretell you the time of great blessing and the bounty of the evening on our eyelids that endure not . . ." Then a very simple but essential human act ends this penultimate part of *Anabasis*. Immediately before this is mentioned, we are told of "the shining edge of the day, on the threshold of a great land more chaste than death". Then comes the basic human need which concludes Part IX: "The girls made water straddling and holding aside the painted cloth of their gowns."

It seems appropriate to ask here what is the ultimate purpose of the transcription and sharing of this vision? Certainly, it is not a mere whim of a poet who has a powerful gift of language and imagery. I would say that it is a partial vision proffered to us with great imagination, the vision of a man who has exceptionally strong senses combined with a most acute mind. In one way, *Anabasis* is a seamless garment; in another, to change the metaphor, it is revised notes on a journey whose end the poet cannot penetrate. We shall see this in Part X, the last section of the poem.

This section is longer than most of the others and is full of celebration. "Living things", "excellent things" are seen. Then comes this vivid piece about the actual celebrations: "Celebrations of open air festivals for the name-day of great trees [even trees have a special day of rejoicing] and public rites in honour of a pond; consecration of black stones perfectly round . . ." And there is still also discovery, for example, "discovery of springs in dead places . . ." What is so astonishing about this whole poem, or series of prose poems, is the way in which Perse makes material things take on a kind of sacredness; this is done partly by detail, but mainly by the poet's excited imagination. He summons up a world, a world full of richness and beauty, but he never forgets very simple things—both actions of men and women, and also objects. All this adds to the sense of satisfaction the reader feels, as well as the excitement.

In Part X, we are told of "sheep-shearers, well-sinkers and horse-gelders". There is talk of harvest and hay and also of building. The tiny mention of building is especially beautiful, "building of enclosures of rose red terra cotta . . ." And, to give us the indication that this journey is not going to end, we read of "the firesmoke of man everywhere".

Perse has the kind of imagination which the tiniest thing can set alight and, apart from his very highly-developed senses, he has a vast accumulation of knowledge of many things. But he never "overloads the rift with ore"; he always knows when to hold back. The result is that he is a master of both the small thing seen or smelt, as well as of the richly ceremonious; the mingling of these two things is always masterly, and especially in this last section.

The poet is full of joy at the prospect of all he sees preparing for yet another journey: "he who fashions a leather tunic, wooden shoes and olive-shaped buttons he who dresses a field; and the man of no trade [this is an enchanting, compassionate touch]: the man with the falcon, the man with the flute, the man with bees; he who takes delight in the pitch of his voice, he who makes it his business to contemplate a green stone . . ." Perse loves all these people; they are precious to him with their varied tasks and trades. So he continues later to tell us of "he who has opinions on the use of a gourd; he who drags a dead eagle like a faggot on his tracks . . . he who gathers pollen in a wooden jar (and my delight, says he, is in this yellow colour) . . . he who dreams of green pepper, or else he who chews fossil gum . . . he who thinks of the flesh of women, the lustful; he who sees his soul reflected in a sword blade . . ."

We are carried away by all this activity, by the excitement, by so many fascinating things going on. These are Perse's people, but he is sharing them with us. He mentions "the lustful" but it is not a judgment; yet I think that to follow it with the words about the man seeing "his soul reflected in a sword blade" is a stroke of sheer genius.

It is true that St-John Perse travelled widely and held high office, but it is the poet who is paramount in this last section of *Anabasis*. One marvels at the wealth of the poet's knowledge, and also of how much he has seen and remembered: "Those who hunt among the furze for green-speckled eggs" or, "all sorts of men in their ways and fashions" who hold as deep an interest for him as the "genealogist upon the market-place". As we near the end of this poem, the more ecstatic Perse becomes, but he is a seer who has everything under control, his own excitement never overwhelms him when he is writing, but reading his words is a beautiful intoxication for us.

Perse has seen "many omens on the way, many seeds on the way, and under unleavened fine weather, in one great breath of the earth, the whole feather of harvest!" Something very important has been concluded and just before the end of the poem, which is followed by a short *Song*, we have these lines of exquisite simplicity: "until the hour of evening when the female star, pure and pledged in the sky heights . . ." And, in a moment of absolutely untarnished glory, Perse ends *Anabasis* (*Song* is a kind of coda) thus: "I have seen the earth spread out in vast spaces and my thought is not heedless of the navigator." The last few words make it clear that although the world of this particular vision has vanished, others will follow.

Now we come to the *Song*. It is not a song in the conventional sense, not a lyric. Perhaps we should call it a hymn both of triumph and gratitude. It has also a personal and gentle note,

a sense of the purity of the joy of the vision Perse has so elo-
quently experienced and passed over to us:

> I have halted my horse by the tree of the doves [doves are
> always everywhere a symbol of peace], I whistle a note so sweet,
> shall the rivers break faith with their banks?

Then we are told that a man, clearly the poet, may behold "at
the end of the fasting sky great things and pure that unfold
to delight".

Perse continues by ending this scintillating prose poem with
a kind of prayer, a prayer almost of gratitude for what he has
seen.

> Peace to the dying who have not seen this day! But tidings
> there are of my brother the poet: once more he has written a
> song of great sweetness.

The poet is humble before his vision and so speaks of himself in
the third person—"my brother the poet".

In this very beautiful and majestic poem, there is great range,
great sensuous beauty and an intuitive feeling for the precise
word or mood. There is little doubt that it is a masterpiece; but,
and I think this is more important, its value lies more in the
realm of ecstasy than of enormous poetic skill. The poet has
carried us into his own world; we are completely convinced by
it.

The next poem of St-John Perse's which is translated by Louise
Varèse, is called *Praises*; the parts to be looked at most closely
are those which celebrate childhood.

Part 1 is, in fact, entitled *To Celebrate a Childhood*. It is of
particular interest that much of this entire poem is written in
the third person. It may, in certain respects, be compared with
Traherne's *Centuries of Meditations* and Richard Jefferies' *Story
of My Heart*. Here are some fragments of Part 1:

> Palms ... !
> In those days they bathed you in water-of-green-leaves; and the
> waters were of green sun too ...
> Palms! and the sweetness
> of an aging of roots ... ! the earth

in those days longed to be deafer, and deeper the sky where
trees too tall, weary of an obscure design, knotted an inextricable
pact . . .
(I dreamed this dream, in esteem : a safe sojourn among the
enthusiastic linens.)

The completely recalled pleasures are given here, and the most
effective use of alliteration is made. The latter is sometimes
reminiscent of D. H. Lawrence's use of it, but it serves a rather
different purpose with Perse.

Part 2 is an ecstatic evocation of the poet's childhood and,
as in *Anabasis*, it is full of the most vivid detail :

And my mother's maids, tall glistening girls . . . And our
fabulous eyelids . . . O radiance ! O favours !
Naming each thing I proclaimed that it was great, naming
each beast, that it was beautiful and good.

We recall how Adam and Eve gave names to everything in the
Garden of Eden, and it is also an important part of the development of a child to give names to things, sometimes to learn the
familiar ones, sometimes to find his own. Just as Traherne does,
Perse raises this innocent, eager state of mind and imagination
to the level of a vision :

. . . vegetable fervours, O radiance, O favours !
. . . I remember the salt, I remember the salt my yellow nurse
had to wipe away at the corner of my eyes.

Soon, after expressing the depths of his gratitude for all that
he was given and observed, the poet proceeds, "I shall not know
again any place of mills and sugar-cane, for children dream, that
in living, singing waters was thus distributed."

Perse knows that childhood is transitory but he has caught a
vision of it on the wind. It has not eluded him, not one tiniest
detail of it.

There is more about childhood to come; Part 3 ends, "Other
than childhood, what was there in those days that is here no
longer ?" Just as Wordsworth knew and wrote about the "shades
of the prison-house" which "begin to close upon the growing
boy", so too does Perse, and he writes about it like this, speaking

of his mother, his grandmother and his nurse and others, but only briefly:

> And I never knew all Their voices, and I never knew all the
> women and all the men who served in our high
>   wooden house, but I shall still long remember
>   mute faces, the colour of papayas and of boredom that paused
> like burnt-out stars behind our chairs.

Perse is re-creating with rich nostalgia a privileged childhood spent in the East. He has forgotten nothing; it lives with him not simply as a memory, but a detailed, joyful memory. In Part 5, he cries out with gratitude,

> O! I have cause to praise!
> My forehead under yellow hands,
> my forehead, do you remember the night sweats?
> . . . . .
> O I have cause! O I have cause to praise.

In these words, which are like prayers, Perse brings back his childhood, his happiness, to himself and to us. Part 5 has another very beautiful passage which begins

> Palms! . . . In those days a more credulous sea and haunted by
> invisible departures . . .

and ends "(O I have cause to praise! O bountiful fable, O table of abundance!)".

Every word Perse uses seems absolutely spontaneous yet, when we look closely at *Praises*, we see the carefully touched-in descriptions, the memory which recalls and joyously shares with us the many glories of the sensuous world, the world which the poet sees with such clear eyes and celebrates in paeans of praise.

Thus, in childhood, "voices were a bright noise on the wind . . . Reverently, my father's boat brought tall white forms: really wind-blown angels perhaps". Here, we are reminded of some of the ecstatic flights of language, on very different subjects, in Rilke's *Duino Elegies*. There are passages, such as the following from Part 6, when the reader is so caught up in the poet's vision that he is not sure whether he is sharing in a child's imaginings or in things that were seen and happened; this effect is very like much of the *Duino Elegies*—nostalgia raised to vision:

> ... I saw Princes walking, and
> their Kinsmen, men of high rank, all well
> dressed and silent, because the sea
> before noon is a Sunday where sleep
> has taken on the body of a God
> bending his knees.
> And torches, at noon, were raised for my flights.
> And I believe that Arches, Halls of ebony and tin were lighted
> every evening at the dream of the volcanoes.

A little further on, Perse ends this section of *Praises* with a further salutation to the palm trees:

> Palms! and the sweetness
> of an aging of roots! ... the breath of the trade winds, wild
> doves and the feral cat
> pierced the bitter foliage where, in the rawness of an evening
> with an odour of Deluge
> moons, rose and green, were hanging like mangoes.

Praises is written in sections and the second section or part is much concerned with food, and the many different jobs of men, and all this is seen through a child's eye even though the poet-visionary sometimes interrupts to give a cry of thanksgiving. So, Part 1 of the second section of *Praises* (and how well-named this poem is) begins thus:

> Meats broil in the open air, sauces are brewing ...
> Then the Dreamer [the child?] with dirty cheeks
> comes out of
> an old dream streaked with violence,
> wiles and flashes of light,
> and jewelled in sweat, towards the odour of meat
> he descends
> like a woman trailing ...

The dream-like air of so much of *Praises* is never vague, just as child's games are never vague, but always specific and precise. Perse has caught this state with great artistry.

The visionary poet, in Part 1 of this section, remembers this, for example:

> I loved a horse—who was he?—he looked me
> straight in the face, under his forelock . . .
> When he had run, he sweated: which means
> to shine!—and under my child's knees I
> pressed moons on his flanks.

The imagery here is perfect. I can think of nothing quite like this part of the poem in English literature except, perhaps Dylan Thomas's *Fern Hill* where the poet begins his poem,

> Now as I was young and easy under the apple boughs
> About the lilting house . . .

and where, later, comes the beautiful phrases about "fields of praise" and horses "flashing into the dark". In method and style, the poems are quite different, but both Perse and Thomas have captured those moments in childhood when reality and imagination meet and become visionary. There is no vagueness in either poet, only a handing on to us of their experience which we may, or may not, have shared in a minor degree.

Perse's passion for detail is given a great deal of scope in Part 3 of this section, but it always has a purpose—to enlarge and make more vivid for us what he has known. This part begins,

> Rhythms of pride flow down the red mornes [*sic*].
> Turtles roll in the narrows like brown stars.
> Roadsteads dream dreams full of children's heads.

In Part 4 of this section of *Praises*, Perse reveals fully the different levels on which he is writing. After "I awake dreaming of the black fruit of the Aniba . . ." he goes on, a little later, to descriptions far beyond a child's compass or knowledge: "And there is the good odour of sex. Sweat makes a cool path . . . Those shores are swelling, crumbling under a layer of insects celebrating absurd nuptials."

The rich pulse and movement of life are felt and rejoiced in, everywhere. Nothing is static. Nor is anything Puritanical. *Praises* is often like movements in a concerto or a symphony;

the mood changes deliberately and perfectly. So we have the gentleness of Part 5 which begins

> ... Now these calm waters are made of milk
> and everything that overflows in the soft
> solitudes of morning ...
>   ... And the adorable childhood
> of day, through the trellis of furled canvas,
> descends along my song.

> Childhood, my love, was it only that? ...

> Childhood, my love ... that double ring of the eye and the ease
>   of loving ...
> It is so calm and then so warm,
> so continuous too,
> that it is strange to be there, hands plunged in the facility of day.

So Perse equates dawn with day. But he is recalling childhood; it is the past, brought to life again in his vision. The spaces between lines and the repetitions are extremely important, part of the technique of a prose poem, but here so controlled, so mastered, that they are never felt merely as technique or literary devices.

Part 6 of this section of *Praises* is also almost elegiac:

> Childhood, my love ! it is morning, it is
> gentle things that implore, like the hatred of singing,
> gentle as the shame that trembles on the
> lips of things said in profile ...
> . . . . .
> And now I am asking you, isn't it morning
> ... a freedom of breath
> and the aggressive childhood of day,
> gentle as the song that half closes the eyes?

Perse's own childhood and dawn are brought together and celebrated. Nothing is overdone or over-written; always there is decorum. Such a great, all-embracing vision needs decorum in order to be communicable and coherent. We are so intoxicated by all that the poet is telling us that we forget how skilfully we are being drawn into and allowed to share his ecstasy.

Part 7, Part 8 and Part 9, speak of the sea, always an inspiring subject for Perse. We should examine some lines and paragraphs from them for they too are part of "the full view", essential to this whole poem. Ships also are mentioned and birds, as in this piece from Part 7 :

> And great leisure then for all those in the stern, surges of silence ebbing over our foreheads . . .
> A bird that was following, his flight sweeps him overhead, he misses the mast, he sails by . . . And the youngest of the travellers, sitting on the taffrail : "I want to tell you about the springs under the sea . . ." (they beg him to tell).

Journeys always fascinate Perse, whether they are by sea or land. The concreteness of his language makes what are mythical, magical voyages seem like real ones; they are part of his vision, in which nothing is too small to be noted and mentioned, and where the language is now rich, now spare but always clear, original and felt to be right.

So Part 7 continues :

> Meanwhile the ship casts a green-blue shadow; peaceful, clair-voyant, permeated with glucose where graze
> in supple and sinuating bands
> those fish that move like the theme along the song.

In Part 8, Perse writes, "This ship is ours and my childhood knows no end. I have seen many fishes and am taught all their names." He admits also that he has seen many things "that are make-believe". When he then speaks of "the peacocks of Solomon" and Montezuma, the mood has changed, and the tempo too. Here, the grown man is talking.

Part 9 is more dramatic than Parts 7 and 8. Orders are given and arguments are going on between unnamed sailors :

> . . . Oh be quiet ! If you speak again of landing,
> let me tell you right now,
> I'll throw myself overboard under your eyes.
>
> . . . Cast off the ship's boat
> or else don't, or decide
> to go swimming . . . that suits me too.

Then the mood changes to one of ecstatic excitement:

> Acts, feasts for the forehead and feasts for the nape! . . .
> and those clamours, those silences! and those tidings on a
> journey and those messages on the tides, O libations of the day!
> . . . and the presence of the sail, great restless soul, the sail, strange
> there, showing warm, like the presence of a cheek . . . O
> gusts! . . . Truly I inhabit the throat of a God.

The vision becomes more sublime; Perse is quite literally carried away by these sails; they remind him of man's soul and the existence of a God. Marvellously as he always describes material things, they are never merely material to him. Parts 10 and 11 are about quays and landings, and in Part 12, "priests" and "Notables" of a city are spoken of. Perse is constantly in search of some unattainable city; we could see this in *Anabasis*. It was the whole purpose of the journey in that poem. In Part 13, the poet returns to childhood again:

> A child sees it all,
> so beautiful
> that he can no longer close his fingers . . . But the coconut
> that's been drained and tossed there, blind clamouring head set
> free from the shoulder,
> diverts from the gutter
> the metallic splendour of the purple waters mottled with grease
> and urine, where soap weaves a spider's web.
> On the cornelian quay, a girl dressed like a Lydian king.

Memory, actuality and vision fuse "And the child coming home from the Fathers' [monks'] school, affectionate", is "hugging the affection of the Walls that smell of hot bread . . ." Perse often mentions jewels, but he is equally at ease with the simplicity of bread and fish and oil. Now "in the center [sic] of the Market of bronze", "a hairless man in yellow cotton cloth gives a shout: I am God! and other voices" say "he is mad". This man could be a Hindu priest, mistaken for a lunatic.

Amongst all this tremendous excitement, the poet quietly ends this section, Part 14, with these simple words, which draw us as well as him down to earth: "As for me, I have drawn back my feet." Some things are too magical, too mysterious to be lingered with for long, and so Part 15 returns to the happy safety of childhood, the vision of the poet's own childhood with which he is in love:

> Childhood, my love, I loved evening too: it is the hour for going out.
> Our nurses have gone into the corolla of their
> dresses . . . and glued to the blinds, under our
> clammy hair, we have
> seen as smooth, as bare, they lifted at arm's length the soft ring of the dresses. Our mothers will be coming down perfumed . . . Their necks are beautiful. Run ahead and announce: My mother is the most beautiful!

Perse can move with what appears to us extreme ease from one world to another, from one viewpoint to another. The spacing of lines in his prose poems is a vital part of his technique, too; it is never arbitrary. In *Praises*, we have the secret magic of a fairy story with the completely concrete, adult vision of a man whose memory of childhood and senses serve that vision. The poet's vocabulary is rich, his knowledge profound, but these things are a means, never an end, a means to show forth to us both his vision and his gratitude for the splendour of the world. His vision gives the smallest detail an importance and, in its context, even a grandeur.

Part 16 of this section of *Praises* speaks of age—"Those who are old in the country are the earliest risen . . ."—but it does not linger long with thoughts of longevity. Soon we are back with the immediate pleasure of the child which is heralded by the very appropriate line, "Suddenly it is day! and the tin of the roofs lights up in a trance . . ." Then the purest, innocent joy comes:

> Children run to the shore! horses run to
> the shore! . . . a million children wearing their lashes
> like umbels . . .

Perse has the unique power to give a sense of speed while at the same time placing the precise phrase of description. He proceeds a little later with these words about the wind:

for a wind, the coolest of the year, rises in the sounds between
the islands, growing blue . . .
> And the day is begun, and the world
> is not too old to burst into laughter . . .

So the cool season is coming. And then with one of those
wonderful apt juxtapositions, Perse turns from Nature to a
delicious smell which almost all men and children love : "It is
then that the odour of coffee ascends the stairs."

The blending of the purely material and sense-enhancing with
the almost numinous is one of Perse's great gifts. He satisfies
our minds and senses, he makes a complete world which we may
enter; some things in it are familiar to us, others strange, strange
with a curious magic. His own rejoicing in life lifts everything
to the level of a vision. In *Praises*, we sometimes feel that the
evil and sickness of the world do not exist—but not for long,
for this poet is essentially a realist.

Part 17 returns us to childhood and what many of us call the
real world. It is brief and much of it is conversation; a very
homely, charming touch is thus introduced at the beginning.
Such moments as these are rare in *Praises*:

> "When you stop combing my hair, I'll stop hating you."
> The child wants his hair combed on the doorstep.
> "Don't pull like that. It's bad enough being touched. When
> you've finished my hair, I'll have hated you."

This is perfect child psychology. The great dignity of the lines
which immediately follow this nursery talk highlights the whole
visionary world into which we have been drawn. It is,

> Meanwhile the wisdom of day takes the shape of a fine tree
> and the swaying tree,
> loosing a pinch of birds ["pinch" is absolutely right here],
> scales off in the lagoons of the sky a green so beautiful, there
> is nothing that is greener than the water-bug.

Part 17 then immediately returns to and ends with the child's
talk: "Don't pull on my hair so . . ."

But all these sections of *Praises* do not end here, nor even with
Part 18, which is certainly, again, like the end of a movement

in music. The mood has changed entirely. The poet says, "And now let me be, I go alone . . .", but he has vague plans for what he is going to do, where his vision appears to him to be carrying him: "I shall go out, for I have things to do: an insect is waiting to treat with me." And so this gentle yet powerful Part ends,

> Or else I have an alliance with the blue-veined stones: and also you'll let me be,
> sitting, in the friendship of my knees.

In this last line, Perse is surely speaking of human love, yet he leaves the reader with precisely the right sense of expectation and suspense.

Praises ends with a sequence on various subjects, with the overall title of *Pictures For Crusoe*. The first two sections are called *The Bells* and *The Wall*, but we shall examine the third, which is called *The City*, because it bears some relation to *Anabasis*. It begins with great activity and excitement:

> Their breath blows out through the chimneys.
> Grease!
> Odour of men in crowds . . .
> O City against the sky!
> The City like an abscess flows through the river to the sea . . .

> Crusoe!—this evening over your Island, the sky drawing near will give praise to the sea . . .
> Draw the curtains; do not light the lamp:
> It is evening on your Island and all around, here and there, wherever arches the faultless vase of the sea . . .

So Robinson Crusoe's island is drawn into Perse's vision. He sees it, and shows it to us with all its beauty. The Plant and Animal Kingdoms are lively but man, man the solitary, is here at peace. So,

> . . . bats stipple the soft evening with little cries
> Joy! O joy set free from the heights of the sky!
> . . . Crusoe! You are there! and your face is
> proffered to the signs of the night like an upturned Palm.

The use of the word "stipple" in this context is masterly. However, Crusoe is not to be left alone for long. The next section of the Crusoe part is about Man Friday. He is greeted by the poet with delight:

Laughter in the sun ...
Friday! how green was the leaf, and your shadow how new, your hands so long towards the earth when, beside the taciturn man you moved in the light the streaming blue of your limbs!

Once again, we are back in a new kind of Garden of Eden, and how lucid and fresh the vision is. Perse says more of Man Friday (oddly, there now appear to be more people on Crusoe's island):

... you leer at the skirts of the cook who is fat and who smells of fish; you see in the mirroring brass of your livery your eyes grown sly and vicious your laughter.

The vision has come down to earth and we now have sections called *The Parrot*, *The Goatskin Parasol*, *The Bow*, *The Seed*, and finally, *The Book*, which is truly almost prophetic. So, *Praises* closes with these words:

You would open the book [probably *The Bible*] and letting your worn finger wander among the prophecies, your gaze far away, you awaited the moment of departure ...

Perse's vision is full of departures; he cannot hold the moment of illumination for long, but, on the other hand, on a lower level, his is a world packed full with every aspect of life. Everything is seen deeply and written of deftly. Our eyes are continually being opened, and continually we wonder at this poet's power.

Before we go on to an examination of some more of St-John Perse's poems, this seems a fitting place to put down what he himself said about poetry in the Citation he gave when he was awarded the Nobel Prize for Literature; the Citation is beautifully and exactly translated by W. H. Auden. Perse placed a very high value on poetry and stated that it was on a level, perhaps a higher level than science and history. These are some of his words: "The high spiritual adventure of poetry need yield nothing in drama to the new vistas of modern science . . . As far as the frontiers of science extend and along their whole stretched arc, we can still hear the hounds of the poet in full cry." He also declared that "Poetry is not only a way of knowledge; it is even more a way of life—of life in its totality". He went on to declare that "A poet already dwelt within the cave man: a poet will be dwelling still within the man of the atomic age" (how right he was); "for poetry is a fundamental part of man." Perse went so far as to say that "Out of the poetic need . . . all the religions have been born . . ."

Having examined two of St-John Perse's poems, we can see that their visionary nature lived up to the high place he gave to poetry in the life of man; his own practice as a poet lived up to his lofty theory of the art. Then, close to the end of his Citation, he said, ". . . in spite of himself, the poet also is tied to historical events. Nothing in the drama of his times is alien to him". For Perse, present and past were one, and both were the raw material of poetry.

We have already noticed this poet's deep attachment to journeys, cities, everything on the move. These preoccupations may be taken as analogues or a very original use of allegory for the restlessness of our own age. It is not surprising, then, to find that he has written a prose poem called Exile, very well translated by Denis Devlin. It is in seven parts. Out of the terror and miseries of partings, exiles, of always being on the move, Perse can often draw a splendour while, at the same time, observe and depict the beauty of countries, seasons and elements. Part 1 of Exile begins:

Doors open on the sands, doors open on exile,
   The keys with the lighthouse keepers, and sun spread-eagled out on the threshold stone . . .
   I have chosen a place glaring and null as the bone-heap of the seasons.
   And, on all the shores of the world, the ghost of the god in smoke abandons his bed of asbestos.

In Part 2, we have the real beginning of this poem:

Dedicated to no shores, imparted to no pages, the pure beginnings of this song . . .

Others in temples seize on the painted altar horns: My fame is on the sands! my fame is on the sands! . . . And it is no error, O Peregrine,

To desire the barest place for assembling on the wastes of exile a great poem born of nothing, a great poem made from nothing . . .

Whistle, O slings about the world, sing, O conches on the waters!

I have built upon the abyss and the spindrift and the sand-smoke. I shall lie down in cistern and hollow vessel . . .

So, from nothingness, the poet draws his vision. Often this poem is like an incantation. At times someone is speaking, as in the following lines:

"Where the sands go to their song, there go the Princes of exile . . .

Where there were great military actions, there lies whitening now the jawbone of an ass . . ."

The vision is built up and revealed to us by the greatest care for detail. Perse has a wonderfully strong visual sense.

The poet himself now proceeds to speak of wisdom

"Wisdom in the foam . . .
I learn a science from the soul's aggressions . . .
. . . . .
I watch in this vast arena signs of good omen soaring.

And Part 2 ends with these words:

Says the Stranger on the sands, "The whole world is new to me . . ." And the birth of his song is no less alien to him.

Perse has a powerful feeling for the dramatic; he knows precisely when great flights of eloquence are needed and when a simple phrase is most effective, as in the last few words of Part 2 of Exile.

Part 3 opens with richness, wonder, and excitement; the reader is caught up into this vision. Again, someone unnamed is speaking, and the voice tells us

"One long phrase without pause forever unintelligible . . .
There has always been this clamour, there has always been this furor [sic]."

138

All the ages are gathered into a few words. The many activities of man are seen freshly. Even though there is "lamentation" and "too many deserted beds", the tone of the poem does not alter. Then, the poet speaks quietly thus: "And all at once all is power and presence for me, here where the theme of nothingness rises still in smoke." Even out of nothingness, a kind of joy is brought forth. Part 4, though its subject-matter is desolate, contains a line like this: "And who is that wandering before dawn at the ends of the earth, crying out for me?"

No major poetry can be entirely negative; the reader feels that Perse is intoxicated even at his vision of things that are "null and void". It is, after all, part of the poet's task to give life to what seems lifeless; this is especially true of the visionary poet. With his perfect and precise view of the world, Perse can intoxicate us, make a splendid world. He does this over and over again, but here is a particularly beautiful passage from Part 4 of *Exile*:

> With the plovers' complaints departed the plaintive dawn,
> departed the showery hyades in search of the pure word,
> And on most ancient shores my name was called . . .

It is rare for Perse to mention himself; he is the least subjective or personal of poets. So, when he does say "my", his words gain an added force. As with all his poems, his use of alliteration is so skilful as scarcely to be noticed above.

Part 4 is much concerned with the actual transcription of visions, the making of poems:

> Ah! all is vain in the winnowing of memory . . .
> And night's poems disowned before the dawn, the fossil wing
> entrapped in great amber vespers . . .

But there is no despair and this Part ends on a note of great hope: "Now I have once more the design for a great, delible poem . . ."

Perse has a unique gift for imparting a kind of glory even to tragic things such as exiles and departures. The glory is part of his vision and shines all the more radiantly because he never evades the most homely event; he remembers always that man is

limited, but he recognizes too his splendid aspirations. In Part
5 of Exile, a voice is speaking again and saying such things
as,

> "My hands more naked than at birth, and lips more free, ear
> to the coral reef where sounds the lament of another age . . ."

and

> "Midday sings, O sadness ! . . . and the wonder is announced
> by this cry : O wonder ! and it's not enough to laugh through the
> tears . . .
> But what is it then, O ! what is it that in everything is suddenly
> wanting? . . ."

and (here the poet is speaking) "Many a century veils itself
before the lapses of history".

To see above and beyond history and all that history means
as a question of centuries passing, one must first possess a sense
of history; this Perse does possess in abundance. Part 5 of Exile
ends, "At these great limestone leaves on their shelves level with
the abyss, lace on the mask of death . . ."

There is great beauty here even in sadness. The tragic beauty
of the transcience of all things is a part of the vision which
Perse reveals to us in this section of Exile.

Part 6 is long and is a paean of praise to all those who help
in times of crisis. The language has a crystalline quality. Again,
a voice is speaking and his words are like a litany. The man
behind this voice rejoices in the man who "ranges the stone
galleries assessing the title-deeds of a beautiful comet [a magnificent conception in itself]; he who, between two wars, watches
over the purity of great crystal lenses; he who rises before day-
light to clean out the fountains, and the great epidemics are at
an end . . ." Countless people are evoked and praised for their
labours from those who soothe "the insane in the great blue-
chalk asylums" to those who paint "a landmark on the brow
of high headlands" or wash "the great shadow-filled casemates
[sic] at the foot of the semaphores" or walk "across the earth
towards the great grasslands" or give advice "about the treat-
ment of a tree grown very old".

There is magic and vision here, but also precise, concrete

instructions or examples. Simple things are charged with splendour by the magnificence of language and the passion of the poet. Nothing is neglected, from "iron towers" to "boneyards and sewers below the city" and "the great fetid hothouses of the Botanical Gardens". Government is mentioned, and so are armies and stud-farms. Special praise is given to the man "who, in time of crisis, arranges for the safeguard of the tall liners held under sail" and for "He who opens an account in the bank for the researches of the mind".

That last detail is anything but materialistic. In fact all through this inspired catalogue we are being swept into the poet's vision. Everything is dynamic, nothing static. Then, there is praise for the man "who leads his mount to the spring and does not himself drink" and, among so much else, for the one who "puts on the poet's robe to pay homage to a beautiful terrace". There are no hierarchies here. All labour has virtue, decorum and honour. The words which come closest to the poet actually speaking (and even they are put in the mouth of another man) are " 'he who is shown, in a most high place, great stones glazed beneath the insistence of flame . . . Those are the princes of exile; they have no need of my song.' "

Yet the poet salutes them nonetheless and as Part 6 draws to a close, Perse writes, now as himself again: "Stranger, on all the shores of the world, without audience or witness, lift to the ear of the West a shell that has no memory . . ." But he is contradicting this great vision by putting it into memorable language. Humility always shines out of visionaries or mystics, whether they are sacred or secular, and Perse is no exception.

Part 7 is the last section of *Exile* and it is brief. It is also, which as far more important, pure incantation, the prayer of a mystic at the height of his mystical experience. Words, phrases, lines spring, dart, leap, yet there is no incoherence. We are reminded of the Ash Wednesday ceremony in this line. "Two women, their foreheads signed with ashes by the same thumb . . ." and then Perse speaks of prayers themselves: "O heart of prayers about the world." Soon, he returns to the subject of exile and writes, "Exile is not of yesterday! exile is not of yesterday."

Exile is itself now something to rejoice in and the poet continues,
a little later:

> Wandering all over the shores, wandering all over the seas, be
> silent, gentleness, and your presence, arrayed with wings at my
> saddle's height . . .
>
> Know that on the sands of exile there hiss the high passions
> coiled beneath the lightning's whip . . . O Prodigal in the salt and
> foam of June! Keep alive in our midst the occult power of your
> song!

So the vision is not mystical now, in the Christian sense of
union with God. It is full of action and delight in action; it is
also full of gratitude for all the wonder of the world and for all
that man can do. Perse ends this magnificent poem with these
almost prophetic words. They are simple and full of promise:
"And the time is come, O Poet, to declare your name, your birth
and your race." We know, from his Citation, how lofty a place
St-John Perse assigned to the poet. Here we see it in action, as it
were. But it is not mere rhetoric, it is belief and passion crying
together.

Among Perse's poems are ones called *Rains* and *Snows*. Here,
we shall consider *Snows*, which is also finely translated by Denis
Devlin. As in all these prose poems men are subject to climate
yet also, entirely by means of the poet's view of it, transformed
by it. He celebrates all climates and the celebration is one of the
chief elements of his vision. In Part 1 of *Snows*, beauty and
sadness are mingled:

> . . . the first snows of absence, on the great linens of dream and
> reality interwoven . . .
>
> And it was at morning, beneath the gray salt of dawn, a little
> before the sixth hour, as in a chance haven, a place of grace and
> of mercy for releasing the swarms of the great odes of silence.

So poetry can also be silence; here it is contemplation as
well. In "this lofty feat of feathers", Perse finds peace and
wonder. He declares that the memories of men which are
"uncertain" understand the mysteries beneath the visible world
covered by snow. The rest of us only see the delicate purity of
the snow: "The first light touch of this thing, fragile and so

trifling, like a fluttering of eyelashes."

In Part 2, the poet tells us what *he* sees and knows:

> I know that ships in distress in this wide, pale oyster-spat
> thrust their lowing of deaf beasts against the blindness of men
> and gods; and the whole world's wretchedness calls the pilot off
> the estuaries.

And he says that now he has "the vision at last without
fault or flaw". The poet is both seer and guide. As always, the
smallest tangible things are radiant to him. Part 2, thus ends
like an incantation:

> It is snowing outside Christendom on the youngest bramble and
> on the newest creature. Spouse of the world, my presence! . . .
> And somewhere in the world where silence illuminates a larch-
> tree's dream, sadness raises its servant mask.

Nothing is missed, not everything is glorious. Perse sees sadness
(it is part of his vision) and shares it with us. To omit it would
be to omit an important part of the mystery of the very existence
of the world with all its intricacies, natural and man-made.

In Part 3 of *Snows*, Perse speaks specifically of "all this plain-
chant of the snows" and later of the Virgin Mary, Mother of
God-made-Man. He writes:

> And She whom I think of among all the women of my race
> [this is mysterious for Our Lady was a Jew, but she was also the
> Mother of all mankind, or this may be one woman praying],
> from the depths of her old age raises to her God her face of gentle-
> ness . . .
> And like a great *Ave* of grace on our path, there sings low the
> pure song of our race.

Here, Perse is, of course referring to the *Hail Mary*, the prayer
to Our Lady which is spoken in many languages throughout the
world. He then says of her (this is certainly Our Lady) with
great reverence: "A Lady of high lineage was your silent soul
in the shadows of your Cross . . ."

Then Perse sees Our Lady as an old woman. The following
words speak for all holy mothers:

. . . a grieving woman's flesh in her old age was your living heart of a woman agonizing in all women . . .

And who is it will lead you, in this greater widowhood, to your Churches underground, where the lamp is frugal and the bee divine?

Here, in *Snows*, Perse shows us a Christian vision. He speaks now in his own voice:

And all this time of my silence in a far country, I have watched on the pale bramble roses your worn eyes become paler. And you alone were spared that speechlessness that is like a black stone in the heart of man.

Perse goes on to speak of "a great *Ave* of grace on our path". He shares his awe with us, he speaks in simple words but they carry a mysterious grandeur.

The poet then continues, remembering the snow which gave him the gift of this vision:

Did it snow, this night, on that side of the world where you join your hands? . . .

Spouse of the world, my presence, spouse of the world, my vigil! . . . in men is the sadness of men, but also that strength which is nameless and, at moments, that grace at which they surely must have smiled.

This is how Part 3 ends, and Part 4 returns to a less exalted vision of the snow. This section is written in the first person, and the poet calls himself "the only accountant, from the height of this corner room surrounded by an Ocean of snows" and "Precarious guest of the moment". A little later on he declares that it is his "design, now to wander among the oldest layers of speech, among the farthest phonetic strata". This likeness of language to geology is a brilliant touch.

As we reach the end of *Snows*, we find that prayer and the very concretely expressed vision of snow come together. Snow is "like a great *Ave* of grace on our path, the great white rose-garden of all the snows all around". But the snow is also an illusion because it conceals rivers which are "still fordable".

With the utmost simplicity, Perse ends *Snows* with this single line, saying so much, telling us how many visions can never be put into words at all; it is also like the end of a prayer: "Henceforth this page on which no more is written." Perse values silence as much as the wealth of words, and he stops when words are no longer adequate to convey a vision.

Though there are many other poems by St-John Perse, this study will end with an examination of *Birds* which has been admirably translated by Robert Fitzgerald, the American poet. This poem, which is a consideration and celebration of all birds, begins by telling us that "The bird" is "the most ardent for life of all our blood kin" and that "on the cross-beam of his wing is the vast balancing of a double season".

Perse knows all the biological facts about the habits of birds and these habits are incorporated into the honour which he pays them. He cries out at "The austerity of flight!" and then declares:

> A man at sea, feeling noon in the air, lifts his head at this wonder: a white gull opened on the sky, like a woman's hand before the flame of a lamp . . .

The poet has observed all his birds most carefully but, after the observation, the splendour of what he has seen brings him, and us, true exaltation. Part 1 (this poem is written in thirteen Parts) ends with this beautiful line: "Sickle-shaped wing of dream, you will find us again this evening on other shores!" Part 2 is largely a consideration of the study which French naturalists have given to birds; Perse rejoices in their findings.

Part 3 is quite different. In it, Perse examines how painters have depicted birds and, after speaking of the "rapture" they know before beginning to "report", says:

> So from a "territory" vaster than that of the bird, the painter takes to himself, by violence or by a slow detaching . . . this pure fragment of space made substance, made tactile . . .

Here we have one artist identifying himself with another, and doing this with understanding and wonder. Braque is mentioned in the line, "Such, for the bird painted by Braque, is the secret strength of his 'ecology'." Perse makes Braque's painting part

of his own vision, and he continues to write of painting in
Part 4. He says: "The lightning 'strike' of the painter, ravisher
and ravished . . ." "Ravisher and ravished" are words which
might well be applied to Perse in all his poems. His vision becomes almost philosophical at the end of Part 4 when he speaks
of "unity recovered under what seemed diverse".

Braque is mentioned again in Part 5; Perse then proceeds to
speak of what birds have meant to mankind throughout the
ages, but he still mentions painting:

> Man has rejoined the innocence of the wild creature, and the
> bird painted in the hunter's eye becomes the hunter himself in
> the eye of the creature, as it does in Eskimo art. Wild thing and
> hunter together cross the ford of a fourth dimension.

This is speculation amounting to vision. We are a long way now
from description. Towards the close of Part 5, Perse's vision
mounts further. The thinking mind and the seer are at one in
the following words:

> We are a long way now from decoration. Here is knowledge
> pursued as a research of the soul, and nature finally joined by
> spirit after surrendering all to spirit. A moving and long medita-
> tion has rediscovered here the immensity of space and time . . .

While showing us his vision, Perse can at the same time explain
the steps towards it. He knows the great value of meditation,
something entirely different from observation or introspection.

Braque is carried through Part 6 also; he is at the service of
Perse the seer and, paradoxically, at one with him. This Part
begins,

> Now that the hour of liberation has come, here is more than a
> rising flight of birds: it is a silent launching of great painted
> images . . .

Most fittingly, the poet ends this brief part by references to
China and Arabia and their sages: "Just so the old pilots of
China and Arabia used to watch their painted bird . . . as it held
its bearings on the surface of water in a bowl." East and West
are brought gently together.

In Part 7 Braque's birds are again referred to and we also have repeated the phrase "Austerity of flight!" Part 7 ends with a very profound line: "It is a poetry of action that is entered with passion here." Philosophy, entering into a picture, contemplation, all play their part in Perse's vision. There is clarity and exactness. The poet has experienced something almost ineffable and, in ecstatic yet simple, always entirely comprehensible words, he hands it to us.

The same spirit is maintained in Part 8 which begins:

Birds, birds, held by long affinity close to man's frontiers . . .
Behold them armed for action, like daughters of the spirit . . .
On the white page with infinite margins, the space they measure is all incantation.

These birds would be symbols or allegorical figures were it not for the fact that they are so clearly described as part of the natural world. Yet Perse *does*, of course, also give them a meaning of his own, otherwise his writing would be merely descriptive and there would be no vision. Towards the end of Part 8, he illustrates this by declaring:

Happy birds, ah, may they extend towards us, from one shore to the other of heaven's ocean . . . May they bear the full honour of it among us by strength of soul!

So, birds represent the liberation of the soul. At the very end of Part 8, Perse not only speaks of "Braque's bird", but also mentions "a particle of rock in Cézanne's geology". The visual arts help him to pass over his art of words to us; they assist the sharing of his vision.

Part 9 is almost entirely devoted to telling us why birds are so important to Perse. He ends this Part thus:

Of all the forms of life that still dwell in man as in a living ark, the bird alone, with his long cries calling to flight, endowed man with a new audacity.

There is something of D. H. Lawrence's attitude towards the natural world in such a paragraph as this. Part 10 begins with sheer incantation: "Gratitude of flight . . . These made of it their joy." Perse takes great delight in the sheer flight of the birds, much in the way St-Exupéry finds ecstasy in flying an aeroplane. Just as he can be one with his plane, so Perse feels united with the birds' flight:

> They more than fly, they come wholly to the delight of being...
> They fly past, and so endure, or soar, and so reign . . . Nourishing space opens to them its carnal depth, and their maturity awakens in the very bed of the wind.

Then a repetition occurs—"Gratitude of flight!" and the poet later speaks of "the failing armature of the Southern Cross . . ."

In Part 10, Perse also speaks of "Long luxuriance and long muteness . . . No whistling of slings or scythes up there." and of "clearing the way of eternity". He also tells us that the flying birds are "mediators for us and strive with all their being to the utmost of being . . ." And at the end of Part 10, the poet compares the birds to "kings and prophets" who "shield their grieving hearts".

All this time, Perse has been thinking of Braque's painting of birds because he brings them into Part 11 thus: "Such are the birds of Georges Braque, whether sea birds or birds of the steppe, coastal birds or birds of mid-ocean." These birds exist "Over the spread of a day longer than the one born of our darkness". *Birds* is a very mysterious poem; Perse has watched birds and he has looked at Braque's pictures of them; so, from art and life, a great vision has grown. One art helps another, one medium links with another; but Braque's birds are not simply described to us, they are transformed by the close scrutiny of Perse's view of them. He makes his own use of them; he gathers them into his poem. So, he speaks of the "eye of a Braque"; it could be another painter who has shown him this vision of birds, combined with his own knowledge of them but Braque's painting made him exult particularly. At the end of Part 11, Braque is paid tribute to; the poet shows his gratitude in these words: "Braque you are sowing the space of the West with holy species."

Perse sees the hand of a divinity in the shaping of a work of art. He continues, in Part 12, to say more of this French painter. At first he declares:

These are the birds of Georges Braque: closer to the genus than to the species, closer to the order than to the genus: quick to rejoin in one stroke the mother stock and the avatar, never hybrid and yet millennial.

And the poet goes on to say that these birds are not "cranes of the Camargue or gulls of the coasts of Normandy or Cornwall", or any other specific birds. "They are all birds of one same race and one same vocation, belonging to a new caste and an ancient lineage." Unity is essential to a vision, and here we have it, but we must be given the particularities first. Perse now tells us that his birds have nothing to do with abstraction, myth or symbol; "they are an immediate creation". They are, in short, real birds transfigured by the poetic imagination. They have nothing to do with "Noah's dove", "the vulture of Prometheus", or any birds mentioned in *The Koran*.

Yet, perhaps a little paradoxically, Perse insists that they are "Birds . . . of a true bird race", "Braque's birds, no other's . . ." He says they have nothing to do with birds associated with Pindar or Poe, Baudelaire, or "the tortured bird of Coleridge". And, though they are Braque's birds, they are "Inallusive and pure, free of all memory", followers "of their own destiny", as well as actual birds. Here, Perse is also affirming the autonomy of every work of art. Just as he has seen something visionary in Braque's birds, so he changes those birds *in* his vision. What we share comes from Perse, not from Braque. That is another kind of autonomy.

And so Part 13, the last Part, celebrates all birds: "Birds, lances lifted at all the frontiers of man!" A little later, Perse's vision reaches its apotheosis in this poem:

> With all things that wander over the world and exist in the stream of time, they go where all the birds of the world go, to their fate of created beings . . . Ignorant of their shadow, knowing of death only that immortal part which is consumed in the distant clamour of great waters, they pass and leave us and we are no longer the same . . .

So the birds have an immortality in our minds and imaginations. But there is a great hope in the last line of this very wonderful poem : "And from that dawn of freshness, as from a very pure aspersion, they have preserved for us something of the dream of creation."

Creation is an event, something concrete which Perse observes around him in all its multifarious detail, but the birds have brought him to a point of ecstasy where a "dream" is a vision. And this dynamic vision has been passed on to us; we have partaken of it.

V

DAVID JONES

A Vision of War

When you look at David Jones's pictures or when you read
what he has written about art and literature, you realize at
once that he is presenting you not with fantasy, not with a
form of escapism, but with history transformed by a poet. Both
Jones's painting and his writing are steeped in history; if a
suggestion of fantasy ever enters those delicate water colours, it
is not there for its own sake but simply because it is part of
man's mind, part of his history; and there is always some element
of myth in history recaptured, not because a poet and painter
like this wants to avoid the facts but precisely because he wants
to enter men's minds, those of men in the past, and go much
deeper than merely into their actions.

This David Jones does. In his long poem *In Parenthesis* he
starts from his own horrific experiences in the trenches in the
1914–18 World War. The book is distilled from a vision and
view of a particular time in this man's life; like all poets or
writers of poetic prose, Jones moves from the particular to the
general. His is not a scientific way of looking at the world, but
it is just as true in its findings, often much more true, because
it deals with matters which even the most delicate scientific
instruments and enquiries cannot reach or touch—the imagination of man, the battle-ground of the human mind, always
changing, never to be photographed, X-rayed, pinned down or
fed into a computer. Important art, and especially visionary
art, is always concerned with the individual, his place in time, his
sense of wonder at his very existence. Visionaries pass on to us

their enlarged sense of the marvellous and mysterious, and so awaken, deepen and heighten our own. The process is always a two-way one.

In Parenthesis was not published until 1937, and in later editions was given a short introduction by T. S. Eliot, who considered it to be a work of genius; in his *Introduction* he makes a singularly enlightening remark:

> . . . to study even the best commentary on a work of literary art is likely to be a waste of time unless we have first read and been excited by the text . . . even without understanding it. For that thrill of excitement . . . is itself the beginning of understanding.

This study of David Jones's *In Parenthesis* is not intended to be merely an exegesis; it is meant to pass over to you the sense of joy—and occasionally of fear, a fear which is usually more like awe than terror—which this writer's work provides, and to lead you into a strange, wonderful but also terrible world.

In Parenthesis is an epic poem, carefully wrought and using every kind of poetic device, though rhyme is rare. It owes some debts to Eliot, Joyce, Pound and Hopkins, though these influences are thoroughly assimilated; this piece of writing is original and it is inimitable. It is inimitable, just as Jones's more difficult poem, *The Anathemata*, is, because the personal element, though completely generalized, neither ends nor begins a tradition. David Jones has his own sources, but when he uses, for example, Malory's *Morte d'Arthur*, or words from the Mass, they are part of his own personality, his nationality, his whole experience of life and, most important of all, of his vision.

Although we know that *In Parenthesis* is based on personal experience, David Jones assures us in his *Preface* that "none of the characters . . . are real persons". That is his way of telling us that the generalizing process has gone on consciously in the mind of the writer while he was making this book. The individual soldier is never forgotten, but his predicament is seen as every man's predicament.

Part 1, the shortest of the seven parts into which the work is divided, depicts, in telling detail, the embarkation of Jones's battalion in December 1915, after a long march when the soldiers were laden with all their baggage, and their arrival in France. This Part, which is called "The Many Men So Beautiful" (a quotation from Coleridge's *Ancient Mariner*) ends on a note of simple sadness, as the men emerge from the cattle-trucks in which they have travelled in France, "You feel exposed and apprehensive in this new world". There is fear here and later this fear will have to be exorcized .

In Part 2 they reach

> . . . a place of scattered farms and the tranquillity
> of fields, in a rest area many miles this side of the
> trench system; a place unmolested and untouched so far,
> by the actual shock of men fighting (p. 13).

We are given a strong impression of the contrast between the impersonality of the drilling of the men and their off-duty comradeship, their need for one another:

> They rested cosily at night in thick straw. They crowded together
> in the evening—hours full of confused talking; the tiny room
> heavy with the haze of smoking, and humane with the
>   paraphernalia
> of any place of common gathering, warm within small walls
>   (pp. 13–14).

We are here shown the short, peaceful passage that existed for these men in a war that was to become more and more like carnage.

Jones tells us in his *Preface* that "It was a place of enchantment" (p. x). This enchantment comes partly from the soldiers themselves, the mixture of Welshmen and Cockneys, with their different forms of wit and humour, their names and nicknames and individual quirks of character, but also from their sharing the same fear and courage. What Jones calls the initial "amateurishness" of this war gave its first phase a personal quality which the later stages of it lacked. By then, new kinds of weapons were being used, and also the crowding together of men who hardly ever got to know one another before they were slaughtered made any individual contact almost impossible.

Much of the power of David Jones's writing in *In Parenthesis* lies in the fact that he always tones down, holds in check the experiences which he is transcribing. What is left unsaid thus becomes almost as memorable as what is actually stated; we read not only between the lines but also between the so beautifully chosen words. Nothing of importance is omitted, whether it is the use of the latrines or eating a soldier's rations, but all is transformed; a different world, where such things do not take place, is never forgotten: here are a few examples from Part 2:

> Only some animal's hoof against her wooden stall made a muted knocking, breaking from time to time upon the kindly creature's breathing (p. 16).

> The full day was clear after the early rain . . . It was not that the look of the place was unfamiliar to you. It was at one to all appearances with what you knew already . . . the same astonishing expanse of sky. Truly the unseen wind had little but your nice body for its teeth . . . (pp. 18–19).

> He marvelled at these foreign clouds. There seemed in the whole air above . . . a strong droning, as if a million bees were hiving to the stars (p. 20).

The bringing together of the transient and the lasting is marvellously sustained throughout this book, but the craftsmanship never shows.

Part 3 of *In Parenthesis* describes the moving up of the battalion to its own position in the trenches, and takes its title from a phrase in a poem by Hopkins ("Bugler's First Communion"); it is called "Starlight Order". This section of the poem is terse, tension is mounting but, most strangely, as war becomes more terrible, so David Jones's vision of it becomes more luminous; Part 3 is, in some ways, the most perfect section of the poem, for in it David Jones gives us both the vividness and also what he calls "The ritual of their [the soldiers'] parading [which] was fashioned to austerity, and bore a new directness". Particularity and immediacy are never lost but the sense of the numinous is always present as well, as in this line about the moon:

> Cloud shielded her bright disc-rising yet her veiled influence
> illumined the texture of that place, her glistening on the
> saturated fields; bat-night-gloom intersilvered where she shone
> on the mist drift (p. 27).

We marvel that such a horrific, a terrifying war should have
lodged in one man's mind yet not stayed there as a wound or
a nightmare, but have been turned by his assiduous craft into
a complete, a palpable vision, something full of light which is
handed on to others.

What the war meant to David Jones as a man is only
sifted through his unique poetry and his painting. No important
artist ever reveals his complete suffering, the moments so very
near to despair. And this is true for Christians, such as this
genius, as well as for unbelievers. Darkness is discovered in the
thoughts of men of the finest faith and character, just as a
stoical courage helps a heathen to withstand death, not out of
fear but out of bravery.

Suspense is everywhere apparent in *In Parenthesis*, but it is
not, as with casual adventure stories, a suspense imposed by the
author on his material, but what arises from his characters, his
setting the entire *milieu* out of which his vision emerges. Tension, a subtler thing, is present too :

> Far thuddings faintly heard in the stranger-world : where the
> road leads, where no man goes, where the straight road leads;
> where the road had led old men asleep on wagons beneath the
> green, girls with baskets, linen-palled, children dawdling
> from the Mysteries on a Sunday morning (p. 30).

The fear and expectancy of the soldiers is here contrasted with
the every-day life of the French peasants; the tension is all the
more potent for not being over-stated.

Now the soldiers are waiting for orders. Nature carries on its
usual activity, but it affects the men :

> The rain increased where they miserably waited, there was no
> sound at all but of its tiresome spatter . . .
>   Wind gusts rose to swirl and frisk half-severed, swung
> branches; jammed wood split to twisted screechings. Away some-

where, gun with lifted muzzle, Jaguar-coughs, across the rain
(p. 30).

Then the men are on the move again, and an officer is likened
to a "western-hill shepherd",

> In virid-bright illumining he sees his precious charge, singly
> going, each following each, fleecy coated, and they themselves
> playing the actor to their jackets on sheepwalk's lateral
> restricting, between the lopped colonnade.
>
> Shuts down again the close dark; the stumbling dark of the
> blind, that Breughel knew about—ditch circumscribed; this all
> depriving darkness split now by crazy flashing; . . . his
> little flock, his armed bishopric, going with weary limbs (p. 31).

Here there is much drama, and there is also the painter's eye
seeing war, recording every detail. Soon, the writing becomes
almost surrealist; one impression passes quickly to another,
reason is almost, but never quite abandoned:

> Obstacles on jerks-course made of wooden planking—his night
> phantasm mazes a pre-war, more idiosyncratic skein, weaves with
> stored-up very other tangled threads . . .
> carry you on dream stuff
> up the hill and down again
> show you sights your mother knew,
> show you Jesus Christ lapped in hay . . . (p. 32).

The writer maintains control because he recognizes and makes
vivid the waking nightmare of the soldier, John Ball, the poet's
own self or *alter* ego. Here I should stress that Jones's end-
stopping of lines, except, of course, when he is employing the
prose poem which has different rules, is never arbitrary. No
one but Wilfred Owen, and he in conventional verse form, has
so brilliantly placed before us, so filled our imaginations with
the very feel of this kind of war. The moments of comradeship
and tranquillity emphasize the moments of dread.

It is truly wonderful the way in which battle orders are linked,
locked, by David Jones with climate, stars, all scenery. Words
such as "faery-bright a filagree with gooseberries and picket-
irons . . ." seem perfectly in keeping with army slang like "It's
cushy mate, it's cushy".

The inner thoughts of the men are also depicted.

> So they would go a long while in solid dark, nor moon,
> nor battery, dispelled.
> Feet plodding in each other's unseen tread . . .
>   Half-minds, far away, divergent, own-thought thinking, tucked
>   away
> unknown thoughts; feet following file friends, each his own
> thought-maze alone treading; intricate, twist about, own thoughts,
> all unknown thoughts, to the next so close following on (p. 37).

When a shell bursts Jones writes:

> The night dilapidates over your head and scarlet lightning
> annihilates the nice adjustment of your vision, used now to,
> and cat-eyed for the shades (p. 47).

Here are some other vivid lines, about a quiet interval in the night:

> You can hear the silence of it;
> You can hear the rat of no-man's-land
> . . . . .
> When it's all quiet you can hear them:
> scrut scrut scrut
> when it's as quiet as this is.
> It's so very still.

When comes this

> Your split knuckles fumbling, foul some keen, chill-edged
> jack-spike jutting . . .

after which Jones suddenly uses this simple line

> You could weep like a child . . .

The effect on the reader is almost Shakespearean. One thinks not only of *Henry V* but also of *King Lear*.

Yet, through all this horror one soldier can sing the nursery rhyme "Johnny's so long at the Fair". In this context, the old, well-remembered rhyme takes on an almost epic quality.

Part 3 moves towards its end inexorably and with a mingling of horror and acceptance.

And always, during this preparation for battle, the world which has nothing to do with it is remembered and included. Thus we have lines such as these:

He heard, his ears incredulous, the nostalgic puffing of a
locomotive, far off, across forbidden fields . . .

> And the rain slacks at the wind veer
> > and she half breaks her cloud cover (p. 51).

When you read this book you will note the importance of the
actual arrangement of lines on the printed page.

As *In Parenthesis* proceeds, we become increasingly aware
that David Jones is also a painter. His visual sense is extraordinarily sharp and luminous; this does not mean, though, that
his writings are secondary to his paintings or the other way
about. Rather, he is a genius who is equally eloquent in two
different media; perhaps only Blake, another seer, shares this
unique combination. But David Jones is as careful with a word
as with a colour, perfectly precise with both.

Part 4, entitled "King Pellam's Launde", takes its title from
Malory's *Morte d'Arthur*, to whom Jones owes a good deal,
though all that he has taken from that book is so thoroughly
assimilated that it is usually only noticed when particular names
arise, as with Part 4.

The men are now in the trenches, and so we have this kind
of writing, highly visual, taut but never hysterical; if anything,
the poet is understating, or using a kind of short-hand in lines
like these describing daybreak:

The flux yields up a measurable body; bleached forms emerge and
stand.
. . . grey wealed earth . . .
Her fractured contours dun where soon his ray would show more
clear her dereliction . . .
The filtering irradiance spread, you could begin to know
that thing from this; . . .

Then we are reminded, fitfully only, of *Macbeth*, when these
words come:

To their eyes seeming a wood moving,
> a moving grove advisioned.
> Stand-to.
> Stand-to.
> Stand-to-arms (pp. 59–60).

The poet's vision is, as it were, held down, kept always in human terms by military orders such as these. And the men themselves are described as follows:

> An eastward alignment of troubled, ashen faces; delicate mechanisms of nerve and sinew, grapple afresh, deal for another day;
> . . . . .
> As grievous invalids watch the returning light pale-bright the ruckled counterpane, see their uneased bodies only newly clear; ... (p. 61).

It is amazing that a man who was actually one of these soldiers could have observed so closely and remembered so much. Again, curses and exquisite descriptions are mingled with perfect decorum:

> Cloying drift-damp cupped in every concave place.
> It hurts you in the bloody eyes, it grips chill and harm-
> fully and rasps the sensed membrane of the throat; ...
> With each moment passing—the opaque creeping into every crevice creeping, whiter—thick whitened, through-white, argent wall nebulous ... (p. 61).

The repetition of words, the frequent alliteration and the use of adjectives as nouns increase the sense of urgency and danger which all are feeling.

Later, once more a single, utterly simple line, "They stood miserably" (p. 63), makes an enormous impact. And then the helplessness of the soldiers, their lack of essential things, is written about:

> How do you get hot water in this place of all water—all cold water up to the knees. These poured quickly lest it should cool off, ... one way and another they cleaned their rifles—
> . . . . . .
> Night-begotten fear yet left them frail, nor was the waking day much cheer for them (p. 64).

A little further on a snatch of "Green grow the rushes O" is recalled in "all a green-o", and childhood comes back in the mention of children who "look with serious eyes on brand-new miracles . . ." (p. 65). Meanwhile, John Ball is on duty and

F   159

"looking upward" from the trench "sees in a cunning glass the image of: his morning parapets, his breakfast-fire smoke, the twisted wood beyond".

The whole of *In Parenthesis* is a magnificent feat of memory and imagination. The truth of war is ever-present—but it is illuminated constantly by the steadfast imagination of the poet. The battlefields become a microcosm of the world, and are stated to be such in this sentence:

> To the woods of all the world is this potency—to move
> the bowels of us (p.66).

Here the spiritual, the visionary are again linked, and linked acceptably, with the physical. It is this sort of linking that gives such unity to the book.

In Parenthesis is written on many levels. The more we explore it, the more strata we discover, the concealed crystals among the dark events. The first and most obvious level is the life and fighting of the men in the dug-outs; the second is the memories of John Ball, the protagonist; the third, the associations of all that happens in history and legend; the fourth, the wide view of nature from the formations of stars in the night sky to the trodden grass.

The writing is often syntactically difficult, elliptical, unpunctuated; repetition is constantly used as a deliberate device. Allusions to literature of a number of countries and centuries give the effect of a rich, entrancing tapestry. David Jones's ear is— and this must be emphasized—as flawless as his eye. He also provides us with notes, elucidating many of the allusions and sources, but as Eliot insisted, we should not read them until after we have let his text work upon us, and perhaps not necessarily even then.

Though this artist has literary allegiances (what important writer has not?), they are never overt. He is, as he must be, ruthless in what he ransacks from Malory, from Icelandic sagas, from Roman history, from Hopkins, Eliot, Joyce and Pound. But his own voice is always unmistakable; when he experiments, the trials and errors of experimentation are his own. In what he has published we see only the assimilation of the influences, only the successful experiments; we are never shown into the study or the studio.

Some of the alliteration throughout *In Parenthesis* is reminiscent of Anglo-Saxon verse, but the influence is only remotely felt. An example of this is: "Where a white shining waned between its hanging rents, . . ." (p. 38). Again, a little of Hopkins can be sensed in: "Now when a solitary star-shell rose, a day-brightness illumined them" (p. 42). But this star is not one of Hopkins's "airy abeles" or "firefolk" in the night sky, but a flashing, killing shell.

The endurance of the men on the battle-fields of France in 1914–18 is reflected in the writing; the pressure, the feeling of men under pressure, is never allowed to flag, yet there is also a story, a very carefully woven design.

Part 4 proceeds with telescoped writing, followed by more prosaic, but never prosy, details of the soldiers' daily, simple doings:

> Two men in the traverse mouth-organed;
> four men took up that song . . .
> Which nearer,
> which so rarely insular,
> unmade his harmonies,
> honouring
> this rare and indivisible
> New Light
> for us,
> over the still morning honouring.
> . . . . .
> The others sat solitary; each one about his own thoughts, except
> for the two music makers, . . . till these too became silent and
> wrapped their little instruments in Paisley handkerchiefs
> against the damp (pp. 67–68).

In between these lines and words, we feel the men's stoicism and also the tension mounting within them. One senses that there is no hatred for their enemies or for the politicians and generals who have brought them to this place at this particular time.

As this section of the book proceeds, allusions multiply. A Welshman says:

My fathers were with the Black Prince of Wales
at the passion of
the blind Bohemian king.
They served in these fields . . . (p. 79).

We enter now into a world of a "maimed king" and a "blessèd
head" which held "the striplings from the narrow sea". Then
a suggestion of Christ enters, in a mention of

the Tree
whose Five Sufficient Blossoms
yield for us (p. 83). [These are His wounds on the cross.]

And this memory and moment of history then fall into the
charmed rhymes of childhood:

I saw cock-robin gain
his rosy breast (p. 83).

(a legend tells how this happened when the robin tried to peck
out the nails holding Christ to the cross).

No one but a very great artist could compare, by subtle impli-
cation, two such disparate things. But the world of David Jones
is a complete world; what at first glance may seem haphazard
is deliberate. Nothing is ever arbitrary. The lines continue thus

I heard Him cry:
"Apples ben ripe in my gardayne"
I saw Him die (p. 83).

In the old nursery rhyme in which the red-breasted robin is
killed, the fly says "I saw him die". The amazing thing is that
these many levels and subtle meanings and comparisons never
seem to us blasphemous. The reason for this is, of course, that
the whole universe is in the care of God, and children's games
and even swear-words have a place there just as much though
perhaps in a different way as the Crucifixion or the unspoilt
night sky. And the Roman soldiers who pierced Christ's side and
gambled for His seamless garment are the same kind of men as
David Jones's soldiers; the only important difference is that the
1914 War soldiers were not killing a God-made-Man. But,
because "The Kingdom of Heaven is within us", all killing is
evil, however ignorantly it is performed. No one is completely

innocent on any battlefield or at any killing. This is what David Jones is telling us, drawing mystery and history together.

Part 4 goes on with its carefully accumulated and timed events. The ordinary soldiers' ironic reactions are put to us like this:

> You live by faith alright in these parts.
> You aren't supported as you spend yourself in this blind
> doubling on your bleedin' tracks by the bright reason for it,
> they know about back there.
> You know no more than do those hands who squirt cement till
> siren screams . . . (p. 87).

It is the poet who knows "the bright reason", but he is living a kind of dual existence; one part of him is registering events, the other enduring them: thus "You are moved like beasts are moved from upper field to pound . . ." (p. 87). David Jones knows that the coming battle is going to be like a slaughtering, an *abattoir*. Most fortunately for us, he was not among the thousands killed; he is the spokesman of these men.

When the soldiers are left to their own devices, "each one of them disposed himself in some part of their few yards of trench" and some talk of the "morning's affairs", some sleep, some "search for some personally possessed thing", some "re-read yet again the last arrived letter". One's compassion is deeply roused by all these attempts to find a little simple, homely comfort in this lonely place of terror. Private Ball finds a much-worn anthology in his pack but even such ancient, tender lines as

> Takis, on the motheris breast sowkand,
> The babe full of benignitie . . . (p. 95).

cannot bring him any ease, so he eats some chocolate instead, a tiny fact which increases our awareness of his character and feelings. All the soldiers are on the alert, and one is reminded more and more of the night before Agincourt, only here there is no king to rally his troops and take their responsibilities upon himself. Darkness falls; "The first star tremored . . ." (p. 98) and then Part 4 ends with these words:

> Solitary star-shells toss as the dark deepens.
> Mr. Prys-Picton's patrol came in, well before midnight (p. 99).

What seems like an anticlimax is really a tremendous feeling of tension which leads the reader into Part 5, whose title "Squat Garlands for White Knights" combines echoes from Hopkins and Lewis Carroll. This part tells how the men move up to the front line, and bears the epigraph "He has brought us to a bright fire and to a white fresh floor-hide". (This, like the epigraphs of all the parts, is drawn from an early Welsh epical poem.) Part 5 begins simply, "Roll on Duration". (The soldiers had signed on for the duration of the war.)

It is impossible to exaggerate how strongly the delicately placed contrast between normal activities and preparations for battle strengthens the power of this entire book; the cumulative effect is almost overwhelming. We are told of fright and food, a luminous star, drill and digging, and all is written of with an amazing accuracy and decorum. Especially visionary moments come in Part 5, as when the following is said of Sergeant Ryan:

> You suppose the texture of his soul to inform the dark and
> exact contour his buff coating describes against the convulsed
> cones of light . . . —he who is an amiable cuckold— . . . Jump on
> these
> fag-ends (p. 109).

The sublime and the absurd are at one; man is a creature of infinite possibilities, yet also a sinner and a clown. And no judgment is ever passed anywhere in this book.

The soldiers are still able to find enjoyment; as Eliot wrote in a different context, they

> Rejoice
> Having to construct something on which to rejoice.

But they quarrel too because they are becoming more tense yet trying desperately not to show it. But there is, fortunately, much to occupy them, "wiring fatigue", "kit inspection", "short arm parade" and so on. But now, real danger is coming closer—"long-distance shells crawled from far over like interminable rolling stock", though Private Ball can still receive " a satisfactory parcel from his aunt in Norwood". And, among all this military activity, a few remember God, and the poet speaks of "the resurrection of the flesh" which will be at the end of the world.

The consistent interweaving of orders, small pastimes, descriptions of the weather begins now to become more and more intense.

> It roused your apprehension that the third halt should so
> exceed the allowed five minutes . . . and with Brigade cyclists
> about at this hour, you gathered they were up to their antics
> (p. 123).

But still the lovely details, which are usually part of a quite different world or of the past, enter. A plane is noticed as,

> Barely clear the poplar top
> at cant and obliquely
> as Baroque attending angels surprise you with their airworthiness
> (p. 124).

And then a little later, after mention of a long list of weapons, comes this beautiful line: "One thousand a hundred and one unicorn horns for a pride of lions . . ." (p. 125). This is truly magical.

We are next reminded of

> the essential foot-mob, the platoon wallahs, the small men
> who permanently are with their sections, who have no
> qualifications, who look surprisedly out from a confusion
> of gear, who endure all things . . . (p. 126).

Those last lines are stark in their simplicity and they tell us with complete conviction that these men are the real heroes of *In Parenthesis*. Then suddenly the pace of the narrative becomes faster still:

> The buzzer, all the time, tapt out its urgencies . . . the new
> operator . . . got fussed because the line wasn't clear (p. 127).

A runner is urgently needed:

Runner Runner Run-nerr!

. . . . .

Runner Runner!—rapt like a proper marm.

Very short lines indicate emergency:

Runner.
Yes sir.
Tell 'em not later than 4.55.
Yes sir.
Tell them to note the correction.
Yes sir.
And find first the Reg'mental.
Yes sir.
I want him now.
Yes sir.
I want him now—I want him here now—he ought to be here now.
Yes sir (p. 129).

Yet the poet still has time to give us a landscape and remind us of the unchanging natural things:

They moved within the hour, in battle-order, . . . where the road cut a face of downland chalk.
And grass-tufts, too, were like they grow on seaward hills— with small wiry flowers against the white, and with the return of summer's proper way, after the two days storm, blue-winged butterflies, dance between, flowery bank and your burnished fore-sight guard, star gayly Adams's dun gear (p. 131).

This Part of *In Parenthesis* ends on a note of disquiet with one simple sentence which is entirely lacking in melodrama:

Now in this hollow between the hills was their place of rendezvous (p. 131).

Part 6 of *In Parenthesis*, called "Pavilions & Captains of Hundreds", deals with the last preparations for battle. Its epigraph contains the words "death's sure meeting place, the goal of their marching," and the Part opens with a quotation from Malory: "And bade him be ready and stuff and garnish him . . . and laid a mighty siege about . . . and shot great guns . . ." We read:

the terrain of bivouac was dark wrapt; the moon was in her most diminished quarter (p. 135).

The men cannot sleep. A "battery opened out with its full complement . . . eight bright tongues licked, swift as adder-fangs darted" (p. 135).

When day comes there is much activity in the valley, and

> ... it was a cert they were for it to do battle ...
> to-morn in the plain field.
> Corporal Shallow said he didn't like the sound of things (p. 138).

The increasing discarding of punctuation helps to bring the state of emergency vividly before us:

> ... engines positioned for the assault and the paraphernalia of
> the gunners and all that belongs to the preparation toward a
> general action and corrugated tin shelters and hastily contrived
> arbours and a place of tabernacles and of no long continuing nor
> abidingness, yet not by no means haphazard nor prejudicial to
> good-order (p. 144).

But though the writer is recording mass carnage he cares for each man with great compassion; at this stage, for example, a man called Joe Donkin, who never spoke to anyone,

> ... said outright and before them all that this was what he had
> 'listed for and how he would most certainly avenge his five
> brethren from the same womb as himself on these miscreant
> bastard square-heads and sons of bitches ... (p. 145).

Yet even now, while presenting us with dread and chaos, David Jones has time to show us the continuous activity of Nature. Thus he writes:

> The other slope was still sun-lighted, but it was getting
> almost cool on this east-facing hill, and the creeping down and so
> across so gradually, gathered to itself, minute by minute, the
> lesser cast-shadows, the little glints and smallnesses, garnered
> all these accidents of light within a large lengthened calm
> (pp. 145–6).

The vision is entire, slang and decorous language go hand-in-hand.

The tension is becoming almost intolerable, and this Jones conveys, but he also conveys something more profound and more universal. His great art, his painterly perceptions, his love of words enable him to make out of a terrible and futile war a whole vision of the world; and it is usually by his juxtaposition of mood and place as well as by his detail that he gives us his world picture.

At the end of this penultimate Part of *In Parenthesis*, comes this: "They lay with little sleep one more night in bivouac" and were finally moved "into their own assembly positions" (pp. 149–150).

Part 7 is called "The Five Unmistakable Marks", which is another reference to Christ's five wounds on the Cross. Although we have now reached the most acute stage of this account of war, the epigraph has a hopeful note: "It is our duty to sing: a meeting place has been found." And now we have this highly-charged, more than merely descriptive passage:

> The memory lets escape what is over and above—
> as spilled bitterness, unmeasured, poured-out,
> and again drenched down—demoniac-pouring:
> who grins who pours to fill flood and super-flow insensately,
> pint-pot—from milliard-quart measure (p. 153).

The men move forward at dawn, and soon there are casualties:

> No one to care there for Aneirin Lewis spilled there . . .
> . . . . .
> And the little Jew lies next him
> cries out for Deborah his bride
> and offers for stretcher-bearers
>   gifts for their pains
> and walnut suites in his delirium
>   from Grays Inn Road (p. 155).

And now comes this momentous line: "But already they look at their watches and it is zero minus seven minutes" (p. 155). Jones deliberately draws out these minutes by such words as: ". . . and seventy times seven times to the minute this drumming of the diaphragm" (p. 156), and also with this beautiful re-creation of the scene:

> The returning sun climbed over the hill, to lessen the shadows
> of small and great things; and registered the minutes to zero
> hour. Their saucer hats made dial for his passage: . . .
> cut elliptical with light
> as cupola on Byzantine wall . . . (pp. 156–157).

Then there are only "two minutes to go". And the compassionate vision of Jones sees each dead or wounded man as an individual,

such as Wastebottom, who "married a wife on his Draft-leave",
and Talacryn, who "leaps up & says he's dead", and very soon
is indeed lying "quite still" (p. 158).

And now, "Last minute drums its taut millenium out" (p.
159), and the attack is launched. The fighting which goes on
throughout the day and night is described precisely as Ball and
his companions endure it. These pages should be read with great
care. I can only try to indicate their power by giving you a few
quotations from them.

Thus, "sweet sister death has gone debauched today and
stalks on this high ground with strumpet confidence", and "leers
from you to me with all her parts discovered" (p. 162).

David Jones has such an intuitive sense of when to turn from
one mood or comment or event to another, that he can intersperse
descriptions of horror with the most gracious writing such as
the following: (The reference is to Cain and Abel)

> Each one bearing in his body the whole apprehension of that
> innocent, on the day he saw his brother's votive smoke
> diffuse and hang to soot the fields of holocaust; neither
> approved nor ratified nor made acceptable but lighted to
> everlasting partition (p. 162).

Not abruptly but with speed and an important and decorous
immediacy, legendary figures and ancient battles are recalled:
Tristram and Lamorak de Galis, "strait Thermopylae", and

> Jonathan my lovely one
> on Gelboe mountain
> and the young man Absalom (p. 163).

Or spoiled natural beauty is sharply noted in these lines: (the
scene is a thicket of "scared saplings" [sic])

> There between the thinning uprights
> at the margin
> straggle tangled oak and flayed sheeny beech-bole, and fragile
> birch whose silver queenery is draggled and ungraced
> and June shoots lopt
> and fresh stalks bled
> runs the Jerry trench.

And cork-screw stapled trip-wire
to snare among the briars
and iron warp with bramble weft
with meadow-sweet and lady-smock
for a fair camouflage (p. 165).

What is becoming more and more noticeable as we reach the end of *In Parenthesis* is the acceptance of the soldiers and their lack of bitterness and enmity. They are fighting, yes, but fighting because they are patriotic and also, which is more important, because this is a job they have to do. War is a kind of craft to them. Desperation goes strangely hand in hand with innocence.

The men allude to death in an almost offhand manner; we are told that Bobby Saunders was seen to "get it early on" (p. 173). But when dignity is needed, David Jones provides it in perfect language and with a tender particularity, as when he writes,

but O Dear God and suffering Jesus
why dont they bring water from a well
rooty and bully for a man on live
and mollifying oil poured in
and hands to bind with gentleness (p. 173).

Suddenly a question is asked: "But why is Father Larkin talking to the dead?" Father Larkin is of course administering the last sacrament of all, Extreme Unction. Amid all this horror and chaos, God's Grace is being given to dying men, and that Grace illuminates the whole of this part of the book. And we also have this invocation to Our Lady:

Maiden of the digged places
            let our cry come unto thee.
Mam, moder, mother of me
Mother of Christ under the tree ... (p. 176).

The texture is rich with allusion, repetition, alliteration, Latin and Anglo-Saxon derivations, and they are all used with enormous care, they all help, with a genius's inevitability of statement, to cast light on the darkest places.

Turmoil is everywhere except in the actual writing, for David Jones has found a unique way to express turmoil without tumbling into it himself.

And so we come to the last pages. The enemy is "through on the flank" (p. 180); the poet, or Private Ball, is among the many wounded; when he tries to crawl away his rifle hampers him, "You're clumsy in your feebleness . . .", and he thinks "Let it lie for the dews to rust it, or ought you to decently cover the working parts" (p. 186), and concludes (only here is the faintest trace of bitterness in the whole of *In Parenthesis*),

> But leave it—under the oak.
> leave it for a Cook's tourist to the Devastated Areas and crawl
> as far as you can and wait for the bearers (p. 186).

Ball and the others are having half-delirious thoughts of nurses and of home,

> . . . and on the south lawns,
> men walk in red white and blue
> under the cedars
> and by every green tree
> and beside comfortable waters (p. 186).

There is a deliberately psalm-like quality about these lines. But then exasperation is expressed,

> but why dont the bastards come—
> Bearers!—stret-cher bear-errs!
> . . . . .
> But how many men do you suppose could bear away a third
> of us:
> drag just a little further—he yet may counter-attack (p. 187).

This is real heroism, not heroics, and David Jones tells us that the dead must lie together, German and Briton side by side,

> Lie still under the oak
> next to the Jerry
> and Sergeant Jerry Coke (p. 187).

The play on Jerry as an English name but also the soldiers' name for a German soldier carries great weight here.

The only moral, if it can be said to be such, which the writer draws comes in the last few lines; they are more than a moral, they are words spoken out of great anguish and profound understanding. They are taken from the *Song of Roland*:

The geste says this and the man who was on the field . . .
and who wrote the book . . . the man who does not know this
has not understood anything (p. 187).

There is a coda to the book which enshrines the poet's entire
vision. The words are printed large in the exquisite lettering for
which this artist is famous, and all are quotations from the Bible.
The last of all, from the *Song of Songs*, rightly and perfectly
sums up the whole purpose of *In Parenthesis*; it is this:

THIS IS MY BELOVED AND
THIS IS MY FRIEND (p. 226).

War may have been futile but love has strangely, magically
emerged from it. So this great work of art ends on a note of
comradeship and charity.

VI

ANTOINE DE ST-EXUPÉRY

A Vision of Space

When we think of flight, our first thought tends to be of speed. We equate it in our minds, also, with motor-racing, skiing—in short, sport in its most spectacular forms. But flight is different, at least for a few chosen men, to whom it can become something more even than a mystique; I mean a way towards a vision. For, in the air, man is quite unconnected with the ground; he is among clouds, stars, the caprice of winds and all weathers. He is releasing himself, losing himself, often forgetting danger, moving beyond sheer exhilaration or the wish to prove something or break a record. He is trying to become one with the universe, but without strain and with his only support an aeroplane which is frail before fierce weathers.

St-Exupéry was a man for whom flying meant just this and as we examine *Wind, Sand and Stars* and *Flight to Arras* we shall see the great vision into which he soared and which made him feel so humble. Flight was for him a kind of prayer, an offering, a vocation. It is true that, in *Flight to Arras*, St-Exupéry is writing of the terrible hazards of flying during the War in 1940, but, even so, his exaltation became even greater then. Patriotism is one more factor in his vision. In a few matters, he may be compared with Richard Hillary who, dreadfully burned during the Battle of Britain, wrote, quite without self-pity, of his experiences. From his wounds, he learnt much, but, though full of courage and with a scarred body he returned to the air, to be killed, he was not a visionary. The best account of him is to be found in Arthur Koestler's *The Yogi and the Commissar* where the bravery, which Hillary refuses to admit, is told to us completely. But, primarily, flying was a way of self-realization for Hillary (later, it became almost completely selfless), while for St-Exupéry it was always something greater. In *Wind, Sand and Stars* he says,

> . . . we have all known flights when for a sudden each for himself, it has seemed to us that we have crossed the border of reality . . . I remember, for my part, another of those hours in which a pilot finds suddenly that he has slipped beyond the confines of this world.

Flying in wartime, flying also in peacetime has an olden sense of both the duel and the elemental about it. For St-Exupéry it became more and more of the latter. As we shall see, he took great interest in other flyers and in the landscape above which all of them flew, but for him, the great, lonely, empty skies gave him a sense of ecstasy; it was not power he wanted but a sense of union with all that surrounds this relatively tiny globe. But his writing is never vague; every detail of his plane and his surroundings is fresh and detailed. Thus he writes in *Wind, Sand and Stars*, which describes the carrying of African mail over the Sahara, of braving the sky above the Andes and of flying over Spain during the Spanish Civil War, as well as much else; he reveals to us the accepted terror of flight in these words which appear early on in the book: "And suddenly that tranquil cloud-world, that world so harmless and simple that one sees below on rising out of the clouds, took on in my eyes a new quality. That peaceful world became a pitfall." This is courage. The wonder of St-Exupéry's experience and vision resides largely in the way he can transmit the essence of his vision while always remembering the details—of the characters of the other flyers, of the intricacy of their machines, of the different countries and climates. Always there is humanity, compassion, expert knowledge, and from this a vision of great simplicity and beauty emerges. The details fuse with a total world-picture.

More than with the other visionaries in this book, we need to know a little of St-Exupéry's life and work; they are really one and the same thing. He was born in 1900 in Lyons. Before he did his military service in the Air Force, he studied at a naval school. His first flying job was with a private company. A little later he was charged with planning the civil air services of Patagonia. He became a test pilot and undertook dangerous reconnaissance flying in 1940. After fighting during the fall of France he went to America and then joined the Allies in North Africa in 1942. St-Exupéry led a remarkably active and daring life; he was dedicated to flying and there seems something strangely fitting about the fact that his body was never traced.

His two books, *Wind, Sand and Stars* and *Flight to Arras* reveal his courage, vigour and also the mystical quality of his character. Writing of his flights in Africa and Spain, St-Exupéry has this to say:

And when the hour is at hand the pilot may glue his forehead to the window with perfect assurance. Out of oblivion the gold has been smelted: there it gleams in the lights of the airport.
And yet we have all known flights when of a sudden, each for himself, it has seemed to us that we have crossed the border of the world of reality . . .

It is doubtful whether many other air crews shared this feeling. Yet St-Exupéry thinks that because all that is connected with flying (even the tedious waiting at airports) has this mysterious feeling for him, then the other men must experience the same thing. But this is his humility; he never for a moment thinks that he is unique, that flying and all it entails does not impart this sense of wonder to all who have jobs in connection with flying. With true visionaries, we always find that they are surprised, if they ever discover it, that they are unique; they regard themselves exactly as if they were like all men. And this, of course, makes them at ease with all who work with them.

Always St-Exupéry is intensely interested in the men he works with, and with peasants and the simplest joys of life. So, a little later in *Wind, Sand and Stars*, he shows delight in being given a bowl of coffee and a roll and says of them: "Even as an old peasant woman recognizes her God in a painted image, in a childish medal, in a chaplet, so life would speak to us in its humblest language in order that we understand." Here, sensuous pleasures and human needs are summed up for the writer in such things. Yet he is never rhetorical. He sees what is precious in the simplest things and so can write:

> All the treasures of the world were summed up in a grain of dust now blown far out of our path by the very destiny itself of dust and of the orbs of night.
> And Néri still prayed to the stars.

We become so carried away by this vision that we fail to see immediately what grandeur is expressed in these simple words. We move with the writer, he carries us along on all his journeys and, as he is a seer, we become aware of a wonder in the most commonplace things because he has seen it first.

Néri, St-Exupéry's co-pilot, is often with him in these flights to Casablanca, Dakar or Toulouse. He becomes transformed by the writer into one who shares his vision; so, in a sense, he is us. The difference is, of course, that he did not know what was going on in the exalted moments of flying which St-Exupéry wrote down for us.

Here are some more passages of the same period, the early flying trips of this remarkable man. It is amazing that he could pay the most careful attention to the mechanics of flying and yet see and record later such things as the following:

> The face of the sea is as variable as that of the earth . . . The surface of the sea appears to be covered with great white motionless palm-trees . . . The hours during which a man flies over this mirror are hours in which there is no assurance of the possession of anything in the world . . .

St-Exupéry exults in flying yet he is fully aware of its dangers. He continues, "Even when the flight is an easy one . . . the pilot navigating at some point on the line is not gazing upon a scene". Yet the words which this seer then uses really contradict what he is saying. Here they are: ". . . these clouds golden in the afterglow are not objects of the pilot's admiration but of his cogitation." We are then told that all that the pilot is observing so carefully is merely a guide to keep his flight safer. But, I repeat, the words in which they are expressed show us that cogitation and vision are linked. This becomes clearer towards the end of this section of the book, which is entitled *The Craft* when St-Exupéry declares, "The machine which at first blush seems a means of isolating man from the great problems of nature, actually plunges him more deeply into them". It is precisely this "plunging", this loss of self which is such an important part of St-Exupéry's whole world view.

The second part of *Wind, Sand and Stars* is overtly concerned with the men with whom the writer works and flies in South America. Each man is lovingly delineated and deeply understood. St-Exupéry has this to say about what death in the air means to a pilot. About a particular pilot he writes: "Mermoz had done his job and slipped away to rest, like a gleaner who, having carefully bound his sheaf, lies down in the field to sleep."

On this particular death, so beautifully expressed and profoundly felt, this visionary writer goes on to say this about death and flying in general for all men who are pilots:

> When a pilot dies in the harness his death seems something that inheres in the craft itself . . . Assuredly he has vanished, has undergone his ultimate mutation . . . They [pilots] land alone at scattered and remote airports, isolated from each other rather in the manner of sentinels between whom no words can be spoken.

St-Exupéry knows this isolation himself in a special way and so he becomes the spokesman for all other such courageous men. But he is a rare, most unusual man and can go on to write, "Thus is the earth at once a desert and a paradise, rich in secret hidden gardens . . ." He never forgets his fellow men—they are "comrades—silent, forgotten but deeply faithful". But St-Exupéry does not forget them and there is in his remembrance of them a very deep charity. These other men are part of his vision, and he mourns that "One by one, our comrades slip away, deprive us of their shade". He greatly values human relationships and says that the memory of them has left "an enduring savour" with him. Then, passing to other matters, he tells us that none of the wonders of life can be bought: "There is no buying the night flight with its hundred thousand stars, its serenity, its few hours of sovereignty . . ." These are gifts, appreciated fully and only by the rare man who is in love with a world where "a concert of little things" can "sustain us and constitute our compensation". So the wonders of flight must be paid for in suffering, fear, endurance.

In speaking of the men who play a great part in his total vision, St-Exupéry is sure that "human relations must be created" and that the "apprenticeship" for this is partly "games and risk". But he also speaks of "the pathetic chant of the human voice". This is a wonderful thing, but there are other wonders too. In speaking of another old friend, St-Exupéry tries to express what Eliot has called "the inexpressible". He speaks thus, as he tries to hand over to us what the friendship of this man meant to him: "There exists a quality which is nameless. It may be gravity, but the word does not satisfy me, for the quality I have in mind can be accompanied by the most cheerful gaiety. It is the quality of the carpenter face to face with his block of wood."

Other visionaries in this book have thought of the craftsman when they have tried to express what they have seen. It is a good metaphor for it shows us that this heightened sense of life can only be accompanied by ardour and by simplicity. At the end of the section in *Wind, Sand and Stars* entitled *The Men*, St-Exupéry recalls these words he once heard spoken by a gardener: "A man is free when he is using a spade." The writer comments on this, speaking of this particular man, "He was bound by ties of love to all cultivable land and to all the trees of the earth. There was a generous man, a prodigal man, a nobleman!"

The quality of St-Exupéry's sensibility is delicate yet strong; his values are firmly established. His vision encompasses both the great spaces of the sky and also the way an aeroplane works. We now come to the section which deals with the latter; it is called *The Tool*. That is what St-Exupéry thought a plane was: "What a spade is to a gardener, or a hammer to a carpenter, so an aeroplane is to a pilot. It is a means, not an end." To most pilots it merely serves the purpose of carrying things in peacetime and of confronting the foe, shooting down or bombing the enemy in wartime. To St-Exupéry, at all times it is a means to a vision, though he does not choose it for this with the full knowledge of what he may attain. Even so, his attitude towards his plane always, before and during the war, has a reverence about it; the plane has dignity and must be cared for.

St-Exupéry's "Tool", his aeroplane, has been designed and made with the utmost care. He is fully aware of all that went into its making. It has needed "computations and calculations . . . working draughts" to "culminate in the production of a thing whose soul and guiding principle is the ultimate principle of simplicity". There must, also, "be the experimentation of several generations of craftsmen". Here, again, we have this admiration for the craftsman, someone who is much more than an engineer for St-Exupéry because he cares so much about what he is making. And when some smooth, perfect part of a plane has been made, "effortless delight" is given, and this most unusual pilot feels that the made thing had been "simply discovered", not just "invented", had in fact, "in the beginning been hidden by nature and in the end been found by the engineer".

The writer then compares the making of an aeroplane to the ancient myth in which the sculptor found "the image asleep in the block of marble" and then "carefully disengaged it". He adds that "The sculptor must himself feel that he is not so much inventing or shaping the curve of breast or shoulder as delivering the image from its prison." It is a little vision of his own that St-Exupéry should feel that, "In this spirit", all engineers, physicists and draughtsmen "tackle their work".

The writer attacks those who think that we have spoilt Nature by designing machines; he is very firm about this and declares that "the machine does not isolate man from the great problems of nature but plunges him more deeply into them". St-Exupéry knows that man was made to make, so, to make a machine well, with loving care, is of great importance; for him, "the machine is certainly as irresistible in its advance as those virgin forests that encroach upon equatorial domains". People who think otherwise are for this writer "pseudo-dreamers".

Gifted with another very different vision, St-Exupéry shows a realism about all this, a realism which we find in all true seers. And he also acknowledges that this "tool" helps his release into space. "It begins by annihilating time and space", he tells us. And, later in this section, still speaking of the manufacture of aeroplanes, he writes, "We take no heed to ask ourselves why we race: the race itself is more important than the object." He is speaking of air races but he says that "this holds true of other things than flying". It applies to colonists and to those who make ships. Had he lived, St-Exupéry would have rejoiced in our reaching the moon. At the end of this section, he speaks with great feeling when he says of the pilot: "He closes his hands over the controls, and little by little in his bare palms he receives the gift of this power . . ." And he ends "The Tool" with these exquisite, precise words: ". . . when his power is ripe, then, in a gesture gentler than the culling of a flower, the pilot severs the ship from the water and establishes it in the air."

The marvellous simplicity, exact knowledge and strong feeling shown in "The Tool" section reveal even more of the visionary ecstasy St-Exupéry knew and thought all pilots knew. Power and gentleness join together, self is forgotten and we are handed an absolutely new attitude not only towards flying but towards the whole world. Unity is achieved. The next section of this book is called *The Elements* and many passages of it resemble prose poems.

St-Exupéry speaks of Conrad at the beginning of this section and says that "It was this human drama that Conrad described when he painted a typhoon". The French writer is not only well-read but he avoids the obvious trap that awaits a visionary writer when he is speaking of the elements—namely, vagueness. But St-Exupéry does not solve this problem by constant reference to other writers; he speaks from the clarity of his own mind as well as from the strength of his sensuous joy. Thus, he declares, when speaking of any writer's difficulty in conveying horror convincingly, that "The reason why writers fail when they attempt to evoke horror is that horror is something invented [that last word is important in this context] after the fact when one is re-creating the experience over again in the memory. Horror does not manifest itself in the world of reality." And the writer goes on to tell us that in "beginning his story of the revolt of the elements" he does not feel that he will write anything which the reader will find "dramatic".

What precisely is meant by this? I think St-Exupéry is revealing the truth to us that any "revolt of the elements", such as a thunderstorm, for example, comes upon us, flyers or men on the ground, with such abruptness and ferocity that we can only be shocked; in this shock lies the "unreality". What is written down later is bound to be a little melodramatic, not merely dramatic. And so St Exupéry, when he writes of the aftermath of storms, of all the elements can do with which we cannot compete, he is detailed, visual, clear, simple and concrete. So he writes: "Towering over the round hills on which the winds have left a residue of stony gravel, there rises a chain of prow-shaped, saw-toothed, razor-edged mountains stripped by the elements down to the bare rock." This is more than observation, it is pure fact wrought to a vision by the eyes and mind of the man who has seen and remembered it. This most exceptional pilot is giving us what he sees in beautifully chosen, precise words; because he is humble, he thinks all men can see like this. We know he is wrong.

Continuing with "The Elements", St-Exupéry writes:

> The blue sky glittered like a new-honed knife . . . Give me a good black storm in which the enemy is clearly visible . . . Very soon came a slight tremor . . . No rolling, no pitching. No swing to speak of. The flight continues horizontal and rectilinear. But you have felt a warning drum on the wings of your plane . . .

Then a crash begins of which the pilot can remember little, had "no impression of tragedy". Later, everything comes to life for him and he says, "Horizon? There is no longer a horizon. I was in the wings of a theatre cluttered up with bits of scenery . . ." Then St-Exupéry realizes that he had been unable to distinguish between the veering planes and the stationery mountainsides. All this time, he remains fearless; it is what he is experiencing that holds his fascination. "I was wrestling with chaos", he declares. There is an almost epic quality about all this. The pilot sees the peak of Salamanca; then he says "It cheered me to think I was about to escape out to sea" for "the peak of Salamanca was a giant".

None of this is cowardly; it is almost unbelievably brave. St-Exupéry feels ecstasy in the battle with the elements and natural objects, he rejoices in it although he is completely aware of all the dangers around him. Of the wind, he says, "When a wind like this one attacks a tropical forest it swirls through the branches like a flame, twists them into corkscrews, and uproots giant trees as if they were radishes." The writer always finds the perfect imagery to describe everything; it is always strong, simple, and even homely. Hence the spell it casts over us, just as all he is doing is filling him with the most intense awareness and excitement. He writes as well of the sea as of the wind; here is an example: "Now and again the water went incongruously transparent between the white pools, and I could see a green and black sea bottom."

Soon, St-Exupéry's hands grow numb and he is angry about this and wonders what has happened. Soon he writes, almost with pure joy, "What a discovery! My hands were not my own . . ." He admits now to fear, though it is not an ordinary fear because he quickly decides how to cope with it:

> "I shut my hands. I shut my hands. I shut my hands." All of of me was condensed into that one phrase and for me the white sea, the whirling eddies, the saw-toothed range ceased to exist. There was only "I shut my hands". [This is a kind of charm worked by this pilot in the middle of great danger.] There was no danger, no cyclone, no land unattained . . . I had no thoughts. I had no feelings except the feeling of being emptied out.

The pilot is fully aware of all the dangers which surround him, yet he can merge himself with them. Afterwards all this violence that has come so close to him recedes, St-Exupéry can say, "There is nothing dramatic in the world, nothing pathetic, except in human relations". He has returned from great peril and been changed by it and learnt something from it. These flights took place in Spain. At the end of "The Elements", St-Exupéry speaks lightly of them, though he does ask, "How can one tell an act of the will from a simple image when there is no transmission of sensation?" What he has felt can never be communicated in the precise way *he* experienced it. He ends this part by stating that "Every week men sit comfortably at the cinema and look on at some Shanghai or other, some Guernica and marvel without a trace of horror" at the terrible things they are seeing. This is what he meant when he said earlier that such real experiences become unreal when they are written about, spoken of or shown in photographs only in order to shock others. To this extent, there is an ultimate loneliness in the cyclone which St-Exupéry experienced and grappled with. The last statement of "The Elements" is very important. As always with this writer, it is absolutely direct. "The physical drama itself cannot touch us until some one points out its spiritual sense." This is the visionary speaking, and that one sentence, though it may not communicate the battle with the elements, speaks sparely and clearly and, in short, communicates with us immediately. We are given the meaning of all that this seer has gone through if we are willing to accept these last words. It is very difficult not to.

Section 5 of this book is entitled "The Plane and the Planet". In it, St-Exupéry tells us what the aeroplane has revealed to us about "the true face of the earth". Pilots, he says, "were like that queen who determined to move among her subjects so that she might learn for herself whether or not they rejoiced in her reign". This is beautiful imagery because it recalls to us the never-forgotten stories of childhood. Later, having flown over the Straits of Magellan, the pilot-poet-writer gives us these reverberant lines about volcanoes:

> This day, as I fly, the lava world is calm. There is something surprising in the tranquillity of this deserted landscape where once a thousand volcanoes boomed to each other . . . In the soft and yellow light, the plain appears as luxuriant as a garden . . . A hare scampers off; a bird wheels in the air . . .

St-Exupéry always sees skies, rocks, plains with a radiant simplicity and as if they were new; when he writes, he makes us too feel that they are new. This is part of the sharing of his vision. When he has flown over Chile, he can declare,

> The earth is smooth, the slopes are gentle . . . We have reached the most southerly habitation of the world, a town born of the

chance presence of a little mud between the timeless lava and the
austral ice . . . how thrilling it is to feel the miraculous nature
of man.

The writer never ceases to wonder at whatever he sees. He cries
out, "What a strange encounter!" after he has depicted the lava
and the ice.

But St-Exupéry expresses what he feels in an even more visionary way when he writes, "I landed in the peace of evening . . .
Standing near a couple of feet of their grace [some girls standing
beside a fountain], I felt more poignantly than ever the human
mystery." There is much that St-Exupéry observes but because
he is a seer, everything is surrounded by wonder for him. The
smallest detail of life is never taken for granted; it is always flar-
ing and fresh. Nothing becomes tarnished and his feeling for
human beings, whether he has known them or not, is one of
reverence. He is grateful for them and that he should be per-
mitted to share their world, their lives.

There are many passages in "The Plane and the Planet"
which read like pure prose poems. Here are parts of some of
them:

> What can one know of a girl who passes, walking with slow
> steps homeward, eyes lowered, smiling to herself, filled with
> adorable inventions and with fables? . . . I feel her to be locked
> up in her language, in her secret, in her habits, in the singing
> echoes of her memory.

St-Exupéry puts a ring of magic round the simplest things; this
is his kind of vision. Like Traherne, a mystic in the seventeenth
century, he would say, "You never enjoy the world aright . . .
till you are filled with the heavens and crowned with the stars."
St-Exupéry knows this experience too but he also explores the
simple human things, as well as the intricacies of what makes
a modern aeroplane. Here are some examples of the former where
he reaches, through what most would consider entirely commonplace things, a true ecstasy:

> I lean against a fountain . . . A child, his head against a wall,
> weep in silence: . . . I know nothing [almost the "nada" of St
> John of the Cross]. I do not enter into their empires. Man in the

presence of man is as solitary as in the face of a wide winter sky in which there sweeps, never to be tamed, a flight of trumpeting geese.

Nature is to be observed and loved and enjoyed, but man can never enter its essence; nor can he do so with men, women or children. A seer's task is to watch and be filled with a heightened wonder at the simplest things; it is not his task to change such things. As St-Exupéry now says, "How shallow is the stage on which this vast drama of human hates and joys and friendships is played!" And, because he knows of the vital importance of friendship—has indeed received it—he asks, and he is really asking himself most of all,

> Whence do men draw this passion for eternity [my italics], flung by chance as they are upon a scarcely cooled bed of lava, threatened from the beginning by the deserts that are to be, and under the constant menace of the snows?

Here, St-Exupéry can find no comfort or reason in God or religion. Even men's "civilizations are but fragile gildings". Man is, then, at the mercy of the elements and all the dangers which lie in wait for him on this planet.

But he has found an answer, not a panacea, not an easy comfort, something he can hand on to others only by his words. It is this:

> But by the grace of the aeroplane I have known a more extraordinary experience than this, and have been made to ponder with even more bewilderment the fact that this earth that is our home is yet in truth a wandering star.

This is more than a provisional solution. And it is very far from seeking out pleasure in order to hide from the terrors and dangers of this planet. St-Exupéry loves this planet, from mountain to sea-shell. About flying and exploring, he feels, "Without question, I was the first human being ever to wander over this . . . iceberg . . . I was thrilled by the virginity of a soil which no step of man or beast had sullied . . ." Now comes the essence of the writer's vision: " . . . very naturally, raising my eyes, I said to myself that from the height of this celestial apple-tree there must have dropped other fruits." He feels that he will find them "exactly where they fell, since never from the beginning of time had anything been present to displace them". So there is hope. There has been desolation and darkness but now St-Exupéry exults; he feels that he is the first man who ever appeared on this planet, and he has the humility not to ask why *he* should be given this sense of purity, newness and wonder.

Then this visionary, who so honours and values the world, does a strange thing. He picks up one or two stones and declares, "here is where my adventure became magical, for in a striking foreshortening of time that embraced thousands of years, I had become the witness of this miserly rain [the stones] from the stars". It is a "marvel of marvels" to him that between this planet, which he calls "this magnetic sheet" and the stars "a human consciousness was present in which as in a mirror that rain could be reflected".

In all this wonder, this ecstasy, there is also something of the philosopher. But the poet is foremost in the visionary experience because, once again, St-Exupéry feels, with extraordinary power, as if he were the first man, the first being to be aware of the whole intricate universe. He had another similar experience when his plane had been forced down in the Sahara. He says that he "was taught that a dream might partake of the miraculous". The attempt to land was a great struggle but, when he did, he found "there reigned a peace as of work suspended and a silence like a trap". He fell asleep and it seemed to him that "Gravitation had become as sovereign as love". Lying on the sand, wondering what to do, he feels at times "like a galley-slave". Then suddenly the following dreams come to him:

> They came to me soundlessly, like the waters of a spring, and in the beginning I could not understand the sweetness that was invading me. There was neither voice nor vision [because this was a dream], but the presentiment of a presence, of a warmth very close and already half guessed.

Full details of the dream are given, mostly connected with entering what seemed like a house. And in this great house, St-Exupéry was sure that he "had found out at last the origin of the feeling of eternity that came over [him] in this wilderness". We all know that dreams are an important part of our life and it is not surprising that such a rare man as this should have such illuminating dreams.

In this dream St-Exupéry sees an old woman who worked in his home; he sees her sewing, he remembers how he was always rushing about as a child, trying to discover things, tearing his shirt. But when he wakes from his dream, he realizes that these are little things, mere "shadows . . . beside the sands, the granite, the virgin forests, the vast swamp-lands of the earth". Thinking of the old woman he recalls how when he grew up he tried to shock her with tales of all the savage wonders he had seen, but she remained unmoved. He used to pity her, thinking her "blind and deaf". Now, isolated in the desert, he sees her stillness as that of faith, and says "that night in the Sahara, naked between the stars and the sand, I did her justice". He pays her further homage in the last line of "The Plane and the Planet" in these words: "Sahara, my Sahara! You have been bewitched by an old woman at a spinning-wheel!"

The more we read of Wind, Sand and Stars, the more remarkable St-Exupéry appears to us. He has a complex mind, a potent imagination, a clear eye for the everyday details of things, and also a marvellous directness.

This visionary writing continues in the sixth part of the book which is called "Oasis". Before he describes an oasis, an oasis, which, for this original mind and character is a house in Paraguay, St-Exupéry says: "One of the miracles of the airplane is that it plunges a man directly into the heart of mystery." Again we see why flying was not a job but a vocation for him. This house in Paraguay, which was for the writer an oasis, was cherished for many reasons, nearly all very simple ones. Thus he says: "A garden wall at home may enclose more secrets than the Great Wall of China, and the soul of a little girl is better guarded by silence than the Sahara's oases by the surrounding sands." This is more than an awareness of the strength of the imagination on the author's part, it is at the heart of his vision. The word "silence" is very important; it occurs over and over again in *Wind, Sand and Stars*, for only in silence can peace, contemplation and a true vision be found.

Even the "dilapidation" he saw in Paraguay filled St-Exupéry with "wonder", while "the waxed and polished over cracks of a house made him feel" "an extraordinary respect". He feels that it would be a kind of sacrilege to intrude on these old broken splendours and try to restore them. At a dinner party, he recalls the candles he saw in his childhood which cast "great wondrous shadows on the walls". He marvels at the innocence of the young girls who "reigned over all the animals of creation"; these girls "knew no vanity". And St-Exupéry ends "Oasis" by wondering what has happened to them—"Have they changed, I wonder?" He remembers the "imbecile" who appeared and thinks, in the last line of this section, that "the imbecile carried away the princess into slavery".

The fairy tale atmosphere of "Oasis" is strengthened by the infinite care and compassion which the writer feels for the people he meets and the house he visits. Whatever happens, he feels adamantly, must not be touched and so spoilt in any way.

Section 7 is called "Men of the Desert". In the Sahara "women have bloomed in their loveliness". In this part, St-Exupéry is concerned with those who live in the desert, his fellow pilots, and with what the wind can do to him personally. He feels that "Time was running through his fingers like the fine sand of the dunes", but he "succumbed to the desert as soon as he saw it". Men give him cartridges; he is supposed to feel afraid and aware of danger, but what, in fact, he feels is

> an immense pride . . . This sea of sand bowled me over. Un-questionably it was filled with mystery and danger. The silence that reigned over it was not the silence of emptiness, but of plotting, of imminent enterprise.

Again and again, St-Exupéry is intoxicated by silence; it is something almost tangible to him. In the sky and the desert it becomes the heart of his vision. In the Sahara "an indefinable bond is established between you and the veneer of gold on the sand in the late sun".

But this contemplative is also a man of action and a very

efficient one. And, as we know, he cares greatly for friendship, for the feeling of men working or relaxing after work together. One of his comrades and co-pilots, Guillaumet, and indeed all with whom he worked, can have known nothing of this strong, essential, secret core of the visionary which is the real St-Exupéry. We have an example of this when he recalls how, left alone in the desert for a little while on his first day in Africa, he saw his first gazelle. When Guillaumet, returning, enquires "You weren't frightened?" St-Exupéry simply says no. "I felt that the sands had shown me the gazelle in confidence, so I said nothing about it and thought 'gazelles are not frightening'."

One night is particularly memorable to him. He suspected a storm ("someone was calling to me from a great distance. Was it instinct?"). He was right but he says, "that was not what excited me. What filled me with a barbaric joy was that I had understood a murmured monosyllable of this secret language, had sniffed the air and known what was coming . . ." St-Exupéry is filled with ecstasy that he can be so at one with the elements. What is extraordinary about his vision is that an old house, a simple girl, a great battle with wind are all alike to him. There is a wholeness about all that he sees and senses.

Then, a little later, comes a beautiful prose poem. Here is part of it.

> Men who have lived for years with a great love, and have lived on in noble solitude when it was taken from them, are likely now and then to be worn out by their exaltation. Such men return humbly to a humdrum life, ready to accept contentment in a more commonplace love. They find it sweet to abdicate . . .

But life is not like this for St-Exupéry; he continues, "Like a ship moving into port, we of the desert come up into the night". I do not mean that St-Exupéry could live on a constant level of ecstasy (in their different ways, even the great religious mystics could not do this, for they too were, after all, men), but that even the commonplace was surrounded with wonder for him; the tiniest detail of living was an important mystery.

Great understanding of the Moors is shown in the following lines:

The first one I saw did not moan; but then he had no one to moan against. I felt in him an obscure acquiescence, as of a mountaineer lost and at the end of his strength who sinks to earth and wraps himself up in dreams and snow.

The imagery here is beautiful, but the understanding, the feeling we have of a oneness with this man so different from ourselves is more important. A lover of solitude, St-Exupéry has this rare gift of entering the lives of others, of feeling almost exactly as they do. Of a dying slave, for example, he says "I could not tell what visions were vanishing in him". Here, the writer shows his understanding by stating a contradiction; he knows only too well that this slave is having visions as he dies, and that shows great knowledge and subtle awareness of another's feelings, especially feelings at the point of death, the most mysterious of all experiences.

Many Mohammedans are mentioned, always with compassion. There is Bark "sitting every night under the same star, in a place where men live in houses of air and follow the wind". Bark would visit St-Exupéry, who was clearly always accessible to anyone and warm with something more than affection—something very like love. He once went to the writer "His body charged with tenderness and mysteriously magnetized, as if the pole of these emotions were very near at hand . . ." He wanted to say "his over-full heart . . . quivering on the brim" that his heart "needed only to find itself back in Marrakesh to be poured out". Many men confided in St-Exupéry. The reason is that visionaries cannot help carrying about with them the exceptional experiences they have known, though this is quite unconscious but is sensed by others.

In the end St-Exupéry bought Bark from the Moors, as was the custom, and set him free "with a flourish of ceremony, in the presence of three Moorish witnesses". He always treated him as a friend, never as a slave. Bark, he tell us, "was free and therefore he possessed the essential of wealth", the right to spend his earnings as he wished, and also to travel as he wished. In short, Liberty.

This "Men of the Desert" part of Wind, Sand and Stars sometimes reminds us of the feelings about the desert which St-

Exupéry shared with T. E. Lawrence. Both men were under its spell; but the former was a visionary in many places and with more kinds of people. Nevertheless, they shared a love of solitude and of comradeship.

Much of "Men of the Desert" is devoted to Bark. After he has been set free, he spends the day in Agadir before going to Marrakesh, his former home. St-Exupéry sets another Arab, Abdullah, to look after him. They wander idly through the town and then Bark suddenly starts buying golden slippers for all the children in the streets. St-Exupéry tells us that "Abdullah was sure he had gone mad, 'mad with joy' he said afterwards", but St-Exupéry finds another explanation. Wandering through the town, Bark had found that his new freedom "had in it a taste of bitterness: what he learnt from it with most intensity was that he had no ties with the world . . . He was free but too infinitely free, not striding upon the earth but floating above it", and so St-Exupéry declares: "Bark went forward lapped in this tide of children as once in his sea of ewes [an utterly simple but surprising image] ploughing his first furrow in the world." For the visionary has seen "hope" in Bark. Although he knows this man who is old must return to "poverty" and "responsibility for more lives than perhaps his old arms would be able to sustain", nonetheless "he felt the pull of his true weight".

St-Exupéry is not imposing his own picture or way of thinking and living upon Bark; he is far too realistic to do that. Bark seems to him

> Like an archangel too airy to live the life of man but who had cheated, had sewn lead into his girdle [another excellent and apt piece of concrete imagery] and had dragged himself forward, pulling against the pull of a thousand children who had such great need of golden slippers.

These last lines are not rhetoric, they are visionary and arise from the depths of the whole character of St-Exupéry.

So this remarkable man comes to the end of this section about the Arabs by saying

> Such is the desert. A Koran which is but a handbook of the rules of the game transforms its sands into an empire. Deep in

the seemingly empty Sahara a secret drama is being played that stirs the passions of men.

The writer has penetrated this secret. He declares, "What a difference in substance between the sands of submission and the sands of unruliness!"

The vision then becomes universal as this section draws to a close. St-Exupéry asks, "And is not all the world like this?" He remembers his childhood and "the dark and golden park we peopled with gods . . . We created a secret civilization where footfalls had a meaning and things a savour known in no other world." But he will not linger in the enchanted places of child-hood. He speaks of returning to these places as a grown-up and ends "Men of the Desert" with this reflection, which is accept-ance, namely the lesson that in the "infinity of childhood . . . we shall never again set foot, and that it is into the game and not the park that we have lost the power to enter". This is not disillusionment for St-Exupéry is telling us that we must grow, and there is affirmation in the statement that "the park" still exists, another part of our lives.

Part 8 of *Wind, Sand and Stars* is called "Prisoner of the Sand". St-Exupéry leaves the desert for three years but tells us that, in 1935, he "had no notion that the sands were preparing me for their ultimate and culminating ordeal". "This", he tells us, "is the story of the Paris-Saigon flight." He admits, though we know he always endured it, that he "was fearful of flying at night in one of those desert storms" when the sky becomes "a yellow furnace" and can destroy "hills, towns, and river-banks drowning earth and sky in one great conflagration". But soon he meets friends. When he takes off now, we see this writer perhaps more clearly than ever before as esssentially the pilot, the explorer of the solitude and, often, silence of the sky. His cockpit has "a particular flavour" and the instruments there seem like "jewels in their panel and glimmering like a constella-tion in the dark of night".

Very quickly St-Exupéry gets to know a new group of airmen, his own crew. They are suffering from engine trouble over a rough sea and between conversations with his crew, St Exupéry reflects ironically, the sea was part of a world I had nothing to do with. Engine trouble here was out of the question: there was not the least danger of such a thing. Why, I was not rigged for the sea ! . . . After an hour and a half of this, the rain died down, and though the clouds still hung low a genial sun began to break through. I was immensely cheered by this promise of good weather.

The mingling of the alert man of action with the contemplative continues throughout "Prisoner of the Sand". St Exupéry is in Italian territory now or, rather, flying over it. Soon, he returns to Tunis and what would, to other pilots, be just an automatic exercise is, for this man, an edge of a vision. He says, "the impalpable eddies of evening air drum softly on the wings and the plane seems to be drilling its way into a quivering crystal so delicate that the wake of a passing swallow would jar it to bits". The active strength and the vivid imagination of this rare pilot astonish us; ordinary flying is transcended by his powerful fusion of action and awareness of something much more important than action.

But St-Exupéry knows too of the danger to other men and his "heart sank" when one's skull had been crushed. He feels deep sympathy yet is aware, "a moment later", that everything has sunk back into a golden silence. The same peace, the same stillness, followed this crash". Some readers might say that this reaction was callous or self-indulgent. It is not, and it is not because of the swift movement of St-Exupéry's mind, which is able to accept and take in so much so swiftly.

Soon, the writer is in Tripolitania where he finds—not seeking it—a new vision. He tells us that "Already this profane world was beginning to fade out . . . I know nothing, nothing in the world, equal to the wonder of nightfall in the air." Here is St-Exupéry's true home; here he is most exalted. But his life is not always like this. We have seen already his care for other people and his vision of other things, but, nonetheless he admits that "My world was the world of flight", and "that those who have been enthralled by the witchery of flying will know what I mean . . ." Flying is not a sport for St-Exupéry, but something much more profound. All visionaries must renounce something, often something very great. This visionary declares, "I, too, in this flight, am renouncing things, I am giving up the broad golden surfaces that would befriend me if my engines were to fail".

There follows a scintillating account of just what it feels like to be on a night flight:

> I have on my side only the stars . . . Earth and sky begin to merge into each other. The earth rises and seems to spread like a mist. The first stars tremble as if shimmering in green water. Hours must pass before their glimmer hardens into the frozen glitter of diamonds . . . In the profound darkness of certain nights I have seen the sky streaked with so many trailing sparks that it seemed to me a great gale must be blowing through the outer heavens.

For this, St-Exupéry thinks it well worth abandoning, renouncing "the profiles of mountains". The whole Universe seems like a vast display of fireworks though it is the plane which is moving, not the stars, the "soundless frolic of the shooting stars" as the writer calls it.

St-Exupéry is always grateful to his fellows, whether they are flyers or ground staff. Thus he declares, "The most helpful ground crew in the world wove in and out of the blinding ray of a searchlight, alternately visible and invisible". These men, too, are part of this whole magnificent picture of the sky; they enable him to be in the air and experience such ecstasy. But he loves the solitude, except for one man, of night flying, and writes thus of a journey from Paris to the Nile:

> There was no moon. The world was a bubble of pitch that had dilated until it reached the very stars in the heavens . . . I might blot the world out of my mind and concentrate my attention upon the slow pulsation of the narrow thread of radium paint that ran along the dark background of the dials.

I think we should state here that St-Exupéry is never flying simply for the chance of the pure joy it may give him; he is always doing a job in peacetime, or fighting in wartime. Like all visionaries, he hopes for exaltation but he is always acting under orders. Neither does he take risks; he watches his instruments most assiduously. So, in this passage, he takes thought of his co-pilot, and also only flies where he "had been told the winds would be favourable". But soon he enters and hands over to us his great joy:

> . . . I wrapped myself closely round in darkness among my miniature constellations which gave off the same mineral glow as the stars, the same mysterious and unwearied light, and spoke the same language. Like the astronomers, I too was reading in the book of celestial mechanics . . .

but "the external world has ceased to exist". All this time, St-Exupéry is intent on the working of his plane. A little later, he flies into a cloud and though "a clean sky would have helped a lot", "light steadied itself in the form of a bouquet of pink blossoms". The pilot realizes that he is "navigating somewhere in the belly of a cumulus whose thickness I could not guess". But the "bouquet" disappears and after searching for lights below and hearing Prévot, his co-pilot, who has been asleep, say "I'll bet we're near Cairo", he begins his descent and then, very suddenly, he crashes, but the two men find themselves safely on the ground.

St-Exupéry assures us that during the descent and abrupt crash, he felt "no emotion". But now the two men have to struggle, lost in the desert. There is no ecstasy for a long time, only anxiety. Yet, even in this condition, St-Exupéry is full of curiosity about what desert animals live on, because he notices the holes of carnivorous sand-foxes. These foxes become friends, "my foxes". And he misses nothing of the eerie desert landscape. The sight of a mirage delights him, but he knows he must find exactly where he is. He writes, "The horizon had stripped itself of its pomp, its palaces, its priestly vestments. It was the old desert horizon again."

At last, Prévot goes away and lights a bonfire, St-Exupéry cannot at first understand this but he walks up to the beacon and, to his great delight, thinks that Prévot is talking to two Arabs. But this turns out to be an illusion, caused by the weariness, and shock induced by the crash of the plane. But Prévot had found an orange which the two men share, and this orange, St-Exupéry says, is "one of the greatest joys he has ever known". St-Exupéry reflects now—having learnt all this from the horrifying experience in the desert—how much "the cigarette and glass of rum" mean to the "criminal about to be executed". Once he had thought that to accept such things "was beneath human dignity"; now he realizes that the "pleasure" they give is enormous.

The men find water but it makes them feel sick; for many more hours they are completely lost. As he lies down to rest, St-Exupéry imagines that he is "at sea. I was on a ship going to South America . . . The tip of the mast was swaying to and fro, very slowly among the stars." More time passes and, though for a moment the writer has experienced a moment of sheer panic, he can now write, "Flying is a man's job and its worries are a man's worries. A pilot's business is with the wind, with the stars, with night, with sand, with the sea. He strives to outwit the forces of nature." And he compares his chosen job with that of the gardener awaiting spring, and then declares that the pilot "looks forward to port as to a promised land, and truth for him is what lives in the stars".

Here is a direct statement of St-Exupéry's dedication, his vocation. He is very brave; he can say, after three days in the desert, that "These are the cares of men alive in every fibre" and adds that he thinks them "more important than the fretful choosing of a night-club in which to spend the evening". He accepts, with absolutely no regrets, what has happened in the desert; he has endured great suffering, suffering of many kinds. All visionaries do, but their sufferings take countless forms. St-Exupéry has gone through much mental, as well as physical, anguish during this endless-seeming time in the desert. When, at last, he is rescued, he can say "Sorrow is one of the vibrations that prove the fact of living". Yet he "felt no sorrow"; instead, he felt that he "was the desert". For a time his old visions seem to have left him for ever. But then, everything suddenly changes and he feels that the desert landscape "had . . . become a kind of stage setting". The earlier exultation returns and St-Exupéry declares, "we had found ourselves alone on earth . . . and here, imprinted in the sand, were the divine and naked feet of man!"

When the men are rescued they are given water; St-Exupéry writes in Biblical language: "Of the riches that exist in the world, thou art the rarest and also the most delicate . . . And the joy that thou spreadest is an infinitely simple joy." And he is full of gratitude to the Arabs of Libya whom he calls "Humanity" itself, as well as "our beloved fellow-man". He goes further and declares,

> You came towards me in an aureole of charity and magnanimity bearing the gift of water. All my friends and all my enemies marched towards me in your person. It did not seem that you were rescuing me: rather you were forgiving me. And I felt I had no enemy left in all the world.

So, after his terrible experiences in the desert, St-Exupéry draws a vision, a vision of the love and goodness of other men. Once more, he is grateful.

Part 9, which is the last part of *Wind, Sand and Stars* is called "Barcelona and Madrid" and deals with St-Exupéry flying there in 1936 during the Spanish Civil War. He begins this section by recalling what he discovered in the desert—namely,

> that in such an hour [of peace and reconciliation in the most terrible circumstances] a man feels that he has finally found himself and has become his own friend. An essential need has been satisfied . . . Never shall I forget that [in the anguish of loss and desolation] . . . my heart was infinitely warm beneath the desert stars.

Before he describes his Spanish experiences St-Exupéry tells us more of what the desert has taught him. Like all visionaries he is constantly both open to pain and also to acquiring fresh knowledge. He thinks that everything is "a paradox", men are not "cattle", and Newton, discovering gravity, weighed "more than a parcel of nonentities". One of the great things which St-Exupéry has learnt, been given, and is infinitely grateful for is "the experience of a sudden joy" which comes "when nothing in the world had forewarned us of its coming". This kind of joy is so "thrilling that if it was born of misery we remembered the misery with tenderness". This seems simple, but in fact it is very subtle.

St-Exupéry has learnt, too, that truth cannot be "demonstrated by the aid of logic". Each man discovers his own truth, a truth which "releases the prince asleep within him unknown to himself". Then, just before beginning to journey to, and flying, in Spain, he states with absolute determination that "it is man and not flying that concerns me most". Here we have another proof of the dignity of St-Exupéry's sense of values and the validity of his visionary awareness of life. His selflessness makes him think of friends who, living lives fraught with danger, found in that very life, "serenity of spirit".

Flying from Lyon, over the Pyrenees, to Spain, St-Exupéry was alone. Over Perpignan, he says that he was day-dreaming, thinking of sitting in a square, sipping a drink and watching the "pretty girls", "carefree strollers" as well as the "pure sky". But soon he is reflecting on deeper matters and says, "Human drama does not show itself on the surface of life. It is not played out in the visible world, but in the hearts of men." St-Exupéry loves and rejoices in the visible world but he knows that there are far more important and profound things. A little later he makes a very wise remark; it is this: "It is another of the miraculous things about mankind that there is no pain nor passion that does not radiate to the ends of the earth." This writer does not put it in these terms, but this is really a large part of the Christian doctrine of *The Mystical Body of Christ*.

Soon this pilot-visionary is near Barcelona. He notices, from the air, the deserted places; he sees smoke and asks himself, "Was this a scrap of evidence of that nearly soundless anger whose all-destroying wrath was so hard to measure?" He cannot believe, immediately, that there is war, with all its attendant violence, in Spain. But quickly he realizes that "A whole civilization was contained in that faint golden puff so lightly dispersed by a breath of wind". To this man of peace it seems "nonsense" that there should be war in Spain, that Barcelona should be "in ashes". He is convinced "of the sincerity" of the Spanish people and, although he sees no "firing line" he is fully aware of the violence now and to come, even though he "saw groups of men and women strolling on the Ramblas [a large square]". But soon he *does* come upon the firing and he says that "a smile was often enough to open the way before him". Then he shows great wisdom when he, caught up and fighting in the Spanish Civil

War, says this about all civil wars: "In a civil war the firing line is invisible; it passes through the hearts of men."

St-Exupéry has landed and, while calmly having a drink, sees soldiers advancing, "four armed men" who, wordlessly, "pointed their guns" at the stomach of a man sitting at the table next to his own. "Streaming with sweat this man stood up", was searched and taken away. For the writer these soldiers have "crossed the invisible firing line". St-Exupéry's guides are, he declares, "anarchists" and now he is really involved with war, but his vision, far from diminishing becomes greater, just as his compassion does. He writes that he and his comrades were "far from the platforms built for tender farewells" and that "this world had lost its human quality", seemed to be made of "iron", and therefore uninhabitable. Then come these wonderful words:

> A ship remains a living thing only so long as man with his brushes and oils swabs an artificial layer of light over it. Leave them to themselves a couple of weeks and the life dies out of your ship, your factory, your railway; death covers their faces.

And now St-Exupéry sees the men who are fighting in this war; he also sees their weapons. But something amazes him: "What is startling here is the silence." There is only occasionally the ominous "thump of a steel plate" as a gun-carriage lands, but "of human voices no sound". Nor are there uniforms. All this reminds the writer of a hospital and he declares that "A civil war is not a war, it is a disease" for there was for these fighters no "going up to the front in the exultation of certain victory; they were struggling blindly against infection.

St-Exupéry sees this on both sides in the Spanish Civil War and he says that the whole thing seemed not like "an invading foreigner" but a struggle "to eradicate a plague". And the silence he now notices is not the beautiful silence of peace with the elements but a silence of men "going off . . . with their instruments of asphyxiation". We already know two good accounts for the Spanish Civil War; the first is George Orwell's very personal but extremely moving *Homage to Catalonia*, written by a man deeply involved with the Republicans, and the second is Hugh Thomas's history of the war, a book written

later and with great impartiality. For St-Exupéry, the war is
something quite different, an event in which "Death . . . is a
sort of quarantine" and where it is not always easy to distinguish
one side from the other.

Much of this last section of *Wind, Sand and Stars* is visionary.
There is something here in common with David Jones's view of
war, although it is expressed in a quite different way. But there
is the same love of men and care for individual people raised to
a point of very great Christian charity (we know that Jones was
a Christian and a Catholic, while St-Exupéry was the same
though he doesn't, in his book, always say so overtly). Now he
says,

> I thought of our respect for the dead. I thought of the white
> sanatorium where the light of a man's life goes quietly out in the
> presence of those who love him . . . Never again will be heard
> exactly that note of laughter, that intonation of voice, that quality
> of repartee.

Here, without resort to literary devices such as alliteration and
much repetition of phrases (though at times he does make use
of the latter), St-Exupéry can, nonetheless, write prose which
is heightened to the form of a prose poem. His vision is such
that something more than straightforward prose is needed. He
continues here, "Each individual is a miracle [something Hopkins would have called "inscape"]. No wonder we go on speaking of the dead for twenty years."

And this war is also unique. As this visionary says, "Here, in
Spain, a man is simply stood up against a wall and he gives up
his entrails to the stones of the courtyard". Of the men fighting
on the ground, St-Exupéry is not committed to either side in
this war but only to men, women, priests, nuns, and so on. The
writer now mingles the observer's attitude of Durrell with the
identifying vision of D. H. Lawrence—a difficult feat but one
achieved with supreme simplicity.

Many facts now emerge, though the writer-pilot has moved
"in a maze of uncertainty". He replies, when questioned, that
he is a Catalan from Barcelona and a Communist (in fact, he is
not a Communist in the Marxist sense). He is, for example,

deeply happy that, at this moment, women are in no danger; he actually sees a girl, about whom he records: "She cast a loving glance round at the countryside, as if stirred by a revelation . . . Everything that went on here seemed as jolly as a picnic." All seems "jolly" to this girl now because she has been accustomed to the monotony of a factory. St-Exupéry's vision of people both widens now and grows deeper; every particularity is important. He himself goes to the Front, then meets friends; and again his vision is passed to us when he writes that "The conscience of the village is tormented by one man"; he has seen this man at a tavern, troubled because he does not yet know whether his fellow villagers see him as "a fascist or not", and whether they will shoot him, but "There was nothing we could do for the man". A little later, St-Exupéry writes, in words like a cry of pure wisdom: "As for me, I wish I understood mankind." He does understand, as we have seen, but he is too humble to admit or, perhaps, too innocent even to know it.

This is proved later when this visionary writes "man's destiny does not reside merely in the destiny of the species: each individual is an empire". Those last five words are of momentous value in themselves, and they also reveal much about the man who writes them. Always particular, St-Exupéry recalls miners "pinned beneath the fallen timber" and says that, in this kind of terrible suffering, "there lives a world". He adds that things ranging from "the hot soup of evening" can change to "perhaps . . . a great universal love" and may "inhabit the skull" of this miner. Now, this writer contemplates mankind from a man who "once drew a reindeer on the wall of a cave" to all men and he states, with a supreme firmness that "we shall bring up that miner from his shaft. Solitary he may be; universal he surely is." This is, without doubt, visionary writing of a very high order indeed.

The Spanish War goes on and St-Exupéry sees horrors (Madrid seems like a place he is staring at "with closed eyes"). Like David Jones, this writer can see and feel and pass on to us experiences on several levels. He suffers but always in a silence of his own at a great depth. He feels for everyone and wishes he could understand what has happened when a "poor child has been stricken"

and when a cathedral is gutted. Involved in war, St-Exupéry, seeing both sides, never loses his compassion, that compassion which
is another important part of his vision, his self-forgetfulness. He
sees men, is always with them, yet he can write of some of them
like this: "Caught in the earth, painted by the earth, their
hands grubby with their gardenless gardening, these men were
raising themselves painfully out of the mud in order to emerge
under the stars."

We should not forget the great courage which St-Exupéry is
showing all the time while in a Spain at war. But his vision
never leaves him; everything is heightened for him and we are
continually given sentences or passages such as the following:

> Crouched behind the stone wall, we listen. No sound of a shot.
> Yet we cannot say we have heard nothing at all, for the whole
> night is singing like a sea-shell.

> Borne on the breeze of a human voice, invisible seeds are
> fertilizing that black earth across the valley.

> "Good night, friend!"
> And the response from the other side of the world:
> "Good night, friend!"
> And silence.
> Their words were not the same, but their truths were identical.
> Why has this high communion never yet prevented men from
> dying in battle against each other?

In this last passage St-Exupéry is wondering why what men
share, which is so much greater than the ways in which they
differ, has not stopped men from warring against each other.
To him, all men are brothers, a truly Christ-like conception, and
a belief which he himself always lives up to with the many men
he meets. We saw this when he was in the desert; now we see
it again in Spain.

Everything is closely observed; he sees as clearly what is on
the ground as he does when he is watching the dials in an
aeroplane, and as always, he has exquisite language for all that
he and other men do. Thus, when he is drinking brandy with a
sergeant, he says "when I had drunk I shut my eyes and saw

behind my lids those ruined and ghostly houses bathed in a greenish radiance as of moonglow under water". Seldom, however, does he see things when he has drunk *anything*; he does not drink much, and always only out of good fellowship. Drink and drugs have no place in his vision of the world. His own strong senses and extraordinarily quick and sensitive imagination give him his fiercely bright view of this planet and the skies.

Watching these fighting Spaniards a little later, St-Exupéry observes, ". . . I saw nothing in their vehemence that made me think it either silly or boastful. I could not but remember that all of them had been ready to die with simplicity." The writer sees immediately what is important about the men in the Spanish Civil War. He always finds simple words and transforms things which many would think trivial. Thus, he continues "Death was abroad, of course, but wandering aimlessly . . . We in the arbour were celebrating life." Then the *De Profundis*, the prayer for the dead, is twice mentioned, but we are told also of "that densely baked bread of Spain" and how a captain doles it out to his men so that each "might receive a chunk as big as his fist and turn it into life. These men had in truth risen *de profundis* [*sic*]. They were in very fact beginning a new life."

Much of this final section of *Wind, Sand and Stars* is reminiscent of *In Parenthesis*; the style is quite different but there is the same swift change of one mood to another, the same identification with the soldiers. Often, St-Exupéry seems like John Ball (who was really Jones himself) in his whole approach to war: one moment, for example, he is seeing and mingled with horrors, while the next he is noticing some natural beauty or observing a great truth about life. A sentence which comes soon is very like the simplicity of David Jones. It is about a wounded man or, rather, the reflection which comes to St-Exupéry when he has seen a man struggling to "reject our universe of dynamite". But the sentence which might almost have been written by Jones is, "Not so much death as the Calvary of a punished child". Here is both clarity, compression and tremendously powerful feeling and understanding.

"Barcelona and Madrid" continues very much in this vein— with such intensely moving insight and vision as the following:

Sergeante R——, let me tell you that we made you a present of your life. Just that. As much as if you had stood at the foot of the electric chair. And God knows, the world sheds ink enough on the pathos of pardon at the foot of the electric chair.

The writing is spare, the imagery never too rich, the style perfectly suited to its subject. St-Exupéry understands when he must be reticent (his tact seems almost endless) even when he desperately wants to ask one of these soldiers a question. He admits to us that he longs to ask this Sergeant what makes him "willing to die", but, instead, asks himself, "what language could be chaste enough for a modest man like you?" But he is so clever that he finds out by asking one or two little questions which would seem to the man to have no bearing on that big one which cannot be asked. From the brief answers, this visionary conjures up the man's whole life and the soldier's "pleasures" and "dreams" "seemed to belong to another age".

Man is the centre of St-Exupéry's vision, but he finds ecstasy in the solitude of flying and in Nature. He can write, "All the ducks on the farm are transformed for an instant into migrant birds . . ." And then, a moment later, he can make a great but not flamboyant generalization about life itself: "Man is overwhelmed by a mysterious presentiment of truth, so that he discovers the vanity of his book-keeping and the emptiness of his domestic felicities. But he can never put a name to this sovereign truth." A conventional Christian mystic would call this truth "God", the God with whom he longs to have complete union. All visionaries desire truth, but they have many ways of searching for it; what is common to every one of them is humility and charity and wonder. And so St-Exupéry is as concerned with that particular Sergeant's search as with his own. He declares, "What Sergeant, were the visions that governed your destiny . . . ?" He adds, that "We compose our creation slowly. And if we die too early we are in a sense cheated out of our share." A little further on he writes of the Sergeant, "But you, by the grace of an ordeal in the night which stripped you of all that was not intrinsic . . . discovered a mysterious creature born of yourself". "Great", says St-Exupéry, "was this creature, and never shall you forget him. And he is yourself."

The writer even goes so far as to say that, since this man has found self-knowledge, he is "the equal of the musician composing his music, of the physicist extending the frontier of knowledge, of all those who build the highways over which we march to deliverance". And he adds with a wonderful simplicity, "Let us say you were happy in Barcelona". In all this kind of writing, we feel drawn into St-Exupéry's vision of the world; he shows us the many things, sometimes very tiny things, we so often neglect; but he also shows us grandeur.

In this war, the writer-pilot never ceases to understand both sides for he says he has also seen it happening in others and marvelled at it. He writes of one man who "having once mounted guard over a flock of terrified little nuns kneeling in a Spanish nunnery, will thereafter know a different truth—that it is sweet to die for the Church". Here the Christian speaks out boldly. The operative word, of course, is "truth". And just before this statement St-Exupéry has said that "Every pilot who has flown to the rescue of a comrade in distress knows that all joys are vain in comparison with this one". This is a joy, but he sees that to be able to learn compassion (in this case that of another man) through seeing those who are supposed to be enemies is a "truth", a profound charity. St-Exupéry soon begins to tell us that all men are right "to hate war" and that, if we are to understand what is "essential in man" we must set aside "the passions that divide us". Again he speaks of science, having told us that "Truth is the language that expresses universality"; he cites Newton and says that he did not "discover" gravity but "accomplished a creative operation".

So we move to the end of Wind, Sand and Stars. In this section, St-Exupéry has told us, shared with us his vision of the world, which is based finally on truth. He says "We all yearn to escape from prison" and that simply to make scientific discoveries tells us nothing "about the human spirit". "To come alive" is to discover the truth within yourself; if that is learnt, suffering and humility cannot help but follow. He declares adamantly that he loathes war; he believes that a simple shepherd "wants to understand". And he will, because he is simple, do his work with love and care. So, here, all St-Exupéry's ecstasies come to this statement—"Death is sweet when it comes in its time and in its place, when it is part of the order of things . . ." He ends "Barcelona and Madrid" with this exhortation: "Comrades of the air! I call upon you to bear me witness. When have we felt ourselves happy men?"

But this book is given a brief "Conclusion", a kind of coda. The writer wants to tell us of the value of the poet, the musician, those "who can break bread with comrades" or open a "window to the same refreshing wind of the sea". To see and understand all this is to "learn a language". But, this visionary is wise; he knows of all the imperfections of the world and writes not with bitterness but with sadness that "too many men are left un-awakened". The book ends with these strong words of faith: "Only the Spirit, if it breathe upon the clay, can create Man."

So, out of all the horrors, the little human details of life, the silences of the stars, the ecstasy of flight, St-Exupéry has him-self learnt through his vision. He was born with all that can make a man a visionary, if he is prepared to learn, and this he has done.

We now turn to *Flight to Arras* which is concerned, at one level, with flying over German-occupied France in 1940. The style of the book is very much like that of *Wind, Sand and Stars*, but the author meets different people, sees different places and is involved in a very different kind of war from the Civil War in Spain. There is one other very vital difference. In *Flight to Arras* St-Exupéry speaks much more often as a Christian (he was educated in a Jesuit school). This book is written in 24 parts and opens with St-Exupéry and other men awaiting orders. He feels while sitting at a desk, like "a schoolboy again" but all these men are in "a time of full retreat", for France has fallen. Typically, this pilot-writer can write "Why should the sweetness of life be a matter for irony?" Then he keeps thinking of clocks, but soon "Orders are given for the sacrifice of the air arm because war must be made to look like war . . . The Staffs appeal to us as if we are a tribe of fortune-tellers." Dutertre, one of St-Exupéry's fellow pilots and comrades, thinks little of the Intelligence instructions they are all being given. He believes that the Germans could be shot down as soon as they crossed into France, but orders are for the airmen to go out on "low-altitude sorties". St-Exupéry himself compares the General Staff to "a first-rate bridge player who is asked what to do with a card by someone playing in another room". He thinks the Staff should "take risks".

St-Exupéry knows they are defeated but he is not afraid; he is surprised to find that, when one would suppose there would be countless problems, "the truth is that for a defeated army the problems themselves vanish". It is, he declares "victory which is like a house in the act of being built", where much activity is going on. But the men must obey. While observing other men—Alias, Dutertre, for example—St-Exupéry is experiencing a wider vision of man's spirit. As in *Wind, Sand and Stars*, he thinks of men's various activities, loving their wives or music for instance; and, for him a nation is "a Being". But, this vision tells him that "Death is a thing of grandeur", though he declares that he does "not like the pretty picture-book of war".

St-Exupéry begins Part IV by saying that "Human anguish is the product of the loss of man of his true identity". Soon he starts flying again and feels he is fulfilling his true function in this situation of a fallen France; "time", for him, "has ceased to run sterile through my fingers". Back at his dials and other instruments, he is at home. He says, very simply, "I was working at my trade". In Part V, St-Exupéry writes, "To know is not to prove, nor to explain. It is to accede to vision." Here, he admits openly his vision, even while he is making sorties over villages which at last he sees very clearly, in great detail. At the end of Part V, he says this, "God suspends the use of things and speech for the period of the nocturnal balance sheet", and the final words of this section are of a profound and poignant simplicity —"I do want to have the right to love. I do want to win a glimpse of the being for whom I die." The human longing here is raised to a desire which is mystical.

There is trouble in Part VI when his plane is chased by German fighters. "We were in God's hands", writes St-Exupéry and tries flying into the sun to shake the Germans off: "It was God's business and the sun's". After the fighters have gone, he nearly faints, but decides "not to mention it", merely remarking to his puzzled navigator, "We are alive". "For the time being", his companion replies, because "there was still Arras", and St-Exupéry speaks of a wounded friend whom, in Part VII, he visits in hospital. St-Exupéry now says "In less than ten seconds a plane can turn into a torch" and that he will not "play Sagon [the terribly hurt pilot] false by talking of his heroism or his modesty". These moments in the hospital are the most powerful, gentle and strangely uplifting so far in *Flight to Arras*.

In Part VIII, the writer becomes more and more concerned with life and death: "To live is to be slowly born." With his own great humility and, of course, denying the truth, St-Exupéry comments, amid all the fighting in fallen France, when another fighter says just " 'A little kick to port, Captain'. There you have reality. But I go back to my shoddy poetry." St-Exupéry has no "shoddy poetry"; he is showing the humility and suffering of all great visionaries. Like David Jones, his lot, or destiny, is to watch men being heroic with a sensitivity of his own that enters their pain, writes of it simply, and so shares it with us.

In Part IX, St-Exupéry is stranded, in bitter cold, with his Group outside Saint-Dizier. To him his "simple bed in that bare and freezing chamber" seems "miraculous". But, so as to make the room warm enough to dress and shave in, he would leap out of bed and light a fire, then return to bed, and as he watched the blaze, "a feeling of quiet jubilation" filled him and the whole room seemed transformed. Here is yet another moment where the visionary sees wonder in the barest, simplest things —and is grateful for them. This fire seems to him like "merry-making [when it] was at its height", shadows dance "and the glowing logs become a rosy architecure". This brief section is ecstatic, "a great adventure". The stringency of his physical conditions make him aware of his body. He says, "How should I possibly have guessed the adventure of the body—first as infant clinging to the tenderness and shelter of the maternal breast, then as soldier made for suffering, and finally as man enriched by the delight of the civilization of fire." There is the greatest simplicity everywhere here.

In Part X, work starts again. St-Exupéry finds "another of the war's absurdities", meaning that nothing is working properly; the planes are not well-equipped. Yet, though this is irritating for a perfectionist and, worse, dangerous, he does not become angry with individual men. Indeed, on the contrary, he declares that they are "for the most part decent and conscientious". He blames "the blind belly of an administration". Most of the sections of *Flight to Arras* are fairly brief. Thus, the eleventh tells us of the horror of seeing, from the air, the villages and land of France burning: "Will that forest recover? Will that forest recover? Seen from this height, France is being undermined by the secret gnawing of bacteria." St-Exupéry is a patriot and the sight of all this is agonizing to him. He regrets deeply that "When a war is on, a village ceases to be a cluster of traditions". Autonomy, individuality go, and this is almost unbearable.

Much of this section, with its repetitions, its quick move from remarks of great wisdom or beautiful description to touching details such as the care St-Exupéry shows for all individual things (we read, for example, how great, old trees must be "annihilated" because they obstruct the view of a "twenty-two-year-old lieutenant") are reminiscent of parts of *In Parenthesis*, especially those parts which present Army warfare at its fiercest. But there is a dreadful apathy growing now among some men since they know they are defeated; the writer says that these "inert men exist" but that "inertia is frustrated despair".

Part XII shows us the writer filled with darkness: "It is hard to exist. Man is a knot into which relationships are tied, and my ties serve me hardly at all." He thinks that something in him has "broken down" and asks himself what it is. He can find no satisfactory answer but asks how "a gesture, a word can give rise to endless ripples in a human destiny". Then he speaks of Pasteur to whom "a slide under a microscope would represent something infinitely more vast than a virgin forest ..."

Now a childhood memory comes to St-Exupéry; he recalls a time when he was five or six and in his family's country house. One night he was frightened by noises and two particular uncles. This memory is part of his vision and relevant here because it shows how much can arise from a small childhood incident, "the apprehension of eternity". It is hearing his uncles pacing the hall of this house "with the patience of a pendulum" that lingers.

There follows a flight of ecstatic visionary writing:

> When chance awakens love, everything takes its place in a man in obedience to that love . . . And now it seems to me that I begin to see what a civilization is. A civilization is a heritage of beliefs, customs, and knowledge, slowly accumulated in the course of centuries . . . [which] open up for a man his inner distance.

St-Exupéry continues, "A civilization that is really strong fills man to the brim . . ." and he gives a profound and simple example; it is this: "There is a density of being in a Dominican at prayer. He is never so much alive as when prostrate and motionless before his God." St Dominic himself, incidentally, used to lie all night at prayer on a stone in the Dominican church of Santa Sabina in Rome. Here, these lines about a man of prayer and a saint are quickly followed by two other particular but different examples of the intensity of a vision. The two other men of vision are Pasteur (mentioned again) "holding his breath over the microscope", and "Cézanne, [who] mute and motionless before his sketch, is an inestimable presence". And now we have the love of silence again which all visionaries share; the man referred to is Cézanne but St-Exupéry intends to apply it to all seers of whatever kind: "He is never more alive than when silent, when feeling and pondering." But the end of this section tells of the world above which St-Exupéry flies, "a world in decomposition".

Part XIII starts with a continuation of this mood, a mood most beautifully expressed:

> All men know where they will sleep when night comes. Ah, but peace dies when the framework is split apart . . . Peace is present when man can see the face that is composed of things that have meaning and are in their place . . .
> But this is war.

The Group of airmen are quartered in various villages now, and Germans seem to be everywhere. There is much action. St-Exupéry and Dutertre see lorries, tumbrils, every kind of thing being packed up. Yet, out of the confusion of war, a prose poem comes. Here is part of it:

> Together, these treasures had made up that greater treasure—a home. By itself, each was valueless; yet they were the objects of a private religion, a family's worship. Each filling its place, they had been made indispensable by habit and beautiful by memory, had been lent price by the sort of fatherland which, together, they constituted.

Even in the middle of grave peril, St-Exupéry can understand such subtle things as these and then put them down with simplicity. He understands perfectly what few recognize—that things become hallowed by use, and also by being held in the memory. He attributes this kind of vision to all men, but all men do not have it. What is important is that he has the magical power to make them seem to us as if they did.

Much action follows and this pilot sees it as pitiful. Evacuation, attempts at escape from the Germans are going on by civilians. An old woman weeps and, we are told she was not weeping for the Group or herself but "crying from exhaustion". Now "Death was a sort of luxury, something like a bit of advice", for the Germans are flying low and shooting incessantly. But St-Exupéry is much more worried about "these workers, these simple people" than his own safety. "How", he asks, "are these people to survive? Man does not eat branches." He sees the death of a "kid" for there is "no milk here. There is only scrap-iron here." Strangely there is no enmity or bitterness in this—only compassion and grief for others.

But St-Exupéry is a pilot in a Group under orders. Again, this section is reminiscent of David Jones with its short sentences, its moments of profound vision, its repeated words. So we have lines like these: "The motor-car. The Army of the East. Western civilization. The chauffeur has been found. England. Bread. What time is it?" This staccato urgency communicates almost the whole of the fall of France to us. It does not matter that Jones's situation was very different, though war was a common factor. What is important is that both fighting visionaries see in the same manner. St-Exupéry is usually much less elliptical, certainly, but he ends Part XIII of this book with words that are far more than simply wise. Here they are: "Treason in our time is a proof of genius. Why, I want to know, are not traitors decorated?" The seer is able to see both sides in this battle, he can enter them and draw great knowledge from entering. What he gives to us in his writing is undoubtedly above war, above all hatred, it is a vision.

Part XIV starts with St-Exupéry's flight to Arras, the title of this book, but only, in that title, is a fleeting glimpse given of what this writing contains. But it is a good one and characteristic of the author that the title should be so simple and direct. At first he feels "peace everywhere" but "this peace, that has become fused with this war, has begun to rot this war". This peace is apathy, defeat and confusion and "spreads apace like a grey leprosy". From the air St-Exupéry sees Germans, French and refugees. Nobody seems to know quite what they are doing. In gentle, most moving words, the writer-pilot tells us that he has seen a dying woman being put into a lorry. He ends this section with three nuns who, making for ". . . God knows what haven invented in a fairy-tale have hustled [off] a dozen children threatened by death". Part XVI moves on in much the same way but, although St-Exupéry says this is not really war, he "will carry on as solemnly as if it were". He will act just like a pilot who has specific instructions, and, though he does not tell us this, like a very brave man.

But he has learnt something more. This is what he has learnt: "I accept death. It is not danger that I accept. It is not combat that I accept. It is death. I have learnt a great truth. War is not the acceptance of danger. It is not the acceptance of combat." The truth is that "for the combatant, it is at certain moments the pure and simple acceptance of death". The word "simple" used here is of great importance.

In Part XVII, St-Exupéry returns to childhood memories, memories which rarely escape from him but are an essential part of his total vision of life. He tries to recall his earliest memory and it seems to be one of a Tyrolian governess; but she is more than a memory; she is "the memory of a memory". Recollections of his talks with this governess are interspersed with description and with people telling the author to fire on the enemy and so we get clear though compressed passages such as this:

> Paula [the governess] knew everything.
> "Captain, they are beginning to fire" ...
> Clouds at two thousand three hundred. Well. Nothing to be done about it. What astonishes me is that beneath my cloud-bank the world is not black, as I had thought it would be. It is blue. Marvellously blue. Twilight has come, and all the plain is blue. Here and there I see rain falling. Rain-blue.

The pilot is caught up in his vision, for him there is no war at all, at least for many intervals, for we quickly have talk like this:

> Interesting, that the road to eternity should be ziz-zag. And so peaceful. The earth here looks like an orchard ... There are trees, some standing isolated, others in clusters. You meet them. And green fields. And houses with red tile roofs and people out of doors. And lovely blue showers pouring all round them.

Throughout this section, St-Exupéry at the dials of his plane is at one with St-Exupéry recalling his childhood. He says, at another point: "Strange, how of a sudden, life has collected in a heap. I have packed up my memories." Soon he sees Arras in flames but this sight is closely woven with the pilot's childhood fairy stories and so he says, "Like that knight, I ride in the blue of the evening towards my castle of flame: and not for the first time". But St-Exupéry soon realizes that complete defeat is at hand and he ends Part XVII thus: "Where now is my vulnerability? Unknown to myself I had been hoping . . ."

Part XVII runs straight into Part XVIII and its first words are, "Despite my lack of altitude I had been hoping". Then come these important lines; they are important because they explain the reasons for St-Exupéry's conception of the way he has been writing: "I had escaped into a memory of early childhood in order to recapture the sense of sovereign protection." Now, in defeated France, he realizes that "for man there is no protection". The writer sees clearly the whole situation "at the heart of the German zone", where he now is. And so he admits his vulnerability, though his courage, vision and reflections on all that is going on never cease. He considers the prospect of his imminent death, and likens himself to a prisoner about to be executed: "You are sentenced: a penalty hangs over you; but the gaol in which you are locked up continues silent . . . Every second that drops is like the one that went before. There is no reason why the second about to drop should change the world. Such a task is too heavy for a single second. Each second that follows safeguards your silence. Already this silence seems perpetual." Then comes this simple, ominous line printed by itself: "But the step of him who must come sounds in the corridor."

He is not, however, shot down. He is still flying. The land has come to life with firing and St-Exupéry asks himself, "Why this sudden springtime of arms?" and later declares, "A nation of jugglers had burst into dance". More simple and expressive imagery follows: "I flew threatened by a vast and dizzying flutter of knitting needles." And he ends Part XVIII with these words: "I raised my head and stared. What I saw was without appeal."

Part XIX continues with this hazardous fighting and opens, "I had been looking on at a carnival of light". St-Exupéry asks Dutertre if they will get through this gun-fire and they both joke about it. The writer has wonderful imagery for all this horror; when the roaring noise stops, the plane's sound is "Like a sigh, almost". When they are "squarely hit by a shell fragment", he says, "The tiger does not do a messy job on the ox it brings down. The tiger sinks its claws into the ox without skidding." To sustain this visionary state of mind amidst such danger seems very close to a miracle. St-Exupéry also continues his reflections on life as a pilot which also widen out into considerations about life in general. So, he declares, "I used to wonder as I was dressing for a sortie what a man's last moments were like. And each time, life would give the lie to the ghosts I evoked." He remembers how he has thought of life in terms of the body, something that has to be taken to the tailor or the surgeon. But now that " 'This is me' " has become an "illusion: and "Your true name [and this means himself] is duty, hatred, love, child, theorem. There is no other you than this."

The following passage reminds one of Gabriel Marcel's Christian Existentialism and also of Hopkins's line, "What I do is me, for that I came". So war and wounds "strip away the flesh and reveal a man's true spirit". The nearer we approach the end of *Flight to Arras* the more visionary philosophy (that is the only name for it) we are given. And St-Exupéry constantly returns to the most vivid memories of his childhood. The child merges into the man in this writing which seems so simple but which is telling us about such complex matters. "Man does not die", says the writer. "Man imagines that it is death he fears but what he fears is the unforeseen, the explosion." And he adds, "There is no death when you meet death . . . I have never known a man to think of himself when dying. Never."

Violent activity goes on and St-Exupéry feels he is "running the plane into a bronze wall". He wonders if he and his crew will "last out" the bombardment. They are not hurt and now come the words, "Shock, relief. Fear, the intermediate step, was missing." Yet St-Exupéry's gas and oil tanks were "pierced". "Otherwise we seemed to be sound", he says. Amazingly, he manages to climb over the blazing Arras, Arras which is "glowing dark red like iron on the anvil". Arras also seems like "a lamp in the nave of a cathedral . . . burning in the service of a cult, but at a price".

St-Exupéry tells us now that there are still "many things [he] was going to find out about". His coolness, courage and above all, his curiosity in these dreadful circumstances, are almost incredible. Part XIX ends with a very natural irritability on the part of St-Exupéry. He is annoyed at the prospect of being questioned about the details of his flight and writes, "Intelligence is Dutertre's business, not mine". His business, he tells us, is "flames, villages burning". But this is not what the questioning major wants. So Part XX begins with a comparison of such questioning with a school examination. St-Exupéry feels that he will "flunk [a slang word for fail] like a schoolboy standing before all the class at a blackboard".

Here, most touchingly *and* courageously, the writer is prepared, willingly prepared, to admit his human weakness. But he is so akin to joy and exaltation in that he still feels like a "flood of affection" and declares, "I am like a housewife whose shopping is done and who is on her way home, her mind on the savoury dinner with which she is about to delight her family". St-Exupéry's vision of simplicity is always a sharing, as this image, and so many earlier ones, reveal. He has reached the rare point where a vision can be continually handed over in the most homely language; but we have seen under and between his lines, the effort and will-power which have been necessary to achieve such a vision of the world. And, also, we can always see suffering not spoken of to his comrades, suffering and anguish. No vision such as St-Exupéry's and David Jones's can be reached without these, for their visions are, in essence, religious, brimful of charity and self-effacement.

Very soon, he is in the air again, flying through a "pallid prison of cloud". The very air seems to St-Exupéry to be "heavy with conspiracy". The ground beneath is not friendly at all; at any second, shells may rise. While flying through a cloud, however, the writer is able to reflect on the nature of his relationships with other airmen. He finds some of their ways with each other strange; what is intended to be amicable often has the reverse effect, and so he concludes, "Truly the human heart is indeed unfathomable". With his Group, he begins the flight back from Arras. He writes that "We in France all but died of intelligence unsupported by substance". One airman in particular is seen in a shining light—Gavoille who "exists. He loves, hates, rejoices, complains. He is shaped and heightened by the strands woven together and constituting his being."

But St-Exupéry is dreading the questions he will be asked (those questions which make him feel like a schoolboy nervous at an examination) when he lands by the major, who is Alias. This does not happen in Part XX. What St-Exupéry feels and imparts to us is a new sense of fellowship with the other men. The last words of this section keep repeating "I am part of" various comrades who are named, and also "I am part of my country, and it of me". This last line shows a very deep patriotism, perhaps something which rises above patriotism as we commonly think of it. It is a loving kindness, a great generosity of spirit.

In Part XXI, St-Exupéry speaks of Major Alias with gratitude

216

and writes that it was he who drove all of them not towards victory, which was impossible, but towards self-fulfilment. He will not take credit for any of this himself. He means by "self-fulfilment" being bound to his inherited qualities ("the springs at my roots") and "to the mob on the highways". He says emphatically that he has become "one of the mob" and "down out of the clouds". Yet what he has seen and felt in the clouds in *Wind, Sand and Stars* as well as in *Flight to Arras* is still valid. A little later, St-Exupéry says "We had grown old in the upper altitudes" and that he had learnt there more than he could have learnt "in ten years in a monastery"; this writer has not, after all, got a vocation for the monastic life. There are other ways of learning about God, others, and oneself than in a monastery. St-Exupéry actually calls the air in which he has seen such visions, "ten years in a monastery". He no longer feels ill at ease with the major; he is part of "the communion of the spirit with the Group". And now the writer utters these very important words "Welcome home from our sortie ready for our silent reward. Its quality is unique, for it is the quality of love." This "veritable love" is "a web woven of strands in which we are fulfilled".

In Part XXII, St-Exupéry, with others, returns to his billet which is a farmhouse where a farmer and his family make much of the men. When the farmer hands round bread, the writer thinks that this may be the last time he will share his food (for the Group do not know where they are going next) and so it is "like an act of worship". He has "learnt to see in bread the essential vessel of compassion for it is bread that is distributed to the miserable". There is no doubt at all that St-Exupéry is thinking of Christian charity, of Christ multiplying the loaves and fishes, and of the Blessed Sacrament itself.

Part XXII is visionary throughout, in different ways. The wind is written of and St-Exupéry says, "The wind in the grain is the caress to the spouse [the farmer's wife], it is the hand of peace stroking her hair". And, almost at the end of this section he says these things, speaking of the way in which his Group had earlier volunteered for service in Norway and Finland:

What were Norway and Finland I used to wonder, to the soldiers and petty officers of France? . . . in some confused way those men were volunteering to die in a human cause symbolized by mental images of snow and Christmas sleigh-bells . . . Had we of France meant a kind of Christmas to the world, the world would have been saved through our being . . . Each is responsible for all . . . Each man bears the sins of all men.

Seldom before has St-Exupéry's vision appeared so openly a Christian one; his experience is like that of a Christian mystic. He has, as it were, now fully revealed himself.

And he opens Part XXIII, the penultimate section, by carrying straight on from those last words in Part XXII; he says "who would call this a creed for the weak?" And he also says, with great simplicity, "I know the meaning of humility. It is not self-disparagement. It is the motive power of action." Now we must examine the philosophical statements which St-Exupéry expresses throughout this section.

He is concerned with Man (he uses the capital letter often, although not always) and with civilization. He declares, "What is true of wheat is true also of a civilization. Wheat nourishes man, but man in turn preserves wheat from extinction by storing up its seed." The fall of France has finally shown him that his "civilization had ceased to be radiant energy". He confesses that he has used the word "Democracy . . . without the least notion that, in respect of the qualities and destiny of Man, I was merely giving expression to an aggregate of wishes and not an aggregate of principles." We know that the very fact that St-Exupéry can say this and many of the things to follow, *and* from what he has seen in his visions presented in both these books, that he has never been deceived. Nonetheless, to have his ideals set out so clearly is of immense value, for men such as he are rare beings.

He blames himself far too much, but this is his humility. Thus, after speaking of the fighting over Arras, he writes, "Because Man inhabited me I had flown homeward to the Group "with the feeling that he was "hurrying to a fire in a hearth". He then asks himself if he was looking for "a sign". Now comradeship enters as a vital factor in all human life, a comradeship which is the very heart of Christian charity. After a beautifully simple

218

image of "two fishermen hailing each other from bark to bark"
he speaks of his strong sense of "the existence of a miraculous
relationship". Then comes the line, "Man, the common denomi-
nator of peoples and nations."

This is more like *The Mystical Body of Christ* than Communism; St-Exupéry loves everyone for their individuality. He
says, a little later on, "My civilization has sought through the
ages to reveal Man to men, as it might have taught us to per-
ceive the cathedral in a mere heap of stones". Now this visionary is speaking of what men share, what they have in common,
and this is not a denial, rather an affirmation, of their individuality. He knows that man was created in the image of God unlike
everything else in Creation; what he shares is a glorious thing
and it is what enables him to love others—their common man-
hood, so simple yet so complex.

And here we come to the Christian revelation seen by St-
Exupéry, lived by him:

> Man was created in the image of God. God was revered in man
> [through Christ by the Redemption]. Men were brothers in
> God . . . It was the contemplation of God that created men who
> were equal, for it was in God that they were equal.

And in clear, soaring words, the writer tells us that man's

> equality in the rights of God—*rights that are inherent in the
> individual* [my italics]—forbade the putting of obstacles in the
> way of the ascension of the individual; and I understand why.
> God had chosen to adopt the individual as His path.

Now with boldness and also a pure, calm assurance, St-
Exupéry is handing to us totally what his lessons, his sufferings
and his visions have shown him. As St Thomas Aquinas said,
"The fruits of contemplation are to be handed on to others".
St-Exupéry, again using beautifully simple examples such as
what the scientist owes to the stoker, speaks of the rights of
men, rights which are due to their dignity as men; he says "the
love of God founded relations of dignity between men . . . As
the inheritor of God, my civilization founded the respect of man
present in every individual."

And now St-Exupéry speaks openly and delightedly of what

he has learnt and suffered, understood. The passages which come at this point are both a litany and a prose poem; paragraph after paragraph begins with "I understand"; here are some of them:

> I understand the profound meaning of the humility exacted from the individual. Humility did not cast down the individual, it raised him up.

> I understand, finally, why the love of God created men responsible for one another and gave them hope as a virtue.

> I understand by this bright light the meaning of liberty . . . It is like a favourable wind. Only by the grace of the wind is the bark free on the waters.
> A man built in this wise disposes of the power of the tree.

And then, like all great and good men, St-Exupéry blames himself for much that is really not his fault at all. This is always the way with visionaries, but such visionaries are rare in modern times. The writer goes on to say that his own civilization had "expended a good share of its genius . . . to preserve the cult of a Prince revealed in the existence of individual men . . ." He praises the Humanism "of the Renaissance and after", for what this "Humanism preached was Man". Then he finds himself momentarily at a loss to define Man by his qualities. But he is soon brimming over with ideas again; speaking of "a country, of a group, of a craft, of a civilization", St-Exupéry says that we can only "clothe ourselves in these higher things" if we begin by creating them within ourselves". Now he writes two sentences deliberately on one line as they are vital: "The essential act possesses a name. It is sacrifice."

Only by sacrifice can Man achieve anything, and when St-Exupéry's civilization "leant upon God it was able to preserve the notion of sacrifice whereby God is created in the hearts of men". But something has gone dangerously wrong and "Instead of affirming the rights of man present in the individual we had begun to talk about the rights of the collectivity". And also sacrifice, the principle of sacrifice which "We still vaguely remember" is alone what "differentiates us from the ant-hill and . . . is the source of the grandeur of mankind".

So, men have taught and promulgated the wrong concepts of liberty and, "As for charity, we have not even dared to go on preaching it". Briefly men have "forgotten both God and Man". We sense the disillusionment in St-Exupéry now. He is profoundly unhappy that men, including himself, have misunderstood charity, the greatest virtue of all, and he says unreservedly that because of this "Man became lost to us". But then he praises "fraternity", which is part of charity, and, with profound feeling, says "We ceased to *give* [my italics]". The words pour forth now:

> Where will I find that rush of love that will compensate my death? Men die for a home, not for walls and tables. Men die for a cathedral, not for stones . . . Men die only for that by which they live.

St-Exupéry in this whole section is not preaching a sermon; he is presenting us with what he has himself learnt through suffering and seeing. His vision enables him to see and understand very clearly. "Collectivity" is man's ruin, and only while "our true civilization . . . still sent forth its dying rays" was man saved. But collectivity is "anarchy" and the reason is this: "They [the anarchists] preached the right of the Mass. The formula cannot satisfy; for if it is intolerable that a single man tyrannize a Mass, it is equally intolerable that the Mass oppress a single man." With a heartrending sorrow, St-Exupéry declares that "The faithful of that new religion [all tyrannies] would object to several miners risking their lives to save a single man entombed, for in that case the rock pile would be injured".

From his vision, St-Exupéry has brought to our times a purity of faith in man and in love. He speaks firmly, he includes himself in those who have ruined, or tried to ruin, our true civilization which means the destiny of every individual man, a destiny which must be honoured and reverenced. But St-Exupéry has not lost another great Christian virtue—namely, Hope, for he cries out,

> I am the stronger provided I am able to find myself . . . I am the stronger because the tree is stronger than the materials of which it is composed . . . I am the stronger because only my

civilization possesses the power to bind into its unity all diversity without depriving any element of its individuality.

St-Exupéry tells us that "Arras unsealed my eyes". But he was never blind; in *Wind, Sand and Stars*, the vision was different in degree, not in kind. The exaltation which this pilot felt in the solitude of the night skies was simply a forerunner of the desolation in the desert and later in the fall of France. In *Flight to Arras* we see the fullness of the vision, the darkness has passed, and now, whatever suffering may come, the light shines and spreads in this man's words. And it spreads to all who read it. St-Exupéry never preaches, never gives us a religious tract, he hands on the truth about life as he sees it so clearly but which other men glimpse only dimly or fitfully. Now we have almost reached the end of *Flight to Arras*.

St-Exupéry reverences both the particular and the universal, the individual and the general. We need to read him closely in this penultimate section (the last one is very brief, a coda really) to understand exactly how he separates and evaluates these things. This is not because he writes obscurely but because his subtle distinctions are written with such a fervent simplicity. So he writes,

> I believe that the cult of the universal exalts and heightens our particular riches, and founds the sole veritable order, which is the order of life. A tree is an object of order, despite the diversity of its roots and branches.

We need to note here that every tree is an individual, particular tree; this is St-Exupéry's meaning. We see this with great clarity when we read the following words: "I believe that the cult of the particular is the cult of death, *for it founds its order upon likeness* [my italics]. It mistakes identity of parts for unity of Being."

These wonderful words now come:

> By my gift of blood over Arras I recreated the love that I feel for my kind as the mother creates the breast by the gift of her milk ... To create love, we must begin by sacrifice.

St-Exupéry also says that "I came back from Arras, having woven my ties with my farmer's family". Here is the shining particular from which the writer has been able to widen and deepen his vision. So now he writes, "I feel the need of a simple Credo so that I may remember". We know of his passionate belief in liberty; the last tenet of his "Credo" is this:

> I believe that what my civilization calls charity is the sacrifice granted Man for the purpose of his own fulfilment. Charity is the gift made to Man present in the insignificance of the individual. It creates Man.

And, finally in Part XXII, St-Exupéry says this: "I shall fight for Man. Against Man's enemies—but against myself as well." Those last five words both sum up the writer's vision and tell us yet again, but also more adamantly, of his essential humility.

And so we come to the extremely brief Part XXIV, the coda to *Flight to Arras*. It is entirely devoted to preparation for flight as St-Exupéry's Group get ready to take off. He himself is half-asleep but when he becomes wide-awake, he remembers his old governess again and writes, "Had air squadrons been issued with Tyrolian nurse-maids we should have been put to bed long ago". Orders are carried out but the men know they are defeated and their spokesman, their seer, ends his book with these words: "The defeated have no right to speak. No more right to speak than has the seed."

But St-Exupéry has told everything, and everything is a vision handed on to us. It seems peculiarly fitting that in 1943, in a reconnaissance flight over the Mediterranean, he vanished. It is thought that his plane was shot down by a German fighter. So the silence this visionary so often thought of and loved came to him in this slightly mysterious way. He disappeared and nobody has ever been sure precisely how. But his vision, all he wanted to say, was finished, and it is preserved for us, rests in our speculations and imaginations.

VII

BORIS PASTERNAK

A Vision from Behind Barriers

During the last few decades a new sort of poetry has risen; it is the poetry of the imprisoned, the work of those who have lost their freedom because of their refusal to conform to the political tenets of Soviet Russia. There are many such people, women as well as men, but not all are articulate. The greatest of the articulate ones is undoubtedly Boris Pasternak who was unable to accept the Nobel Prize for his living classic, *Dr Zhivago*, a novel which has come over into the free world and been translated into countless languages.

I choose Pasternak as a writer in this sort of predicament not simply because he is a great writer but because he is a visionary one, and since his vision is most evident in his poems, it is those which I intend to examine.

One or two things need to be said about all the available poems written by those who have shared, or are sharing, Pasternak's anguish. Firstly, their work is full of words about love and the beauty of the natural world and, secondly, there is never any self-pity. In utter darkness, these brave people manage to see a chink of light. But Pasternak saw more than that; he created a radiant world, often employing Christian subjects.

There have been prisoners in the past who have written out to and for the liberated world but it is this century which has produced the political prisoner and the genius who creates a world within what seems from outside such a narrow, such a narrow, such a circumscribed place. In a sense, then, the modern visionary writer is something entirely new and Pasternak was the forerunner. Out of all his mental and physical afflictions, out of his vivid appraisal of the evil into which his homeland had sunk, he brought a vision, turned it into poetry and gave it to us, the apparently free.

But Pasternak knew, and this is a very important part of his whole outlook, that none of us is completely free; all of us are bound by anxieties of one sort or another, we are all troubled, though only the honest will admit this. Pasternak, however, wrote out of extremity, just as David Jones did in *In Parenthesis*, and since both men were geniuses, they saw beyond the moment; they dealt with the vital and the immediate yet also saw it transcended. What they saw is what we read in their work.

We must understand the special difficulties of anyone who writes under stress, who holds views quite other than those of the official ones of his country and yet refuses to give in to those views. This gives his work an added tension, an increased urgency. If the writer is a visionary, nothing will stop him transcribing what he sees and hoping that, eventually, what he writes will be read by others who have freedom but—and this is of crucial importance—not the knowledge of that vision of the world from which it springs. The vision is a world of its own but it arises from a particular place and time in modern history. A visionary's mind is *never* imprisoned but he is a man of flesh and blood and all his senses contribute towards formulating the making of the world that is far more than the world of his imagination. Perhaps we might recall here that St John of the Cross's mystical writings were written in prison. However, apart from the Christian religious character and subject-matter of many of Pasternak's poems, the two writers bear no other resemblance.

From a writer who is under great stress, one might expect some sign of desperation, even of bitterness, to appear in his work. With Pasternak, there are neither of these things; if there were, they would be blemishes in his writing because one can never separate moral from critical questions when one is discussing writers. The whole man must be considered, since it is from the complete person that the vision experienced arises.

So it is not from imprisonment, the loss of liberty and the

most delicate human rights that dark visions come, or embitter-
ment. On the contrary, in great writers the way in which they
are circumscribed intensifies their genius; diamonds shine most
brightly in complete darkness. Here is part of a love poem called
Meeting by Pasternak which shows not only close observation
but a great compassion :

> A lock of bright hair
> Lights up your face,
> Your kerchief,
> Your figure and your shabby coat.
> . . . . .
> And in my heart the humility of
> > your expression
> Will remain forever,
> And now the hard heart of the world
> Is not my business.

Tenderness transcends "the hard heart of the world", for the
poet but it is a tenderness won from suffering and from caring
deeply about other people. In a most strange paradoxical way,
the régime under which Pasternak had to live made him more
vulnerable to the tragedies of the world, yet also able to treasure
the great beauties of it. So his vision is, in the last resort, a joyful one; he has seen and thought deeply enough to realize that
wonder and love and natural beauty are more important and
lasting than anything a particular ideology can impose on a man
who insists on his freedom, an inward freedom which nothing
can touch or tarnish.

There is no savagery in Pasternak's poems and no disillusionment either. He is a writer placed in an extreme situation but
able to face it, accept it and make great literature out of it. Great
writers have often been in extreme situations in the past but no
such situation is ever quite like any other; objectively, the man
who is behind the Iron Curtain and must exist there, although
he disagrees with everything which it stands for, is in a uniquely
contemporary situation. All places of suffering are different,
whether they are Calvary or Buchenwald. Words from men
who are totally at odds with all that Russian Communism means
send out, almost miraculously, messages of hope and affirmation.

They cannot literally be likened to the dove who carries the olive branch—what *outer* peace can they truthfully offer?—but they most assuredly resemble pigeons who carry messages of affirmation. Always, with Boris Pasternak, this is so.

The sadness we find in Pasternak's love poems is as much the sadness of the loved one as his own. It is a poetry of loss but also a poetry of personal relationships. Its very spareness makes it all the more poignant. *Parting* contains these lines:

> She was as near and dear to him
> In every feature
> As the shores are close to the sea
> In every breaker.

This poem would be too personal, too heartbreaking were not the poet able to use such an image as this. A stanza from *August* shows the same power to generalize loss, but it need hardly be said that there would never have been this profound grief had there not once been supreme joy. So *August's* penultimate stanza is this:

> Goodbye, timeless years
> And woman who challenged
> The abyss of humiliations,
> I am your battlefield.

But it is Pasternak's specifically religious poems which hold the unbreakable vision of his joy. The Communists had the knowledge to see this and what it portended, but they never had the wisdom to understand these lines from *Christmas Star*. I think it was fear that made them scorn them. Why, otherwise, should they wish to suppress this great writer's work. These are the lines:

> In a strange vision all time to come
> Arose in the distance.
> All the thoughts, hopes, worlds of the centuries,
> The future of art galleries and museums,
> All the pranks of goblins and deeds of magicians,
> All the Christmas trees and all the children's dreams ...

Here was something too fundamental for the leaders of the Soviet régime to accept. Their intellects were not sufficiently poisoned or frozen to see the power of this kind of visionary writing; on the contrary, they *did* recognize it and understood what it might do to people, their own, those minds they had already tried to trammel and condition. And so their only way out was to suppress Pasternak's work, to withdraw it from the eyes and minds of others; it was genuine fright which made them do this since they were not even sure just how much they had conditioned their people to utter materialism. First, the writer suffered, and then the people from whom his work was withdrawn. But no true vision can be withdrawn for long; human beings are adept at picking locks, especially locks which lead them to freedom of spirit and body. All the materialism in the world contains a candle lighted by someone, who may be anonymous, but who understands through his own life that "man cannot live by bread alone".

Pasternak always used strictly rhythmical and often classical poetic forms for his poems, though the best translations, the ones which gave the truest idea of his mind, emotions and character are, in general, best translated into freer forms; these make fine English poems while, at the same time, they retain the Russian atmosphere.

Pasternak wrote several books of verse before his great novel, *Dr Zhivago*, but it was that novel which brought his name before the world and his acceptance and then refusal of the Nobel Prize for Literature. He died in 1960 at the age of 70. The most finely chiselled as well as the most visionary poems which Pasternak wrote are those associated with his great novel, but there are many other poems, written, perhaps, under less stress but containing and showing forth the most delicate perceptions. His sister, Lydia Pasternak, who had also translated her brother's poems, considers that *Themes and Variations* "consolidated Pasternak's reputation as a great poet". These must be looked at with consummate care.

Themes and Variations was written between 1918 and 1919. A short poem of three four-line stanzas called *Stars Were Racing* ends

> Sea-breeze from Morocco touched the water,
> Simooms blew. In snowdrifts snored Archangel.
> Candles swam; the rough draft of 'The Prophet'
> Slowly dried, and dawn broke on the Ganges.

Here the poet is looking far beyond his own tormented country. Nor is he enclosed in the prison of his own mind; he is both entering the outer world, the world beyond politics and ideologies, and also giving us adumbrations of a vision which was, under great suffering, to be transcribed later.

Always, like David Jones in this, Pasternak is aware of the changing seasons, the wonder of the stars. So, in a volume called *The Vastness of Earth*, a poem called *Spring, 1944*, gives us these lines:

> A dreamer and a half-night-ponderer,
> Moscow I love with all my power.
> Here is the source of all the wonderful
> With which the centuries will flower.

The translation is not altogether successful but it shows us one very important factor in all Pasternak's later poems—the complete lack of bitterness, the patriotism towards a country which he remembered under a very different régime. But no stones are thrown at the present rulers; bitterness, anyway, is always the death of the possibility of great poetry. Euphoria too is unfitting; it is unreal, cannot last. Pasternak's ecstasies are always in control, at least when they are turned into art to be handed over to us.

This great man also wrote poems for children—always a very difficult task—and a special gift. *Fairy Tale*, though not written for children, has a fairy tale quality, especially in its opening stanza:

> Once, in times forgotten
> In a fairy place,
> Through the steppe, a rider
> Made his way apace.

There is wonder here and the reader's excitement is aroused.

My Sister Life appeared in Russia as early as 1917 and was received with great enthusiasm. One of the poems from this book, entitled *About These Poems*, adumbrates that unique mixture of joy combined with the knowledge that all things are passing and must pass that is unique in this period of Pasternak's life. But *About These Poems* contains more carefree gaiety than most of his work:

The attic will repeat my themes
And bow to winter with my lines,
And send leapfrogging to the beams
Bad luck and oddities and signs.

Here, the vision is wholly sunlit.

The especial vision of Boris Pasternak arises, almost always, out of Christian faith, human love transcended and the beauty of the natural world. There is certainly wide enough scope in these subjects. But his first book, which contains poems written between 1912 and 1914, before the Russian Revolution, there are also poems of place. At this time, Pasternak was a free man, able to travel. About *Venice*, he writes:

Reality was born of dream-shreds
Far-off, among the hired boats
Like a Venetian woman, Venice
Dived from the bank to glide afloat.

There is an acute visual sense evident in this and something else which is even more important. I mean that the poet does not just write a vivid descriptive piece about this famous city; he sees beyond it. From his earliest writings, we can see the visionary in Pasternak; whatever he touches he transmutes: he is a true alchemist.

His next book, *Over the Barriers*, (1914–16) contains poems which show his love of natural beauty and the seasons; a fragment entitled *Spring* gives us these lines, memorable in their fine translation:

And the air, in the oblique
Interlace of twigs and birds, is
Naked, weightless and unique.

Like Hopkins, Pasternak saw deeply into the individuality of everything. He becomes almost ecstatic in *The Swifts*, which also comes from *Over the Barriers*:

There is not a thing that could stop them, up there,
From shrilly, exultedly [sic] crying,
Exclaiming: The earth has vanished off to nowhere,
O look It has vanished—O triumph!

The poet is able to identify himself completely with these birds; his spirit soars with their flight. Their beauty uplifts his heart.

If Pasternak is to be seen as the Nobel Prize Winner who was forced to refuse his prize, we can, by this very act, understand him better. His vision becomes more powerful sheerly on account of the necessity of his refusal. Marxism has no sympathy with the personal or the sublime. So, although *Dr Zhivago* was the banned book, the poems are a gift handed on to us, whether they are the poems which arose from that book or other, earlier ones.

God is in Pasternak's poems, great human love is there, and also a great understanding of seasons, climates, and both the plant and the animal kingdoms. From scientific facts, these latter poems assume a vision, observed by him, transmuted by his imagination, and then handed to us. So now we must look at more of his poems. The next poem concerned with natural beauty which must be considered appears in *My Sister Life*. This book appeared in the summer of 1917 and the poem entitled *Thunderstorm, instantaneous forever* deserves especial attention. Its last stanza is this:

> Then the crumbling mind began to
> Blink; it seemed it would be floodlit
> Even in those distant corners
> Where the light is now intense.

This sort of writing has more of the loving observer's attitude than the man who willingly steeps himself in something. Light to Pasternak is of immense importance; it is nearly always both an inner and an outer one. In *Stars Were Racing*, which appears in the same volume as the poem above, the heightened sense of place and of history appear in the following lines:

> Darkened were the bedrooms; thoughts were racing,
> And the Sphinx was listening to the desert.
> . . . . .
> Sea-breeze from Morocco touched the water.
> Simooms blew. In snowdrifts snored Archangel.
> Candles swam; the rough draft of 'The Prophet'
> Slowly dried, and dawn broke on the Ganges.

Always light or half-light is present in the poems of this period. But Pasternak is not simply interested in the places he mentions for their own sake; they are not separate from each other but linked by the illumination of his knowledge and understanding. More important still, they and all they speak of are illuminated by a visionary's imagination.

I want to return to *Poems for Children* because here, in a poem called *The Roundabouts*, Pasternak shows his ability to identify himself completely with the innocence of childhood. The last stanza runs:

> Whirlwinds fill the roof-umbrella
> Spinning on a centre-prop;
> Slower circles the propellor,
> Slower, slower, slower, stop.

The poet has retained the joyfulness of childhood and here we have an enchanting example of it.

It is timely now to return to the *Dr Zhivago* poems and, in particular, to a poem called *Evil Days* where, without the faintest hint of blasphemy, Pasternak identifies himself with Christ himself:

> And Jesus remembered in the desert,
> The days in the wilderness spent,
> The tempting with power by Satan,
> That lofty, majestic descent.

Pasternak is caught up in a pure Christian vision. He speaks of Christ thinking of his first miracle at Cana—the turning of water into wine at a marriage feast—but he ends his poem with something all Christians have wondered about—namely, the raising of Lazarus from the dead:

> How, startled, the candle-flame guttered,
> When Lazarus rose from the dead . . .

All Christians are left with faith and hope but also with a longing to know what the after-life was like. In a few words, Pasternak recognizes and records this. In *Mary Magdalene*, he equates himself with the sinful woman who was forgiven by Christ and became a great saint. In gratitude, she says, in this poem:

> O what might not have been my fate
> By now, my teacher and my saviour,
> Did not eternity await
> Me at the table, as a late
> New victim of my past behaviour!

Her faith in Christian and in eternal life is complete; so, to express her overwhelming feelings, she pours precious ointment from an alabaster vase over Christ's head.

In the poem entitled *In Holy Week* we have an even closer view of Pasternak's Christian faith. Again he makes the whole scene and the Apostles come to life before one's eyes. Of the latter, he writes,

> Their alarm
> Is understandable.
> Gardens burst through fences,
> The earth's foundations quake:
> God is being buried.

The quiet awe about these lines communicates Pasternak's sense of the numinous, of his very close relationship with God, directly to us. The poem ends on a note of faith,

> ... as soon as the weather changes
> Death can be vanquished
> Through the travail of the Resurrection.

The Resurrection entails "travail" because of Christ's Agony in the Garden, his betrayal by St Peter and, most of all, by the Crucifixion which preceded it. Pasternak sees the drama but he is never melodramatic or rhetorical; the whole situation has a timelessness for him because, with faith and hope, there is no time.

In his *Dr Zhivago* love poems, Pasternak also moves beyond time though he always gives us exquisite details. So in *Meeting*, we have these lines:

> The snow is wet on your lashes
> There is pain in your eyes.
> You are engraved on my heart
> With a chisel dipped in acid.

The poet is moved by the "humility" of the expression on the face of the woman he loves; it fills him with awe. But he ends this poem with a question. Always he wants to know what life, every aspect of it means:

> But who are we, where do we come from,
> When of all those years
> Nothing but idle talk is left
> And we are nowhere in the world?

There is the sense of nothingness, the "nothingness, the "nada" of St John of the Cross, though with Pasternak the love is human. But his humanity is always clothed with an almost divine compassion.

To maintain this sense of closeness of God, to understand Christian doctrines, to write down his vision both of specifically religious subjects and of his love of Nature is a very great triumph. We are fortunate, indeed, that despite all the limitations of the Iron Curtain, they have come through to us and been rendered into such fine English translations.

We should return to the religious poems and examine the beautiful, long, for Pasternak, *Christmas Star*. It has a detail and a simplicity that are almost sometimes more like a painting than a poem. Here are the poem's closing lines, where one feels the poet's presence,

> Out of all the great gather Mary allowed
> Only the Wise Men through the opening in the rock.
>
> He slept in the oak manger,
> Radiant as moonlight in the hollow of a tree
> Instead of a sheepskin,
> The lips of the ass and the nostrils of the ox kept him warm
>
> The Magi stood in the shadow,
> Whispering, scarcely finding words,
> All at once a hand stretched out of the dark,
> Moved one of them aside to the left of the manger.
> He looked round. Gazing at the Virgin from the doorway
> Like a guest, was the Christmas Star.

The sense of wonder here mingled with complete simplicity of approach is very wonderful. Not only the Christmas Star but Pasternak also, we feel, is the guest. Holiness surrounds this poem. The great awe a man feels in the presence of God loses none of its decorum for being so simply expressed; on the contrary, it gains from it. We may, perhaps, think for a moment of Eliot's *Journey of the Magi* but there is a great difference between the two poems. In Pasternak's poem, the poet has entered the past, triumphed over time, and given us far more than a beautiful description. He has, momentarily, had a vision, a very concrete one, of the journey of the Three Kings to the Christ Child, and himself taken part in their visit. In Eliot's poem, on the other hand, the poet is not felt as a presence at all: he is giving a beautiful account of an event in the life of God-made-Man but he himself does not appear upon the scene at all.

The Miracle is a very important poem. It is about Christ walking from Bethany to Jerusalem "with the sadness of presentiment" (almost certainly of The Agony in the Garden, The Betrayal by Judas, and The Crucifixion. For as man, these are terrible things for the God-made-Man). Everything around him seems bitter. And Pasternak writes, after telling us that Christ is walking to meet his disciples,

> He was sunk so deep in his thoughts,
> The dejected field began to smell of wormwood.
> Everything was still; he stood in the middle,
> > alone.
>
> . . . . .
>
> Everything got mixed up: the heat and the desert,
> The lizards, springs and streams.

This is the heart of desolation. Pasternak is going through The Dark Night of the Soul, but he is not describing it in the first person; he is telling us that Christ knew this state and that all who follow him deeply must know a little of his suffering,

Christ speaks to a fig tree, thus:

> What joy have I of you?
> Of what profit are you, standing there like a post?
> I thirst and hunger and you are barren,

> And meeting you is comfortless as granite.
> How untalented you are, and how disappointing!
> Such you shall remain till the end of time.

The tree trembles, and it seems that "The laws of nature would have intervened". Now Pasternak enters as far as any man can into the terrible loneliness of Christ, but he does not lose hope, for the poems ends,

> But a miracle is a miracle, a miracle is God.
> When we are all confusion,
> That instant it finds us out.

At the lowest depths of a man's suffering, Pasternak is saying, if he has faith a miracle will rescue him, he will discover light and joy. It is clear that Pasternak experienced this himself and, from the experience, made one of his finest poems.

Evil Days follows *In Holy Week* in mood very closely. It is about several events in the life of Christ but does not follow the chronological sequel in the *Gospels*. It begins by revealing to us the God-made-Man's entry into Jerusalem on Palm Sunday but after that it reminds us of the Christ's miracle at the marriage feast at Cana and then of Satan's temptation of him. Pasternak presents his vision of these things in this way because he is showing us all these events going through Christ's mind; in the second stanza, he says, "Now was the epilogue, the end". We read of "The Pharisees seeking proofs" who "Fawned on him like foxes". Then come these lines:

> And the dark forces in the temple
> Delivered him to the mob for judgement.

Pasternak becomes one with the whole life of Christ, most especially with his suffering.

Pasternak, with awe not blasphemy, identifies himself completely with Christ's suffering. He knows that his own is nothing compared with the perfect Man who is also God, but this is the unique and only way in which he can express his vision, his utter openness to God. As in the poem just examined, Christ again is shown to be remembering the past. Now, in the bitterest hours, Pasternak puts these words into his mouth:

236

> He now remembered like a dream
> The flight to Egypt and his childhood.

Such touches are most subtle and illuminating. Christ remembers too

> ... the majestic mountain
> In the wilderness, and that pinnacle
> From which Satan tempted him
> With world power.

For God, there is no time and so the poet achieves the effect of timelessness by making some of the earlier events of Christ's life come back to his mind now. As in *Mary Magdalene II*, where Mary speaks for herself, we have this sense of the suspension of time. Thus, Mary says,

> I see the future in detail
> As though you had stopped it.
> At this moment I am able to prophesy
> With the foresight of a Sybil.

And she goes on to tell us in detail some of the events which immediately precede the Resurrection. *Evil Days* ends simply, but the simplicity is momentous:

> ... the gathering of poor in a hovel,
> And the descent into the cellar with a candle,
> And the candle snuffing out in fright
> When the resurrected man stood up.

This, of course, is a reference to the raising of Lazarus from the dead. *Mary Magdalene II* tells us, in her own words, of Christ's Resurrection and, in a few words conveys the dread which the Apostles and the faithful women have endured since the apparent death for ever of Christ on the Cross:

> Those three days will pass
> But they will push me down into such emptiness
> That in the frightening interval
> I shall grow up to the Resurrection.

Mary Magdalene realizes that although her sins have been forgiven and that Christ took away her guilt, she must, to attain

the deepest possible knowledge of him live through those three
terrible days of apprehension. Here, Pasternak enters into her
experience and shows us *his* Dark Night of the Soul by giving us
so briefly and vividly Mary Magdalene's suffering. He is not
simply equating himself with her; the only way in which he can
find to hand over his vision to us is here by re-telling, in a very
original way, parts of the life of Christ. It is a very effective
method.

In *Gethsemane*, Pasternak gives us a vision of the desolation of
Christ, the betrayal by Judas, and the betrayal of a different kind
by St Peter; as always, the language is gentle, simple, but every
phrase is luminous or dark with calamity. The poet, in short,
manages to lead us into the whole historic event. He begins the
poem with complete directness:

> The turn of the road was lit
> By the unconcerned shimmer of distant stars.

Two lines later, he continues,

> The field tailed off
> Into the Milky Way.
> Grey-haired olive trees tried to walk the air
> Into the distance.

The visual sense is sharp, the scene is set for the terrible desolation which is to follow.

Having described "a vegetable garden" and quoted Christ's
own words in the Gospel when he implores his Apostles to "stay
here and watch with me", Pasternak depicts the complete loneliness of The Agony in the Garden. He writes:

> The night was a kingdom of annihilation,
> Of non-being
> The whole world seemed uninhabited,
> And only this garden was a place for the living.
>
> He gazed into the black abyss,
> Empty, without beginning or end.

Two lines later, the poet says that Christ has "tamed his agony
with prayer". Agony of this kind is thus seen almost as some-

thing animate; if yielded to, it certainly can destroy. So the quiet word "tamed" carries great force. Over and over again, and especially in this poem, we can see how Pasternak understood and lived through suffering and, in this way, discovered his vision. He too tamed his many pains, frustrations, misunderstandings and, worst of all, loneliness. But here he tells us, in his own inimitable way what Christ, God-made-Man, endured to redeem mankind; he does not speak of himself.

Gethsemane goes on to tell us of Christ waking his sleeping Apostles. Then the first, terrible betrayal occurs:

> Hardly had he spoken when from who knows where
> A rabble of slaves and thieves appeared
> With torches and knives
> And in front of them Judas with his traitor's kiss.

We are then given a very dramatic, though brief, account of Peter striking off the ear of one of these men and of Christ, the lover of peace, telling him to put back his sword in his scabbard. He says:

> "Could not my Father send a host
> Of winged legions to defend me? . . ."
> . . . . .
> "But the book of life has reached the page
> Which is the most precious of all holy things.
> What has been written must be fulfilled,
> Let it be so. Amen."

Christ as a man with free will has chosen his death; he has accepted every degradation and inner and outer suffering for the redemption of mankind. Pasternak is not simply versifying the Gospel account of this; he is living through it with his imagination, an imagination that can render one man's vision of the most important events in Christianity. And they are rendered with passion as well as the acceptance learnt from Christ himself. So Pasternak ends Gethsemane with Christ declaring,

> "The centuries will float to me out of darkness.
> And I shall judge them."

There it is—utter simplicity, no comment from the poet, but we are never given a moment of doubt what suffering enabled him to write such a poem.

August is written in the first person and mingles very subtly the poet's vision with references to events in the Gospels. The poet is dreaming:

> I dreamed that you were coming,
> One after another through the wood
> To see me off.

After referring to Christ's Transfiguration, the poet proceeds to speak of it again:

> All could clearly hear
> A quiet voice near by.
> This was my own past voice, prophetic,
> Untouched by dissolution:
>
> "Goodbye, azure and gold
> Of the Transfiguration.
> Soften with a woman's last caress
> The bitterness of the hour of my death."

It becomes clearer and clearer that Pasternak is identifying himself with Christ, though, in this poem, in a much more subtle way than in, for example, *Gethsemane*. It is more mysterious, the vision is disclosed more gradually. Thus the general effect is of a great and powerful personal experience, which the poet is only just able to put into words. The poem goes on:

> "Goodbye, timeless years
> And woman who challenged
> The abyss of humiliations.
> I am your battle-field.
>
> "Goodbye to the span of the outstretched wings,
> Free stubbornness of flight,
> Image of the world revealed in speech,
> Creativeness, working of miracles."

These last lines are a little obscure, but they surely refer to The Descent of the Holy Ghost on the Apostles after Christ's Ascen-

sion. Thus, Pasternak has entered more than the human life of
God-made-Man, the Second Person of the Blessed Trinity. He
is also speaking of the Holy Ghost who brought the Gift of
Tongues to the Apostles.

The vision in Pasternak's love poems moves far deeper than
the love of a single person. It fills him with love and compassion
for all things, as we can see most poignantly in the last two
stanzas of *Daybreak*:

> I feel for each of them
> As if I were in their skin,
> I melt with the melting snow,
> I frown with the morning.
>
> In me are people without names,
> Children, stay-at-homes, trees.
> I am conquered by them all
> And this is my only victory.

His "victory", then, is to be caught up in the whole universe,
but most especially with people. His lofty vision is humble, as
all true visions are. He wants to give, to lose himself by giving,
to be the pain that the whole world suffers. In *Winter Night*,
which is largely descriptive, a moment like this can occur:

> A draught from the corner
> Puffed at the candle's flame,
> And like an angel, the heat of temptation
> Raised two wings in the form of a cross.

There is no dichotomy in Pasternak's vision and love. He is
drawn to give to a woman in the same way as he offers himself
to God. In such self-effacement, there must always be suffering;
but Pasternak writes it down and draws us into the intricate
wonder of the world, showing us the beauty and hinting how
to accept the pain.

In his last poems, there is a plea of such quiet faith, for only
a tranquil faith can express a great vision, that moves the
reader to the depths. In a poem called *God's World*, he sees all
the simplicities of the world and how important they are.
Because he is living in a country which is not free, though he

is prepared to carry the burden of tyranny and of a régime in which he cannot believe, these small things become vast. He writes,

> Countries, continents, isthmuses, frontiers,
> Lakes and mountains, discussions and news,
> Children, grown-ups, old folk, adolescents,
> Appreciations, reports and reviews
>
> O respected and masculine letters !
> All of you, none excepted, have brought
> A display of intelligent logic
> Underneath a dry statement of thought.
>
> Precious, treasured epistles of women !
> Why, I also fell down from a cloud . . .

Pasternak has a naked, lucid view of all things; suffering has sharpened it, but it was always there, and we, who are not behind barriers feel the strength of his courage and poetic vision —an intensely realistic vision in which there is no bitterness at all. This poet's gift for recollection, a visionary's more than total recall, he can write with great nostalgia but completely without sentimentality. Thus a poem called *Unique Days* (a very suitable title) contains these lines :

> Of all these days, these only days,
> When one rejoiced in the impression
> That time had stopped, there grew in years
> An unforgettable succession
> . . . . .
> And sleepy clock-hands laze away
> The clockface wearily ascending.
> Eternal, endless is the day,
> And the embrace is never-ending.

This is more than memory; it is the wonderful, simple grasp of eternity, held for a moment even in this world by rare men and women. And it is, with Pasternak, also human; but he knows that great human love has a touch of something more—in short, the divine—about it. Memory puts a brake on time, but strong emotion holds it fast, protects it for brief moments from all the pressures and powers of time.

Time's works are seen and shown to us in the poem called *Ploughing Time* which begins,

> What is the matter with the landscape?
> Familiar landmarks are not there.
> Ploughed fields, like squares upon a chessboard,
> Today are scattered everywhere.

Nature and what man must do to Nature in due season are viewed now by Pasternak's penetrating eyes. Even over so simple but important a matter as ploughing, however, he gives, partly by the brevity of his poem, an extraordinary importance, the kind of importance which, in their different ways, D. H. Lawrence and Lawrence Durrell, invested in it.

This is the place to examine further the poem entitled *God's World*, for, in six four-line stanzas, the poet manages to compress, without any *feeling* of compression the natural world as the world of God. Pasternak believed that God created the world and is present in every part of it. The poem starts,

> Thin as hair are the shadows of sunset
> When they follow drawn-out every tree.
> On the road through the forest the post-girl
> Hands a parcel and letters to me.

These letters have come "By the trail of the cats and the foxes" and they bring news of "countries, continents, isthmuses, frontiers". The poet is full of joy. Why, however, we may well ask is this poem called *God's World*? And why does it bring such special wonder to the poet? First, the letters and parcels come from people whom the poet loves and who so clearly show their love for him by sending him these things; second, and most important, the poem is full of *caritas*, a love between men and women which includes the love and mercy and graciousness of God himself. So, for this visionary, the simple letters and parcels assume a momentous importance.

There are letters from men—"O respected and masculine letters!"—which "display" "intelligent logic / Underneath a dry statement of thought". And letters from women are "Precious, treasured epistles". All these are to be valued as part of the world created by God. So small things are part of a larger vision experienced and passed on to us. The poems which have just been examined are those of Pasternak's last years, 1957–60. From a book published just before those, entitled *When It Clears Up 1945–57*, a deep look at a few of the poems printed there is now relevant. One of these, called *It Is Not Seemly*, tells us some very important things about Boris Pasternak's attitude towards fame. The "It Is Not Seemly" of the title refers to fame, and in the second of seven four-line stanzas, the poet tells us why this should be so. He writes,

> To give your all—this is creation,
> And not—to deafen and eclipse.
> How shameful, when you have no meaning,
> To be on everybody's lips !

Here we see the poet's sense of his vocation and the visionary's realization that to be well-known, honoured, renowned means nothing beside the writing of poems, and of prose, itself. So he goes on to do something he very rarely does—that is to say, he gives advice—but he is also advising himself; this is what is so important. The third stanza of this poem, then, begins, "Try not to live as a pretender . . ." The fourth says this :

> Leave blanks in life, not in your papers,
> And do not even hesitate
> To pencil out whole chunks, whole chapters
> Of your existence, of your fate.

This is of extraordinary interest because it reveals to us, in very simple words, just how much Pasternak valued his writing, how he knew all the technical difficulties, but also that although no poet, visionary or otherwise can hope to lead a perfect life, he can in his writing, which derives from all he has seen and learnt, possibly achieve a perfect poem or a body of perfect work. The poet-visionary owes a duty to his poetry; he has been given a gift which he must not abuse or allow to tarnish. He has not only the desire but the responsibility to communicate what he knows. As a visionary, Pasternak has seen, felt and suffered so much, but he knows that the small details of life deftly stated can open up a whole vision for others.

So he proceeds:

> Into obscurity retiring
> Try your development to hide,
> As Autumn mist on early mornings
> Conceals the dreaming countryside.

This brings us sharply back to the fact that Pasternak was against the Soviet Union's régime. But it also means more than this, the beautifully simple, almost slipped-in pieces of description help to make the poem work on several levels. Only his vision, together with complete control over his poems, could achieve this. And so *It Is Not Seemly* ends,

> And never for a single moment
> Betray your *credo* or pretend,
> But be alive—this only matters—
> Alive and burning to the end.

Here are two of the most important elements in Pasternak's vision—steadfastness and, whatever happens, remain open to life, see what it shows, enter it and then hand over what you have found. In his situation, the handing over, the sharing was difficult, almost impossible, but he did finally achieve it in his poems and in *Dr Zhivago*. It is not surprising that he was considered the best Russian translator of Shakespeare. He would understand every mood from the most lofty tragic speeches to the words of simple, humble men. As Dr Johnson said of Shakespeare, "His story demands Romans and kings, but he thinks only on men", so would Pasternak's attitude be.

We are now reaching the close of the visionary poems, that vision from virtual imprisonment, at least for a writer. A good poem to end with seems to be *The Miracle*; we have looked at this already but its last stanza is worth repeating since it seems a perfect summing-up of Pasternak's Christian vision:

> If the leaves, branches, roots, trunk,
> Had been granted a moment of freedom
> The laws of nature would have intervened.

But a miracle is a miracle : a miracle is God.
When we are all confusion,
That instant it finds us out.

Pasternak never lost his intense faith so that, what to men who
are not visionaries would seem a quite ordinary event, did at
times appear to him to come as a direct insight given by God,
God entering the poet's soul. Even when he was not writing
poems on religious themes, this shines out of Pasternak's poems;
to him nothing was ordinary. Out of his darkness he saw and
communicated a very great light indeed.

LAST WORDS

Writing about these twentieth-century visionaries, I realize that all of them open up ways to the future; they are not static, all of them lead somewhere. Where they lead is not, in general, certain, but that they do lead is. Most of them have seen paths to the moon and to satellites—here, science has entered. None of them is entirely personal, let alone introspective. Perhaps what unites them is hope, a rare quality nowadays—hope and a vivid, concrete awareness of our own world to-day. Finally, what must be said is that, in this context, "awareness" reaches from the secret desires of the human mind and heart to flying into space. Man is a discoverer. In this book, I have tried to show him as a visionary, a kind of prophet. Above all else, I have tried to catch the point, the moment, where the personal and the impersonal join. Here, love, peace-making, excitement, curiosity join hands. Only one thing must be cast out, and that is the vague. There is nothing blurred about the very different visions of the writers in this book. Clarity clings to them, and only true clarity reaches to the heights and the depths of human and more than human understanding.

BIBLIOGRAPHY

Auden, W. H., *Collected Shorter Poems, 1930–1944*, London, Faber, 1950

Durrell, Lawrence, *Collected Poems*, new and revised edition, London, Faber, 1968

Lawrence, D. H., *Complete Poems* . . . collected and edited by Vivian de Sola Pinto and Warren Roberts, 2 vols, London, Heinemann, 1964

Pasternak, Boris, *Dr Zhivago*, translated by M. Harari, London, Collins, 1958

Pasternak, Boris, *Poems*, translated by Eugene M. Kayden, The University of Michigan Press, Ann Arbor, 1959

Pasternak, Boris, *Fifty Poems*, translated by Lydia Pasternak Slater, Allen and Unwin, 1963

Perse, St-John, *Anabasis*, with a translation by T. S. Eliot, London, Faber, 1930

Perse, St-John, *Eloges and other poems*, translated by Louise Varese, New York, Pantheon Books, 1956

Perse, St-John, *Exile and other poems*, translated by Denis Devlin, New York, Pantheon Books, 1949

Saint-Exupéry, Antoine de, *Flight to Arras*, translated by Lewis Galantiere, London, Heinemann, 1942

Saint-Exupéry, Antoine de, *Wind, Sand and Stars*, translated by Lewis Galantiere, London, Heinemann, 1939

Yeats, W. B., *Collected Poems*, 2nd edition, London, Macmillan, 1950